T0305075

Macroeconomics in the Small and the Large

Macroeconomics in the Small and the Large

Essays on Microfoundations, Macroeconomic Applications and Economic History in Honor of Axel Leijonhufvud

Edited by

Roger E.A. Farmer

University of California, Los Angeles, USA

Edward Elgar
Cheltenham, UK • Northampton, MA, USA

Published by
Edward Elgar Publishing Limited
The Lypiatts
15 Lansdown Road
Cheltenham
Glos GL50 2JA
UK

Edward Elgar Publishing, Inc.
William Pratt House
9 Dewey Court
Northampton
Massachusetts 01060
USA

A catalogue record for this book
is available from the British Library

Library of Congress Cataloguing in Publication Data

Macroeconomics in the small and the large : essays on microfoundations, macroeconomic applications and economic history in honor of Axel Leijonhufvud / edited by Roger Farmer.
    p. cm.
  Includes bibliographical references and index.
  1. Macroeconomics. 2. Economic history. I. Farmer, Roger E. A. II. Leijonhufvud, Axel.
  HB172.5.M3357   2008
  339–dc22

Mixed Sources
Product group from well-managed
forests and other controlled sources
www.fsc.org Cert no. SA-COC-1565
© 1996 Forest Stewardship Council

ISBN 978 1 84844 046 3

Printed and bound in Great Britain by MPG Books Ltd, Bodmin, Cornwall

Contents

Contributors

Masanao Aoki is Professor Emeritus in the department of Economics at the University of California, Los Angeles (UCLA). He has held professorial appointments at the Institute for Economic and Social Research at Osaka University, Tokyo Institute of Technology and the University of Illinois. Professor Aoki is past President of the Society for Economic Dynamics and Control, a Fellow of the Econometric Society and a Fellow of the Institute of Electrical and Electronics Engineers (IEEE) Control Systems Society. He is author of a dozen books and numerous scholarly articles.

Roger E.A. Farmer is Professor of Economics at UCLA and has previously held positions at the University of Pennsylvania, the University of Toronto and the European University Institute. He is a Fellow of the Econometric Society, a Fellow Commoner of Cambridge University, Research Associate of the National Bureau of Economic Research (NBER) and the Center for Economic Policy Research (CEPR), and co-editor of the *International Journal of Economic Theory*. In 2000 he was awarded the University of Helsinki medal. He is a specialist on macroeconomic theory and the author of five books and numerous scholarly articles. Professor Farmer is best known for his work on *Self-Fulfilling Prophecies in Macroeconomics*.

Lars Peter Hansen is the Homer J. Livingston Distinguished Service Professor of Economics at the University of Chicago. He is the recipient of the 2006 Erwin Plein Nemmers Prize in Economics from Northwestern University and co-winner of the Frisch Medal from the Econometric Society. He is a member of the National Academy of Sciences and American Academy of Arts and Sciences, a Fellow of the Econometric Society, and a National Opinion Research Center (NORC) Research Associate for the Economics Research Center. Hansen is a former John Simon Guggenheim Memorial Foundation Fellow and Sloan Foundation Fellow.

Daniel Heymann is Senior Economist at the Economic Commission for Latin America and the Caribbean (CEPAL) and Professor of Economics at the University of Buenos Aires and at the University of San Andrés. He is co-author with professor Leijonhufvud of a 1995 book on *High Inflation*.

Peter Howitt is the Lyn Crost Professor of Social Sciences in the Department of Economics at Brown University. Previous positions include

Ohio State University and the University of Western Ontario. He is Fellow of the Econometric Society, Fellow of the Royal Society of Canada, past president of the Canadian Economics Association, Research Associate of the NBER and International Fellow of the C.D. Howe Institute. Professor Howitt is author of five books and numerous articles on macroeconomics and is best known for his work on endogenous economic growth.

Timothy J. Kehoe has taught at Wesleyan University, the Massachusetts Institute of Technology, and the University of Cambridge. Since 1987 he has been a Professor in the Department of Economics at the University of Minnesota where he is currently Distinguished McKnight University Professor. Professor Kehoe is a Fellow of the Econometric Society, a Research Associate of the NBER and an adviser at the Federal Reserve Bank of Minneapolis. His research and teaching focus on the theory and application of general equilibrium models.

B. Zorina Khan is in the Department of Economics, Bowdoin College. She received her PhD from UCLA where she studied as a Fulbright Scholar. Her research examines the economic history of law, litigation, intellectual property rights, and technological change in Europe and the United States. Professor Khan is a Trustee of the Cliometric Society and a member of the National Bureau of Economic Research. In 2004 she was awarded the Griliches Fellowship which is granted every two years to an NBER researcher in empirical economics. Her book, *The Democratization of Invention: Patents and Copyrights in American Economic Development, 1790–1920*, received the Alice Hanson Jones Biennial Prize for an outstanding work on American economic history.

David Laidler is Emeritus Professor of Economics at the University of Western Ontario. He previously held positions at the University of Manchester, Essex University, the University of California Berkeley and the London School of Economics. He is an expert on monetary economics and the author of several books and numerous articles on monetary economics and its history.

David K. Levine is John H. Biggs Distinguished Professor of Economics at Washington University in St Louis. He is co-editor of *Econometrica*, co-editor of *NAJ Economics*, President of the Society for Economic Dynamics, Fellow of the Econometric Society, Research Associate of the NBER, former member of the American Economic Association Honors and Awards Committee, and member of the Sloan Research Fellowship Program Committee. He previously taught at UCLA where he held the Armen Alchian Chair in Economic Theory.

Edmund S. Phelps is the McVickar Professor of Political Economy at Columbia University, the director of Columbia's Center on Capitalism and Society and the winner of the 2006 Nobel Prize for economics. Professor Phelps is a Fellow of the National Academy of Science, a Distinguished Fellow and former Vice-President of the American Economic Association, and a Fellow of the Econometric Society, the American Academy of Arts and Sciences and the New York Academy of Sciences. He is best known for his work on economic growth, the Golden Rule savings rate and the natural rate of unemployment.

Thomas J. Sargent is the Berkeley Professor of Economics and Business at New York University (NYU) and a Senior Fellow of the Hoover Institute at Stanford University. He previously held positions at Stanford University, the University of Chicago, the University of Minnesota and the University of Pennsylvania. He is Fellow of the Econometric Society, the National Academy of Sciences and the American Academy of Arts and Sciences and is President of the American Economic Association, past President of the Econometric Society and past President of the Society for Economic Dynamics and Control. He is the author of 12 books and numerous scholarly articles and has worked on many diverse topics in macroeconomics including the development of rational expectations econometrics and more recently work on robust control.

Kenneth L. Sokoloff was Professor of Economics at UCLA. He passed away on 21 May 2007 shortly after contributing to the conference from which this volume grew. Professor Sokoloff held visiting appointments at Oxford University, École des Hautes Études, the California Institute of Technology, Tel Aviv University, the Russell Sage Foundation and the Center for Advanced Studies in the Behavioral Sciences. He was a Research Associate of the National Bureau of Economic Research and a Fellow of the American Academy of Arts and Sciences. Professor Sokoloff was a renowned economic historian whose work had important implications for economic development.

Festschrift for Axel Leijonhufvud: Preface

Roger E.A. Farmer

Axel Leijonhufvud was born in Stockholm, Sweden and obtained his Bachelors degree at the University of Lund. After coming to the United States in 1960, he earned an MA from the University of Pittsburgh and a PhD from Northwestern University. He came to the University of California at Los Angeles in 1964 and was named Full Professor in 1971. In 1995 Axel was appointed Professor of Monetary Theory and Policy at the University of Trento in Italy although he remains an Emeritus Professor at the University of California, Los Angeles (UCLA).

In August of 2006 the Economics Department at UCLA organized a conference to recognize Axel Leijonhufvud's contributions to the department and to economics at large. It is a remarkable testament to the esteem with which Axel is held in the profession that we were able to attract a star cast of former students, colleagues and friends, all of whom were kind enough to contribute their time and their work to this volume that celebrates a career which spans five decades and shows no sign of decline.

Many people contributed to the success of the conference with both time and resources. Gary Hansen suggested the idea that UCLA should honor our senior faculty members in this way and he provided departmental resources to fund this as the first of a series of similar conferences to honor distinguished UCLA faculty. The then Dean of Social Sciences, Scott Waugh, supported the conference financially as did Al Harberger, David Levine, Ken Sokoloff and the Ettinger Fund, an endowment funded by Robert Ettinger, a 1980 Alumnus of UCLA and President of Flaherty and Crumrine Inc. Gwen Matthews organized the conference events assisted by Michelle Ellis, Lucas Lee and Gloria McBride. I would especially like to thank Masonori Kashinagi who read and commented on the entire manuscript and created the index. Last but not least, the 2006–07 Harvard Westlake Jazz Explorers consisting of Lucas Berman, Leland Farmer, Kurt Kanazawa, Ian Sprague and Ian Stanton provided a memorable evening of entertainment.

Introduction

Roger E.A. Farmer

I first met Axel in the winter of 1987. I was a young Assistant Professor at the University of Pennsylvania and was visiting the campus of the University of California, Los Angeles (UCLA) to present a seminar at the Economics Department. The 1980s were a tumultuous time for macroeconomics. The rational expectations revolution had begun to sweep the profession but its impact was not yet fully appreciated. Macroeconomics at UCLA had not yet fallen to the new classical onslaught and was still dominated by the Keynesian ideas of Robert Clower and Axel Leijonhufvud.

I had studied Axel's (1968) book on Keynes as an undergraduate in Manchester in the late 1970s and at that time it appeared as if the reconstruction of Keynesian economics in the work of Robert Barro and Herschel Grossman (1976) in the United States and Jean Pascal Benassy (1976), Jacques Drèze (1975) and Edmond Malinvaud (1977) in Europe, would be *the* new paradigm for macroeconomics. When Barro repudiated his earlier ideas and embraced new classical economics, the writing was on the wall. Barro was captivated by the writing of Robert E. Lucas Jr. who promoted an alternative in his (1972) article that would replace Keynesian economics with a version of general equilibrium theory based on Chapter 7 of Gerard Debreu's (1959) monograph, *Theory of Value*. Lucas proved persuasive and for the past 25 years the history of macroeconomics has been that of dynamic stochastic general equilibrium theory. To put Axel's contribution into historical perspective we were lucky enough to persuade David Laidler to write the opening chapter of this Festschrift, 'Axel Leijonhufvud and the quest for micro-foundations: some reflections'.

The adoption of rational expectations brought many benefits. Macroeconomists were provided with a consistent theory, and generations of graduate students were schooled in mathematics and statistics that allowed the current generation of macroeconomists to develop theories that have a much more solid technical foundation than those that preceded them. But in my view, something was lost in this process. The introduction of more sophisticated mathematics was accompanied by a shift back to less sophisticated economics as it became prudent to understand the simplest version of dynamic models before progressing to their more elaborate variants. The real business cycle model of Kydland and Prescott (1982) is driven by a single shock to technology, but the nineteenth-century business cycle theorists who preceded Keynes constructed verbal theories that were much richer than this. Pigou, in his (1929) book *Industrial Fluctuations*, included 'errors of optimism and pessimism, harvest variations and autonomous monetary movements' as additional sources of business cycles, and it is only now that we are beginning to reinvestigate these pre-Keynesian ideas with the tools of dynamic stochastic general equilibrium theory.

Perhaps the biggest casualty of the rational expectations revolution was Keynesian economics itself which was swept away as an irrelevant detour in the history of thought. This is unfortunate since there are ideas in Keynes's (1936) *General Theory* that pose fundamental challenges to new classical economics and that have not been refuted by confrontation with the facts. The interpretation of Keynes that appeared in Leijonhufvud's (1968) book was one in which agents trade at disequilibrium prices. The development of this idea by contemporary writers led to characterizations of Keynes's *General Theory* as the economics of nominal rigidities. Axel himself was never comfortable with this characterization and my own contribution to this volume, 'Old-Keynesian economics', is an attempt to provide a microfoundation to the *General Theory* that does not rely on nominal price stickiness. In the subsequent chapter, Edmund Phelps takes up a related theme. A key idea in the *General Theory*, and one that has been largely ignored by new-Keynesian economics, is that the future is unforecastable; a situation that Frank Knight referred to as risk as opposed to uncertainty. In his chapter, 'Interest rate setting in the presence of investment prospects and Knightian uncertainty', Phelps argues that interest rate rules of the kind that have been favored by the new-Keynesians should contain an escape clause to allow them to adapt to events that cannot be foreseen, even probabilistically.

Throughout his career Axel has been occupied with the idea that economists should learn from dramatic events. The Great Depression and the Argentinean hyperinflations of the 1980s are examples of this. His focus on Keynesian economics was motivated by the fact that we do not have good explanations for the Great Depression, and his work on Argentinean hyperinflation, with his student Daniel Heymann, was motivated by the same basic idea. When confronted with the apparent fact that the post-war economy has remained remarkably stable, Axel developed the idea that during normal times the economy sits within a band of fluctuations he dubbed the 'corridor'. In this region classical economics does a good job of explaining market economies. Sometimes however there are large disturbances that move the economy outside of the corridor and at times like this the rules of the game break down and classical economics no longer works well. The chapter by Daniel Heymann, 'Macroeconomics of broken promises', is a description of the kinds of effects that can occur in an economy, in this case Argentina, when normal institutions are eroded.

How should one understand the kinds of events described by Daniel Heymann with economic theory? In their chapter, 'Bankruptcy and collateral in debt constrained markets', Timothy J. Kehoe and David K. Levine provide a microeconomic model of agents who interact in a world where collateral matters. Their model provides a possible microfoundation for Axel's concept of the corridor, since in their words: 'the institution of bankruptcy and collateral that may be well suited for "ordinary" shocks may break down when subject to unusual shocks'.

Axel's work is not characterized by its technical nature, but his ideas have displayed a depth that often appears to be beyond our current capabilities to describe by formal models. To paraphrase a conversation that I recall with Axel: 'Living in Hollywood has made me realize that the developments in modern macroeconomics are much like those in the movies – modern plots are sadly lacking but the special effects are truly spectacular'. It is a testament to Axel as a true master of a good plot that three of the profession's best economists, both as creative economists and as creators of new techniques, agreed to contribute to this volume. In his chapter, 'Growth patterns of two types of macro-models', Masanao Aoki introduces a new class of stochastic process that has not previously been considered in economics as a model of growth. In their chapter 'Time inconsistency of robust control?', Lars Hansen and Tom Sargent respond to parallel criticisms made by Zenghin Chen and Larry Epstein and by Martin Schneider, each of whom had claimed that the previous work of Hansen and Sargent on robust control may not be consistent with the assumption that agents' actions are time consistent.

Axel has long had a deep interest in economic history and he is largely responsible for developing the history group at UCLA which for many years was led by Kenneth L. Sokoloff who sadly passed away in May 2007. In his chapter with B. Zorina Khan, 'A tale of two countries: innovation and incentives among great inventors in Britain and the United States, 1750–1930', Sokoloff and Khan compare the patent systems of the US and Great Britain and argue that US patent law was responsible in large part for different patterns of growth.

In his more recent work, Axel has worked on an alternative microfoundation to the *General Theory* based on the microeconomics of Alfred Marshall as opposed to the general equilibrium foundations rooted in Walras. Axel's recent interest in non-Walrasian foundations is represented in this volume by the work of Peter Howitt who describes in the closing chapter, 'Macroeconomics with intelligent autonomous agents', how economic institutions can develop spontaneously in a world where agents follow simple behavioral rules.

REFERENCES

Barro, Robert and Herschel Grossman (1976), *Money, Employment and Inflation*, Cambridge: Cambridge University Press.

Benassy, Jean Paul (1976), 'The disequilibrium approach to monopolistic price setting and general monopolistic equilibrium', *Review of Economic Studies*, **43** (1), 6–81.

Debreu, Gerard (1959), *Theory of Value*, Cowles Foundation Monograph 17, New Haven, CT: Yale University Press.

Drèze, Jacques (1975), 'Existence of exchange equilibrium under price rigidities', *International Economic Review*, **16** (2), 301–20.

Keynes, John Maynard (1936), *The General Theory of Unemployment, Interest and Money*, London: Macmillan.

Kydland, F. and E. Prescott (1982), 'Time to build and aggregate fluctuations', *Econometrica*, **50**, 1345–71.

Leijonhufvud, Axel (1968), *On Keynesian Economics and the Economics of Keynes: A Study in Monetary Theory*, New York: Oxford University Press.

Lucas, Robert E., Jr. (1972), 'Expectations and the neutrality of money', *Journal of Economic Theory*, **4** (2), 10–124.

Malinvaud, Edmond M. (1977), *The Theory of Unemployment Reconsidered*, Oxford: Basil Blackwell.

Pigou, Arthur C. (1929), *Industrial Fluctuations*, London: Macmillan.

1. Axel Leijonhufvud and the quest for micro-foundations: some reflections

David Laidler*

I think that I first met Axel Leijonhufvud when he was still a graduate student at Northwestern University, and, because I had the good fortune to be Bob Clower's junior colleague during my time at University of Essex, I was kept well aware of the development of his ideas even before *On Keynesian Economics and the Economics of Keynes* (Leijonhufvud 1968) appeared. When it was published in 1968, Harry Johnson made sure that I was an early British reader, and I am proud to say that my copy of it bears an inscription from the author, commemorating a visit he made to University of Manchester in 1974. That, as is evident from Laidler (1974), was at a time when his influence had begun to loosen my previously rather uncritical embrace of monetarism. In short, I have been learning from Axel's work for a long time, and I have sometimes followed it too, usually from a little to the right, but with undiminished admiration over the years.

I have given this essay the sub-title 'some reflections' because it is proba-bly as much informed by (no doubt prejudiced) hindsight and (no doubt inaccurate) memory as by a careful weighing of the published record. The history of macroeconomics in the second half of the twentieth century, and of Axel Leijonhufvud's place in it, largely remains to be written, but I hope that this essay will provoke some of those who were not yet professionally active in those years, and can therefore view them dispassionately, to begin that task. When they do so, I also hope that their work will bear out at least some of the judgements offered here.

1.1 ECONOMIC THEORY IN THE 1950s

Half a century ago, those of us starting out on the serious study of eco-nomics found a great deal to perplex us. The subject, particularly as it was taught at the intermediate level and above, was theory-based, but that theory was divided into two components, the connections between which were, to say the least, obscure. Microeconomics dealt with the maximising

1

behaviour of individual households and firms, how the decisions of these individuals were coordinated by the price mechanism, and how this mechanism might fail properly to allocate the economy's endowment of productive resources without a few well-placed government subsidies and taxes designed to change the structure of relative prices. Macroeconomics, on the other hand, as enshrined in the Hicks–Hansen IS–LM model, dealt with aggregate consequences of the behaviour of those same firms and households, arguing that these would often include a failure of that same endowment of productive resources to be fully employed without help from a steady injection of expenditure from the government that was so coordinated with the flow of taxes paid by the private sector as to provide an appropriate level of aggregate demand.

Microeconomics and macroeconomics thus seemed to be telling possibly contradictory stories about how the economy as a whole worked. To be sure, efforts were made to forge a link between them: for example, Paul Samuelson's neoclassical synthesis, notably as expounded in the third edition of his introductory textbook (Samuelson, 1955) had it that, though the market economy needed some government help designed with the aid of macroeconomics to bring about full employment, once this was achieved its further allocative functioning could safely be left to those devices which were the subject of microeconomics; and Abba Lerner's *Economics of Control* (1944) had earlier found a role for micro theory in guiding the pricing behaviour of publicly owned enterprises in a thoroughly socialised economy whose government made maintaining full employment a priority. But both of these attempted links had to do with the policy applications of received economics; they skirted questions about the logical relations between the theoretical foundations of its two branches and about whether, and if so how, these could be reconciled.

By the late 1950s, IS–LM macroeconomics was beginning to take on the status of an unchallenged orthodoxy, under the label 'Keynesian Economics', and had begun to find its policy feet too.[1] Soon, though belatedly, it would dominate policy-making even in the United States. In 1965, at the height of its influence, but in perhaps the worst call made by an eminent economist since John Stuart Mill's 1848 claims about the completeness of the theory of value (see Mill, 1848 [1909], p. 436) Robert Solow (1965) would proclaim that: 'most economists feel that short-run macroeconomic theory is pretty well in hand . . . All that is left is the trivial job of filling in the empty boxes, and that will not take more than 50 years of concentrated effort at a maximum'.

If we remember this (partly tongue in cheek) claim of Solow's nowadays, that is probably because only three years after it was made, Axel Leijonhufvud would quote it in his book *On Keynesian Economics and the*

Economics of Keynes (Leijonhufvud, 1968, p. 4). This work did more than any other single contribution to energise the search for a cure for the discomfort that many economists were feeling in constructing proper microfoundations for macroeconomics, an endeavour that would end up pushing the IS–LM model from the centre of macroeconomics and replacing it with a new approach whose microeconomic basis was thoroughly transparent. But though what Harry Johnson (1971 [1978], p. 198) would refer to as Leijonhufvud's 'monumental re-interpretation of [Keynes's] thought' was seminal in giving impetus to these developments, the micro-foundations that were eventually established were the very opposite of the ones he had proposed.

In what follows, I shall reflect upon how and why this came about. Specifically, I shall first describe the micro-foundations problem as it appeared about 50 years ago, and how it was then being addressed. Then I shall argue: (1) that, even as Leijonhuvfud was writing his book, the macro-orthodoxy that so disturbed him was already being undermined by monetarism, whose attack was, however, based more on empirical evidence than micro-theoretic considerations; (2) that a by-product of monetarism's success was nevertheless to shift the theoretical concerns of macroeconomists away from just those parts of Keynes's legacy upon which Leijonhufvud sought to build; and (3) that, as a consequence, the search for micro-foundations that he helped set in motion was quickly diverted from his chosen path.

1.2 MARSHALLIANS AND WALRASIANS

The received economic theory, the overall structure of which seemed so puzzling half a century ago, was the product of two intellectual upheavals in the 1930s. Both of these had happened in Britain, but because of the destruction by the Nazis (along with much else) of important and distinct intellectual traditions on the continent of Europe, not to mention because of the accident that English was also the language of the United States, whose universities would soon come to dominate all of economics (again, along with much else), they profoundly influenced the development of the subject as a whole. The first of these was the macroeconomic revolution that surrounded the publication and interpretation of Keynes's (1936) *General Theory of Employment, Interest and Money*, and the second, less noted but just as influential, was an upheaval in microeconomics that saw continental 'general equilibrium' theory, whose principal English language text was John Hicks's *Value and Capital* (1939), largely displace Marshallian 'partial equilibrium' analysis.[2]

These developments were incompatible with each other. General equilibrium analysis stemmed from the work of Walras and the first generation of Austrians, notably Carl Menger, but the short-run macroeconomic theory that sprang from it – Austrian business cycle theory – had failed to catch on in the 1930s, partly as a result of Keynes's success.[3] Partial equilibrium analysis, on the other hand, was one component of a broader Marshallian approach to economic theory that had also provided microeconomic foundations for the macroeconomics of the *General Theory*, as Leijonhufvud (2006) has recently documented. Thus, the root cause of economic theory's troubles in the 1950s was that, in the 1930s, competing Continental and Marshallian traditions had won one battle each, the former on the micro front and the latter on the macro, and that a third battle remained to be fought, over the micro-foundation of macroeconomics.

The most thorough exposition of the tension between Marshallian and Walrasian approaches to economics written at that time was Milton Friedman's (1953) 'The methodology of positive economics'. This essay argued that the main point of contrast between the two lay in the Marshallian use of economic theory as 'an engine of analysis' that permitted empirically testable hypotheses about real-world economic phenomena to be formulated, and the Walrasian quest for an analytic framework general enough to encompass essentially any possibility. Obviously, on this criterion, the economics of Keynes's *General Theory*, with its strong hypotheses about the stability of the consumption function, the volatility of the marginal efficiency of capital, the sensitivity of the demand for money to the rate of interest, and so on, is as thoroughly Marshallian as the general equilibrium theory of *Value and Capital* is Walrasian, and it is hardly surprising that the bodies of literature that followed on from them would prove hard to square with one another.

Even so, by the 1950s, the phrase 'Keynesian economics' had come to refer to a system built not so much around Keynes's own specific empirical hypotheses, but around the IS–LM model, a formal framework which could accommodate those hypotheses to be sure, and generate results that bore a reasonable resemblance to what Keynes had claimed them to imply as well. But the IS–LM framework was a general equilibrium model of sorts that could also accommodate other hypotheses which yielded very different predictions.[4] Though IS–LM was certainly not a model in the tradition of Walras in any strict sense, some of its exponents were beginning to deploy it in ways that any follower of Friedman would characterise as Walrasian, and it was hardly surprising that economic theorists working along such lines would begin to explore its logical relationship to traditional general equilibrium theory. That is how the search for the micro-foundations of macroeconomics, to which Leijonhuvfud contributed so much, seems to have begun, and two names stand out among those who preceded him, Don Patinkin (see for example 1956 [1965]) and Robert Clower (see for example 1965).

1.3 THE PATINKIN–CLOWER CONTRIBUTION

The typical general equilibrium model of 50 years ago dealt with an economy with a given endowment of productive resources, inhabited by utility-maximising households and perfectly competitive profit-maximising firms, and its analysis showed (among other things) that the resources in question would be fully utilised if a set of relative prices ruled in the system that rendered the decisions of each agent compatible with those of all others, this even if the information available to each agent concerned only those prices (as well as its endowments of resources, its own tastes if a household, or the technology available to it if a firm).

The typical IS–LM model, on the other hand, largely devoid of explicit maximising foundations, dealt with a world in which one input, labour (or two if account was taken of an exogenously given capital stock) produced a single good. In that model the nominal wage level was constant, and agents also faced a portfolio decision which was usually reduced to one about holding a stock of nominal money (whose supply was exogenously fixed). Such a model could, and typically did, generate a solution in which some labour remained unemployed.

Two salient characteristics in particular differentiated these systems from one another: the absence of money from the first of them, and the capacity of the second to generate unemployment. Patinkin's main contribution to their reconciliation was to introduce nominal money into the general equilibrium system by including real money balances in agents' utility functions, and allowing a 'real balance effect' driven by a modicum of price flexibility to ensure that the model generated a stable equilibrium price level. But he also showed that the logical properties of his model implied that, if unemployment was to occur, the labour market in his system must have settled at a point of market disequilibrium, off and inside its demand curve for labour.

Clower, on the other hand, emphasised the contrast between the behaviour relations implied by a standard Walrasian general equilibrium model, where quantities responded to prices, and a key relationship of the standard IS–LM model in which one quantity, consumption, varied with another, income. He then argued that the latter only made sense if agents were trading at false prices, prices other than those compatible with general equilibrium. Specifically, he argued that, if households were unable to sell

all the labour they intended at the going real wage, they would simultaneously be unable to fulfil their consumption plans, and that their actual consumption would then be constrained to vary with income. The general
equilibrium model enabled notional demand and supply curves to be generated, but the plans implicit in them could only be accomplished if market
clearing prices ruled. If they did not, then actual behaviour would be driven
by effective demand and supply curves in which quantities figured as
arguments.

Patinkin's analysis of the labour market, and Clower's of the goods
market, were complementary to one another, and implied that microeconomic foundations for IS–LM macroeconomics were to be found, first, in
the hypothesis that trading could indeed take place at non-market clearing
prices and, second, in its implication that an initial shock to the system
would then set in motion quantity dynamics, an income-constrained
process, of which the Keynesian muliplier was the prototype, in which deviations from full employment equilibrium were amplified rather than
damped.

Such interactions were, of course, amenable to explicit modelling based
on maximising premises, and one product of the Patinkin–Clower enterprise was an extensive formal literature whose highlights include Barro and
Grossman (1976), Benassy (1975) and Malinvaud (1977), but whose details
need not concern us in this chapter. Suffice it to say that the easiest way to
build models in which trading takes place at false prices is to hold prices
constant, and that more and more elaborate systems built upon this
assumption rapidly ran into diminishing returns. The literature in question
rigorously established the existence of the linkages between general equilibrium analysis and 1960s style macro-theory that the insights of Patinkin
and Clower had postulated, and generalised them as well. To this extent
it was important, but its significance was to help bridge an existing
gap between two already well-established research agendas, rather than to
create a foundation for any new work.

1.4   LEIJONHUFVUD, KEYNES AND MARSHALLIAN MICROECONOMICS

Leijonhufvud's work should be seen as a search for an alternative and
potentially more fruitful way forward from the Patinkin–Clower
insights. He assiduously avoided the trap of reducing trading at false
prices to trading at fixed prices, so his work had an immediate claim to
relevance when it came to analysing the interaction of money prices and
quantities over time, a problem that was attracting increasing attention

as the great inflation that began the mid-1960s gathered momentum; and crucially, his way of establishing microeconomic foundations for a macroeconomics descended from Keynes's very Marshallian *General Theory* was self-consciously to seek them, not in contemporary Walrasian microeconomics, but in the equally Marshallian microeconomics that Keynes had worked with, and from which IS–LM analysis had become detached.

This Marshallian microeconomics, though already overshadowed by its Walrasian challenger, had not quite disappeared 50 years ago. Indeed it figured prominently in Friedman's (1953) essay on 'The methodology of positive economics' already referred to above, where the main example cited of the advantages of the pragmatic Marshallian approach to economic theory was the theory of perfect competition, whose empirical content Friedman favourably contrasted with monopolistic competition, for him the epitome of Walrasian vacuousness. Nowadays, it seems odd to characterise perfect competition as Marshallian, because we are used to defining it as a state of affairs in which all agents are price takers, who respond to market clearing prices set by an entity known as the 'Walrasian auctioneer'. But Friedman's view made excellent sense at a time when perfect competition's defining characteristic was still regarded as being the absence of any interdependencies among individual firms' roles in the price formation process that would rule out the use of supply and demand analysis at the level of the industry, and when the every-agent-a-price-taker assumption remained to be examined.[5]

Friedman was, that is to say, writing before Kenneth Arrow's (1959) observation that, if every agent was a price taker, then no one was left to set and change prices, and therefore before the above-mentioned fictitious auctioneer became a central player in microeconomics, whose specific task was to resolve this paradox.[6] Leijonhufvud, on the other hand, was writing in the immediate wake of these developments, and was fully conscious that they seemed to render the Walrasian theory of competitive markets totally unhelpful for analysing real-world price adjustment processes. But he was also aware that the older Marshallian conception of competition that had underlain Keynes's macroeconomics left space for prices to be adjusted without the help of an auctioneer; and he saw that modern theories of market search, such as were being developed, among others, by his colleague Armen Alchian, were perhaps able to fill this space and in a way that would allow the Patinkin–Clower insights about the consequences of trading at false prices to be placed on a firmer theoretical footing.

Leijonhufvud summarised the point in an article published shortly before his book, (explicitly citing Arrow, 1959 and Alchian and Allen,

Walras' auctioneer is assumed to inform all traders of the prices at which all markets are going to clear. This always trustworthy information is supplied at zero cost. Traders never have to wrestle with situations in which demands and supplies do not mesh; all can plan on facing perfectly elastic demand and supply schedules without fear of ever having their trading plans disappointed. All goods are perfectly 'liquid,' their full market values being at any time instanta- neously realizable. Money can be added to such models only by artifice.

Alchian has shown that the emergence of unemployed resources is a predictable consequence of a decline in demand when traders do not have perfect information on what the new market clearing price would be. The price obtainable for the ser- vices of a resource which has become 'unemployed' will depend upon the costs expended in searching for the highest bidder. In this sense the resource is 'illiquid' . . . Reservation price will be adjusted gradually as search continues. Meanwhile the resource remains unemployed. To this analysis one need only add that the loss of receipts from its services will constrain the owner's effective demand for other products – a feedback which provides a rationale for the multiplier-analysis of a system of atomistic ('competitive') markets. (Leijonhufvud, 1967 [1981a], p. 6)

The account of the problems associated with finding new equilibrium prices given in the first part of this quotation is more elaborate than those that Keynes frequently offered his readers, but it does not differ in sub- stance from them. Leijonhufvud's claims that the Economics of Keynes was informed by a microeconomic analysis of decentralised markets that did not rely on the auctioneer were thus surely correct, though it is less clear that Keynes was sufficiently aware of the alternative to have self- consciously rejected it.[8] The following passage, taken from the *Treatise on Money* (Keynes, 1930), is typical of several discussions there and in the *General Theory*, of the difficulties faced by agents in such markets when prices must change to keep them cleared:

Under a socialist system the money rate of efficiency earnings of the factors of production might suddenly be altered by *fiat*. Theoretically, I suppose it might change under a system of competitive individualism by an act of collective fore- sight on the part of entrepreneurs in anticipation of impending monetary changes, or by a *coup de main* on the part of trade unions . . . In existing cir- cumstances, however, the most usual and important occasion of change will be the action of entrepreneurs . . . in increasing or decreasing the volume of employment which they offer at the existing rates of remuneration . . . and so bring about a raising or a lowering of these rates. (1930, Vol. 1, p. 141)

1.5 INTERTEMPORAL COORDINATION

As Leijonhufvud was at pains to argue, what mattered for setting in motion cumulative fluctuations in expenditure and employment was not that prices should be rigid, but only that they should move sufficiently slowly to permit trading at non-market clearing prices to get under way. Indeed, as the passage quoted earlier makes clear, it was an essential characteristic of his analysis that the quantitative consequences of trading at false prices would arise from the very same dynamic processes that would drive variations in those prices. It was partly on this basis that Leijonhufvud argued that fixed-price IS–LM exercises not only seriously misrepresented the economics of Keynes but, more generally, were inadequate for analysing the behaviour of any market economy; but only partly. He also strongly criticised the appropriateness of the IS–LM model's treatment of output as consisting of a single good. The distinction between consumption and investment goods was, he suggested, crucial.[9]

Not only did a chronic inability of the price of capital goods to find and maintain its right level relative to that of current consumption lie at the heart of Keynes's explanation of the market economy's inability to maintain full employment, but that explanation was also basically correct. Any shock which required that this relative price should fall to re-equilibrate the system would initially create a shortfall of the nominal demand price of capital goods from their supply price, and set in motion a cumulative contraction of output. However, the required relative price adjustment could not necessarily be accomplished by a fall in money wages (even if these were capable of rapid adjustment) because this would also cause the money price of consumption goods to fall. What was needed was a fall in the rate of interest that would cause the current demand price of capital goods to rise. But, argued Leijonhufvud, 'Once the income-constrained process had been allowed to gather momentum . . . expectations would no longer be such as to sustain full employment even in conjunction with a "metastatically right" interest rate' (1968a, p. 340); and so, in his view:

> Keynes' diagnosis of the conditions leading to a downturn in activity focussed on the relation between the money prices of non-money assets [i.e., investment goods] and the money wage rate. If this relation was out of line, . . . he put the 'blame' on too low asset values as a rule, not on too high wages. The conclusion is that deflation will help *only if* it changes this relative price in the appropriate direction, i.e., *only if it cures the malady that underlies the emergence of excess supply of commodities in the first place*. (1968a, pp. 341–2)

And to repeat, in Leijonhufvud's interpretation of Keynes, that malady lay in a misaligned relative price of investment and consumption goods: with a concomitant failure of market mechanisms to coordinate the allocation of resources over time; and cumulative output fluctuations, driven by income-constrained dynamics, were the market economy's response to this failure. Obviously, a single good IS–LM model could not be used even to formulate this idea, let alone evaluate it.[10]

Now *Keynesian Economics and the Economics of Keynes* presented two challenges for its readers. Firstly, as a work in the history of economic thought, it repudiated IS–LM analysis as an interpretation of Keynes's *General Theory*, and proposed an alternative version of that book's central message. Secondly, as a contribution to economic theory, it proposed the abandonment of this same IS–LM model in favour of an approach which, being based on the analysis of trading at non-market clearing prices, reduced then standard microeconomics to a special and not very interesting case of an altogether broader framework. In short Leijonhufvud argued that macroeconomics had gone off on the wrong track because Keynes's interpreters had failed to understand him, that the perplexing gap between the macro and micro components of then contemporary economic theory referred to earlier in this chapter had been a direct result of this, and that the gap in question could not be bridged without fundamental revisions to both micro and macro theory as they then stood.

A full treatment of this extraordinarily ambitious book's significance for the development of economics would have to assess both the validity of its claims about the discipline's past, and the success of its proposals for the subject's future, and there is not space here to do both. The balance of this chapter will therefore deal only with the latter topic, and only certain aspects of it into the bargain.

1.6   MONETARISM

Coincidentally, the word 'monetarism' was introduced into the mainstream vocabulary of economics by Karl Brunner in (1968), the same year in which *On Keynesian Economics and the Economics of Keynes* was published, and ultimately it would be developments springing from this doctrine that would prevent Leijonhuvfud's ideas having their intended impact on the future course of economic theory. Monetarism was not new in 1968, of course.[11] On the contrary, the appearance in March of that same year of Friedman's American Economic Association (AEA) presidential address on 'The role of monetary policy' (of which more below) put in place the capstone of an intellectual edifice that had been under construction at least since the publication of his *Studies in the Quantity Theory of Money* in 1956.

As Leijonhufvud himself would later note: 'By the mid-sixties . . . macroeconomics was drawing most of its excitement from the challenge posed by . . . the "monetarist" or "new-quantity" theory of Friedman, Schwartz, Cagan, Brunner and Meltzer' (1976 [1981a], p. 316). Monetarism, however, was also an alternative and parallel expression of dissatisfaction with orthodox LS–LM macroeconomics to that represented by his own work; but where Leijonhufvud's research agenda centred on matters of economic theory, monetarism was more concerned with practical policy and the empirical evidence upon which it might be based. Initially too, these competing approaches emphasised different economic phenomena, income and employment fluctuations and inflation respectively, a factor which Harry Johnson would still argue as late as 1971 made monetarism inherently less interesting to mainstream economics.

But there was more to monetarism than the revival and refinement of the quantity theory of money as an explanation of inflation. Thomas Mayer organised his still definitive (1975 [1978]) survey of the doctrine around 12 defining characteristics, three of which are particularly noteworthy in the current context, namely: 'Belief in the inherent stability of the private sector . . . Irrelevance of allocative detail for the explanation of short-run changes in money income, [and] . . . Focus on the price level as a whole rather than on individual prices' (p. 2). In his contribution to the symposium that Mayer's paper inspired, Benjamin Friedman (1978, p. 96, fn. 3) noted in passing that the monetarist debate had not intersected with Clower and Leijonhufvud's work, and this is surely not surprising. Their emphasis on the importance of allocative detail and relative prices for understanding macroeconomic fluctuations, not to mention their insistence on the private sector's vulnerability to income-constrained dynamics that tended to amplify shocks, set their work far apart from that doctrine. Nor did it have any point of contact with the characteristic of monetarism that Mayer put at the very top of his list, namely the deployment of 'The quantity theory of money in the sense of the predominance of the impact of monetary factors on nominal income'.

As we have seen, Leijonhufvud was concerned with the logic of economic theory as it was then expounded, and as it appeared in Keynes's work; but at a time when 'positive economics' was popular and 'monetarism' seemed to be based on its precepts, many among his readers would be bound to judge his work not so much on the basis of its logical coherence and scholarly accuracy, as on its empirical relevance. His version of the *Economics of Keynes* was, however, firmly based on the presumption that the experience of the inter-war years in general, and of the United States in the 1930s in particular, had demonstrated that market economies were inherently unstable, and that it was the task of economic theory to discover just where their flaws lay. Hence, monetarism's assertion of the inherent stability of the private sector challenged not only IS–LM orthodoxy, but Leijonhufvud's work too, and it was supported by (among other evidence) a specific and detailed reinterpretation of the causes of the Great Depression in the United States.

The full impact on economics of Chapters 7–9 of Friedman and

Schwartz's (1963) *Monetary History of the United States*, which dealt with the 1930s, was slow to be felt.[12] Their immediate message about economic history was that the downturn with which the Depression had begun in 1929 had very likely been provoked by monetary tightening, and that the economy's subsequent catastrophic contraction had been caused, not as orthodoxy had it, by some exogenous collapse in the marginal efficiency of capital that monetary policy had been powerless to offset, but by colossal ineptitude on the part of the Federal Reserve. Leijonhufvud did in fact refer to the *Monetary History*'s diagnosis of the role of monetary contraction in bringing on the initial downturn in late 1929:

> Keynes [as author of the *Treatise on Money*] would have concurred with Friedman and Schwartz in all essentials of their critique of Federal Reserve policy in this period [the late 1920s] and in attributing the onset of the Great Depression to the period of tight money preceding the actual downturn in activity, although he would, as usual, have conducted the analysis in terms of interest rates and 'credit conditions' rather than the stock of money. (1968a, p. 286)

But he did not refer to what Friedman and Schwartz had to say about the Great Contraction itself in that book, nor to the broader implications of their reinterpretation of economic history for macroeconomic theory.[13]

Those implications were nevertheless of profound significance, for if the cause of the Great Contraction had been an avoidable monetary disturbance, did not that perhaps suggest that market economies which were not subject to such policy disturbances were well capable of coping with the allocation of resources over time and therefore inherently stable after all? If this was indeed the case, then the conventional interpretation of economic history that had motivated Leijonhufvud's work (and much else) was misguided, and though interesting as doctrinal history and economic theory, was it not also empirically irrelevant?

It was not until the early 1970s that these deeper implications of Friedman and Schwartz's work began to sink in among economists in general, and Leijonhufvud addressed them indirectly in his (1973 [1981a]) paper on 'Effective demand failures'. There he faced up to a weakness of his earlier work, namely that it seemed to make economic instability all too inevitable, and now declared that: 'the central issue of macroeconomics is – once again – the extent to which the economy, or at least its market sectors, may properly be regarded as a self-regulating system? How well, or badly, do its "automatic" mechanisms perform?' as a prelude to exploring the properties of the 'corridor of stability' within which various mechanisms that he had earlier ignored or downplayed might be at work. These included the capacity of inventories, not least inventories of money and financial assets, to interfere with the mechanics of income-constrained processes so as to dampen deviations from full employment caused by various shocks.

1.7 NEW CLASSICAL MICROFOUNDATIONS AND OCCAM'S RAZOR

Effective Demand Failures provoked little direct response.[14] By the mid-1970s, a new approach was beginning to take hold of the micro-foundations research agenda. Where Leijonhufvud's *Economics of Keynes* had investigated the non-Walrasian microeconomics of an economy that was presumed to be unstable, and had perhaps explained more instability than the world in fact displayed, New classical economics went to the opposite extreme. Building upon monetarism – indeed James Tobin (1981) would label it 'Monetarism Mark 2' – it investigated the macroeconomic properties of a system in which Walrasian micro-mechanisms were presumed always to work, and which could only be disturbed by arbitrary shocks administered by erratic monetary policy.

The rise to popularity of this approach has a number of explanations. First of all it had an element of empirical plausibility. Not only had Friedman and Schwartz reinterpreted the Great Depression as a consequence of monetary policy, but by the early 1970s memories of it were fading under the influence of a quarter-century of rather stable expansion at more or less full employment. And closely related to this, inflation, in Harry Johnson's (1971) judgement, the policy problem to whose analysis monetarism was in any event best adapted, was becoming a serious issue.

But these empirical issues were of secondary importance when compared to the influence of theoretical developments, particularly the discovery of the so-called 'expectations-augmented Phillips curve'. This was not an exclusively monetarist creation, for Edmund Phelps (1967) was its co-creator, but Friedman (1968) used it to help establish two quintessential monetarist propositions: namely, that the permanent inflation–unemployment trade-off with which exponents of IS–LM Keynesian economics were by that time routinely supplementing their analysis, was at best a short-term phenomenon, and that monetary policy's only long-term effects were on the inflation rate. In other hands, moreover, though curiously not in Friedman's own, the expectations-augmented curve began to fill the role of the 'missing equation' that monetarist analysis had long needed to allocate the quantity-theoretic effects of money growth on money income between its real-income and price-level components.

The rich literature that in the late 1960s examined potential microeconomic foundations for this relationships still awaits careful attention from historians of economic thought, but it should at least be noted here that

Leijonhuvfud's deployment of Armen Alchian's search theoretic analysis of non-Walrasian market processes was one candidate, although not the one that ultimately won out.[15] Instead Robert E. Lucas's (1972) thoroughly Walrasian aggregate supply curve interpretation of the curve, coupled with his application to it of John Muth's rational expectations concept, found broad acceptance; and this was quickly cemented not just by Lucas's own subsequent work (1976) on its application to econometric policy modelling, but also by that of Thomas J. Sargent (1973) on its implications for Friedman's natural unemployment rate concept, and of Sargent and Neil Wallace's (for example 1975) demonstration that it permitted monetarist scepticism about systematic monetary policy's ability to affect anything other than the inflation rate to be put on firm micro-theoretic foundations.

Citing subsequent papers by Lucas, Harry Johnson (1976 [1978]) explained why Leijonhuvfud's approach failed to catch on in the following terms: 'It is virtually impossible to find a simple and comprehensive mathematical device for converting a general equilibrium system of mathematically formulated relationships into a fruitful technique for the study of persistent "disequilibrium" and "market failure".' (p. 244), and he elaborated the point in a footnote: 'The essential problem is that it is virtually impossible to invent a plausible mechanism that leaves the economy in disequilibrium with unexploited possibilities for profits or increased labour incomes, and at the same time specifies exactly how the economy will respond to a change in profit or labour income opportunities' (p. 244, fn). Johnson's point was a sobering one, for it amounted to saying that to give up Walrasian foundations in order to study macroeconomic phenomena seemed also to require their abandonment when allocative issues were to be discussed, if the analytic consistency of economic theory was to be preserved, and that there was no workable alternative available to permit this shift.

The abandonment of Walrasian general equilibrium theory as a basis for the study of the economics of allocation was too large a sacrifice to contemplate, and perhaps the discipline might have chosen to live a little longer with what was by then an all too obvious inconsistency between its macro and micro branches, had not Lucas's work seemed to render this unnecessary. Here it was not so much its theoretically compelling treatment of information processing as an exercise in maximising behaviour that mattered as its extremely attractive capacity to reconcile the co-existence of fluctuations in quantities as well as prices with continuously clearing Walrasian markets.

In the conventional Keynesian economics that Leijonhufvud had attacked, quantities varied in response to demand shocks because prices did not vary at all, and in his version of the *Economics of Keynes*, they varied because prices did not vary instantaneously. But both approaches simply took it for granted that, if prices were instantaneously flexible, quantities would always remain at their full employment level. In Leijonhufvud's words: 'Perfect knowledge and absence of any costs connected with the act of changing price (or rate of output) would enable the traders in an atomistic market to detect and move instantaneously to the new price equilibrium following a disturbance' (1968, p. 69). Perfect knowledge was to him synonymous with the presence of a Walrasian auctioneer in the marketplace, and trading at false prices the inevitable consequence of his absence.

Lucas, on the other hand, kept the auctioneer in place but limited his activities. Specifically, he still let him set prices that would keep markets cleared but prevented him from informing agents about them. They had to estimate relative prices by applying knowledge of a true model of the economy in which they operated to information about the time series properties of the monetary disturbances to which it was subject (both of which they were assumed to have) and information about particular money prices culled from the markets in which they were sellers. Thus Lucas logically separated the phenomenon of limited information from the mechanics of price formation; and in so doing, he demonstrated that limited information problems that did not imply price stickiness were nevertheless sufficient to generate quantity variations even in the presence of complete price flexibility.

In short, Lucas showed that neither *Keynesian Economics* nor the *Economics of Keynes* was needed to explain what seemed to be the salient facts of macroeconomic experience, because the addition to a Walrasian general equilibrium model of the right assumptions about agents' limited information was sufficient to do so. Lucas's model, if it was to be taken seriously as an 'as if' representation of a real world in which there was no auctioneer, amounted to arguing that markets would be kept cleared, not just by the collective foresight of entrepreneurs acting in anticipation of impending monetary changes as Keynes (1930, p. 141) had suggested when stretching for an example, but also by those entrepreneurs' ability to take account of the errors into which imperfections in that foresight would collectively lead them. But far fetched though it was, even on an 'as if' basis, it implied nevertheless that a separate macroeconomics was logically unnecessary for the explanation of output and employment fluctuations, and that Walrasian microeconomics was sufficient as a basis for all economic theory. Economists in large numbers began to reach for Occam's razor, and both IS–LM-style *Keynesian Economics* and Leijonhufvud's *Economics of Keynes* were quickly cut adrift. In short, Walrasian economics seemed to have won the third and final battle with the Marshallian alternative.[16]

1.8 A POSTSCRIPT ON INFLATION AND DISEQUILIBRIUM

As a matter of logic, to show that it is not necessary to refer to a specific factor when explaining a phenomenon does not also demonstrate that factor's irrelevance, and as Harry Johnson (1965, p. 395) warned in his review of *The Monetary History of the United States* (Friedman and Schwartz 1963): 'Occam's Razor is a fine principle, but there is no need to cut the throat of empirical research with it.' Thus, though in the 1970s and 1980s it was very difficult to get serious attention paid to any analysis of output fluctuations that either relied on price stickiness and/or postulated information problems that did not square with the idea of rational expectations, Marshallian pragmatism turned out still to have some life left in it when it came to coping with the economics of inflation.

As we all know, it is very difficult to find a place for money in an economic model in which markets always clear, which is why work in the new classical tradition expended so much energy on 'cash-in-advance' constraints, and 'overlapping generations' models.[17] For many applications, perhaps this did not matter, but hardly surprisingly, investigations of the consequences of a falling value of money that began from premises that money had no serious work to do in the first place were hardly likely to find these to be important. The best that they could do to capture the idea that inflation was costly – and everyday experience demonstrated beyond any reasonable doubt that it was, extremely so – seemed to be to follow Friedman (1969) in deploying Patinkinesque formulations of the demand for money that relied on putting real balances in the utility function, or to revert to Baumol–Tobin-style models of transaction costs in asset markets; but these rather arbitrary fixes implied that the costs of inflation were merely a matter of 'shoe-leather', barely worth considering when weighted against likely unemployment costs of reducing it, as James Tobin (1972) was quick to point out.

The basic trouble here was that, in a Walrasian framework, the costs of inflation at best could be assessed on the assumptions that it was 'fully anticipated' and that markets for goods and services continued to clear. Because such an approach trivialised money in the first place, it also trivialised any disorder of the monetary system, inflation included. It is surely no accident that Leijonhufvud (1977a and 1977b [1981a]), a recent exponent of a Marshallian approach to microeconomics that left space for market disequilibrium, was quick to recognise these problems, and to propose an alternative line of attack. This started from an institutionalist vision of monetary exchange that encompassed its essential role in the workings of the market economy, and enabled him to organise ideas about how inflation not only undermined the ability of money prices to transmit information and incentives to agents, but also arbitrarily redistributed the property rights on whose security the very workings of voluntary exchange depend in the first place.

There is not space here to give Leijonhufvud's work on the costs of inflation the attention it warrants, but I suspect that a careful study of the subsequent literature on these issues, that finally led to policy-makers taking these costs seriously enough to begin to tackle inflation in the 1980s, will show that it had a seminal influence.[18] I also suspect that a comparison of Leijonhufvud's earlier work on the disequilibrium microeconomics of employment fluctuations with his later analysis of inflation's capacity to disrupt the workings of market mechanisms will reveal close analytic connections between them, though Leijonhufvud himself did not stress these connections. His 1981 paper (Leijonhufvud 1981a) on inflation started from institutions rather than micro-theory per se and when he developed its ideas further in his much underappreciated work with Daniel Heymann on *High Inflation* (1995), it was once more these factors, not to mention a great deal of empirical evidence about what actually happens in markets under such conditions; that took centre stage.

Recall, furthermore, Harry Johnson's Lucas-inspired objection quoted earlier to Leijonhufvud's disequilibrium dynamic reconstruction of the *Economics of Keynes*: 'it is virtually impossible to invent a plausible mechanism that leaves the economy in disequilibrium with unexploited possibilities for profits or increased labour incomes, and at the same time specifies how the economy will respond to a *change* in profit or labour opportunities'. Does not Leijonhufvud's subsequent work on inflation imply a response to this criticism along the following lines? 'Quite so: that is because once disequilibrium takes hold of a monetary economy, markets stop working. If we want a world to which the special case of Walrasian general equilibrium theory can usefully be applied, we had better have policies that prevent either deflationary or inflationary shocks big enough to bring about such a state of affairs'. Let me conclude by asking whether this would not be a very pragmatic, even Marshallian, comment on the limits to Walrasian theory's usefulness, and by expressing the hope that it might also meet the approval of the author of *On Keynesian Economics and the Economics of Keynes*.

NOTES

*   This chapter was presented at a conference in honour of Axel Leijonhufvud held at UCLA, 30–31 August 2006. Comments and helpful questions from Roger Farmer,

Peter Howitt, Pentti Kouri, Axel Leijonhufvud and Tom Sargent are gratefully acknowledged.

1. The publication of Alvin Hansen's *A Guide to Keynes* in 1954 was surely a critical step here. The book both symbolised and cemented the dominance of the IS–LM interpretation of Keynes in the standard undergraduate curriculum.
2. The story of general equilibrium theory's arrival in English language economics is complicated. Walras's *Elements* (1874) itself did not appear in translation until 1954 when William Jaffe's edition appeared. (It is perhaps relevant that, Jaffe held an appointment at Northwestern University, when Leijonhufvud was a graduate student there.) The main source of information about this body of theory available in English in the 1930s was the 1923 translation of Gustav Cassel's *Theory of Social Economy* (1903 [1923]), though Hicks seems to have read Pareto in the original Italian.
3. This history too is beyond this chapter's scope. I have discussed it at length in Laidler (1999).
4. And the fact that Hicks (1937) had a major role in its creation and popularisation makes it tempting to speculate that there was a micro general equilibrium influence at work there from the beginning. Even so, the immediate inspiration for Hick's creation of the famous diagram seems to have been his interactions with Roy Harrod and James Meade about the interpretation of the *General Theory*. On this see Warren Young (1987).
5. The contrast between Marshall's and Walras's approach to economics was much discussed in the 1950s and early 1960s, and I am far from sure that everyone who drew a line between the two did so in the same place. It would be interesting to investigate this matter further. It is also worth noting that partial equilibrium microeconomics retained a strong position in introductory textbooks long after intermediate and advanced microtheory had been taken over by the general equilibrium approach.
6. This entity seems to have got this name some time in the late 1960s, perhaps from Leijonhufvud himself. This author recalls Hirofumi Uzawa referring to the 'market secretary' at about this time.
7. Alchian and Allen were, like Leijonhufvud, members of the University of California, Los Angeles (UCLA) Economics Department. They were probably unwise to publish important and original analysis for the first time in an introductory textbook, if they wanted to maximise its exposure among their professional colleagues.
8. Among his predecessors, however, both Edgeworth and Walras had been very aware of the need to separate the process of price formation from that of exchange in general equilibrium systems which give rise to the need for this entity. On this matter, see Leijonhufvud (1968, section II–2, pp. 67–8.)
9. Leijonhufvud's concern with intertemporal allocation issues perhaps reflects his Swedish training, for it was Knut Wicksell's (1898) who had, not altogether intentionally, set in motion the shift of monetary economics' focus away from the influence of the quantity of money on the price level towards that of the rate of interest on saving and investment. He would later write a seminal study of the influence of these ideas on early macroeconomics, namely 'The Wicksell connection' (1981b). The possible Swedish origins of Leijonhufvud's 1960s insights into Keynes's role in developing the analysis of this problem is yet another important topic which lies beyond the scope of this chapter.
10. The reader will note that Leijonhufvud's interpretation of the essentially dynamic nature of Keynes's central message rests heavily on material that appears in Chapter 19 of the *General Theory* and plays little role elsewhere in the book. As he himself noted, however, though that message was about dynamics, 'Keynes' model was static' (to which this author would add, and was not badly summarised in the IS–LM framework either, which is why so many of the *General Theory*'s early readers found versions of it there; on this, see Laidler, 1999, Chapter 12).
11. Karl Brunner too was a member of the UCLA department in the 1960s, and it is therefore probably no accident that his version of monetarism paid more attention to the information problems that lay at the heart of monetary economics than did Friedman's (see, for example, Brunner and Meltzer, 1971). The history of the UCLA department's contributions to monetary economics during this period would make a fascinating study.

12. As Susan Howson has impressed upon me. Note also that we are now more conscious than were readers of the 1960s of the work of some of Friedman and Schwartz's predecessors, and it is hard now to appreciate just how radical it seemed at the time, and how strong was its impact. Lauchlin Currie's work, for example, had largely been forgotten, though he had published an article entitled 'The failure of monetary policy to prevent the depression of 1929–1932' in the *Journal of Political Economy* in 1934, surely a title that tells its own story. On the reaction of American economists to the Great Depression while it was under way, see Laidler (1999, Chapter 9).

13. He did refer briefly to these matters in later lectures given at the Institute for Economic Affairs in London in 1969 (see 1969 [1981a], p. 42).

14. Peter Howitt's (1978) paper was a notable exception. I am, however, relieved to be able to report that, along with *Information and Co-ordination* (Leijonhufvud 1981a) where it was reprinted, it is cited in some of my own subsequent discussions of money's 'buffer-stock' role (see Laidler 1984, 1987).

15. Such a study should begin with the famous 'Phelps volume' (Phelps et al. 1970). Phelps (1974) characterised the main purpose of Leijonhufvud's book as being to establish a connection to the *General Theory* for the literature in question, surely too narrow a characterisation of its significance.

16. As with Friedman and Schwartz (1963), it took some years for the full significance of Lucas's contribution to be fully appreciated. As we have seen, even so notable a contributor to the New classical literature as Robert J. Barro would later become was still publishing on the economics of fixed-price equilibrium models as late as 1976.

17. The cash-in-advance constraint was originated by Clower (1967), in order to highlight the ideas that, because, in a monetary economy, goods did not exchange for other goods, they were less liquid than money, and that this had consequences for the way in which markets function. These ideas are obviously closely related to those that inform Leijonhufvud's work, and it is therefore safe to say that the uses to which new classical economics put the cash-in-advance constraint were not among those that Clower had in mind.

18. For example, it is cited in Peter Howitt's now classic 1990 paper on the costs of inflation which played a crucial role in the debates that preceded Canada's adoption of inflation targets in 1991.

REFERENCES

Alchian, A. and W. Allen (1964), *University Economics*, Belmont, CA: Wadsworth.

Arrow, K. (1959), 'Towards a theory of price adjustement', in M. Abramowitz et al. (eds), *The Allocation of Economic Resources*, Stanford, CA: Stanford University Press.

Barro, R.J. and H.I. Grossman (1976), *Money, Employment and Inflation*, Cambridge: Cambridge University Press.

Benassy, J.-P. (1975), 'Non-Keynesian disequilibrium theory in a monetary economy', *Review of Economic Studies*, **43** (October), 503–23.

Brunner, K. (1968), 'The role of money and monetary policy', *Federal Reserve Bank of St. Louis Review*, **50** (July), 8–24.

Brunner, K. and A.H. Meltzer (1971), 'The uses of money: money in the theory of an exchange economy', *American Economic Review*, **61** (December), 784–805.

Cassel, G. (1903), *The Theory of Social Economy*, (2 vols), as translated. 1923, London: Jonathon Cape.

Clower, R.W. (1965), 'The Keynesian counter-revolution: a theoretical appraisal', in F.H. Hahn and F.R.P. Brechling (eds), *The Theory of Interest Rates*, London: Macmillan, for the I.E.A.

Clower, R.W. (1967), 'A reconsideration of the micro-foundations of monetary theory', *Western Economic Journal*, **6** (December), 1–8.

Currie, L. (1934), 'The failure of monetary policy to prevent the depression of 1929–32', *Journal of Political Economy*, **42** (April), 145–77.

Friedman, B. (1978), 'The theoretical nondebate about monetarism', in Mayer et al. (eds), *The Structure of Monetarism*, New York: Norton.

Friedman, M. (1953), 'The methodology of positive economics', in *Essays in Positive Economics*, Chicago, IL: University of Chicago Press.

Friedman, M. (ed.) (1956), *Studies in the Quantity Theory of Money*, Chicago, IL: University of Chicago Press.

Friedman, M. (1968), 'The role of monetary policy', *American Economic Review*, **58** (March), 1–17.

Friedman, M. (1969), 'The optimum quantity of money', in *The Optimum Quantity of Money*, London: Macmillan.

Friedman, M. and Schwartz, A.J. (1963), *A Monetary History of the United States 1867–1960*, Princeton, NJ: Princeton University Press for the NBER.

Hansen, A. (1954), *A Guide to Keynes*, New York: McGraw-Hill.

Heymann, D. and A. Leijonhufvud (1995), *High Inflation*, Oxford: Oxford University Press.

Hicks, J.R. (1937), 'Mr Keynes and the Classics: a suggested interpretation', *Econometrica*, **5** (April), 147–59.

Hicks, J.R. (1939), *Value and Capital*, Oxford: Clarendon Press.

Howitt, P.W. (1978), 'The limits to stability of full-employment equilibrium', *Scandinavian Journal of Economics*, **80** (September), 265–82.

Howitt, P.W. (1990), 'Zero inflation as a long-term target for monetary policy', in R.G. Lipsey (ed.), *Zero Inflation: The Goal of Price Stability*, Toronto: C.D. Howe Institute.

Johnson, E.S. and H.G. Johnson (1978), *The Shadow of Keynes*, Chicago, IL: University of Chicago Press.

Johnson, H.G. (1965), 'A quantity theorist's monetary history of the United States', *Economic Journal*, **75** (June), 388–96.

Johnson, H.G. (1971), 'The Keynesian revolution and the monetarist counter-revolution', reprinted in E.S. Johnson and H.G. Johnson (eds) (1978), *The Shadow of Keynes*, Chicago, IL: University of Chicago Press.

Johnson, H.G. (1976), 'Keynes' *General Theory:* revolution or war of independence?' reprinted in E.S. Johnson and H.G. Johnson (eds) (1978) *The Shadow of Keynes*, Chicago, IL: University of Chicago Press.

Keynes, J.M. (1930), *A Treatise on Money*, 2 vols, London: Macmillan.

Keynes, J.M. (1936), *The General Theory of Employment, Interest and Money*, London: Macmillan.

Laidler, D. (1974), 'Information, money and the macroeconomics of inflation', *Swedish Journal of Economics*, **76** (March), 26–41.

Laidler, D. (1984), 'The "buffer-stock" notion in monetary economics', *Economic Journal*, **94** (Conference Papers Supplement), 234–51.

Laidler, D. (1987), 'Taking money seriously', *Canadian Journal of Economics*, **21** (November), 253–79.

Laidler, D. (1999), *Fabricating the Keynesian Revolution*, Cambridge: Cambridge University Press.

Leijonhufvud, A. (1967), 'Keynes and the Keynesians, a suggested interpretation', reprinted in A. Leijonhufvud (1981a), *Information and Coordination*, Oxford: Oxford University Press.

Leijonhufvud, A. (1968), *On Keynesian Economics and the Economics of Keynes*, Oxford: Oxford University Press.

Leijonhufvud, A. (1969), 'Keynes and the Classics, First Lecture', reprinted in A. Leijonhufvud (1981a), *Information and Coordination*, Oxford: Oxford University Press.

Leijonhufvud, A. (1973), 'Effective demand failures', reprinted in A. Leijonhufvud (1981a), *Information and Coordination*, Oxford: Oxford University Press.

Leijonhufvud, A. (1976), 'Schools, "revolutions" and research programmes in economic theory', reprinted in A. Leijonhufvud (1981a), *Information and Coordination*, Oxford: Oxford University Press.

Leijonhufvud, A. (1977a), 'Costs and consequences of inflation', reprinted in A. Leijonhufvud (1981a)

Leijonhufvud, A. (1977b), 'Inflation and the economists', reprinted in A. Leijonhufvud (1981a).

Leijonhufvud, A. (1981a), *Information and Co-ordination*, Oxford: Oxford University Press.

Leijonhufvud, A. (1981b), 'The Wicksell connection: variations on a theme', in A. Leijonhufvud, *Information and Coordination*, Oxford: Oxford University Press.

Leijonhufvud, A. (2006), 'Keynes as a Marshallian', in R.E. Backhouse and B.W. Bateman (eds), *The Cambridge Companion to Keynes*, Cambridge: Cambridge University Press.

Lerner, A. (1944), *The Economics of Control*, New York: Macmillan.

Lucas, R.E., Jr (1972), 'Expectations and the neutrality of money', *Journal of Economic Theory*, **4**, 115–38.

Lucas, R.E., Jr (1976), 'Econometric policy evaluation', in Brunner K. and Meltzer A.H. (eds), *The Phillips Curve and the Labour Market*, Carnegie Rochester Conference Series, Vol. 1.

Malinvaud, E. (1977), *The Theory of Unemployment Reconsidered*, Oxford: Blackwell.

Mayer, T. (1975), 'The structure of monetarism', reprinted in Mayer et al. (1978), *The Structure of Monetarism*, New York: Norton.

Mayer, T. et al. (eds) (1978), *The Structure of Monetarism*, New York: Norton.

Mill, J.S. (1848), *Principles of Political Economy with Some of Their Applications to Social Philosophy*, reprinted in W.S. Ashley (ed.) (1909), London: Longman Green & Co.

Patinkin, D. (1956), *Money, Interest and Prices: An Integration of Monetary and Value Theory*, New York: Row Peterson; 2nd edn (1965), New York: Harper & Row.

Phelps, E.S. (1967), 'Phillips curves, expectations of inflation, and optimal unemployment over time', *Economica*, NS **34**, (August), 254–81.

Phelps, E.S. (1974), *Inflation Policy and Unemployment Theory*, New York: Norton.

Phelps, E.S. et al. (1970), *The Microeconomic foundations of Employment and Inflation Theory*, New York: Macmillan.

Samuelson, P.A. (1955), *Economics: An Introductory Analysis*, 3rd edn., New York: McGraw-Hill.

Sargent T.J. (1973), 'Rational expectations, the real rate of interest and the natural rate of unemployment', *Brookings Papers on Economic Activity*, **2**, 429–72.

Sargent, T.J. and N. Wallace (1975), 'Rational expectations, the optimal monetary instrument and the optimal money supply rule', *Journal of Political Economy*, **83** (April), 241–54.

Solow, R.M. (1965), 'Economic growth and residential housing', in M.D. Ketchum and L.T. Kendall (eds), *Readings in Financial Institutions*, New York: Houghton Mifflin.
Tobin, J. (1972), 'Inflation and unemployment', *American Economic Review*, **62** (March), 1–18.
Tobin, J. (1981), 'The monetarist counter-revolution today: an appraisal', *Economic Journal*, **91** (March), 29–42.
Walras, L. (1874), *Elements of Pure Economics*, trans W. Jaffe (1954), Homewood, IL: Richard Irwin.
Wicksell, K. (1898), *Interest and Prices*, trans Richard Kahn (1936), London: Macmillan, for the Royal Economic Society.
Young, W. (1987), *Interpreting Mr. Keynes: The IS–LM Enigma*, Cambridge: Polity Press.

2. Old-Keynesian economics

Roger E.A. Farmer*

2.1 KEYNES AND THE KEYNESIANS

In his (1966) book, *On Keynesian Economics and the Economics of Keynes,* Axel Leijonhufvud made the distinction between the economics of the *General Theory* (Keynes, 1936) and the interpretation of Keynesian economics by Hicks and Hansen that was incorporated into the IS–LM model and that forms the basis for new-Keynesian economics. In that book, he pointed out that although the new-Keynesians give a central role to the assumption of sticky prices, the sticky-price assumption is a part of the mythology of Keynesian economics that is inessential to the main themes of the *General Theory*. In this chapter I will sketch an alternative microfoundation to Keynesian economics that formalizes this argument by providing a microfoundation that does not rely on sticky prices. I call this alternative microfoundation, old-Keynesian economics.

It is fitting that this chapter should appear in a volume in honor of Axel Leijonhufvud since the ideas I will describe owe much to his influence. Although Axel's thesis was written at Northwestern University, his work on Keynes came to fruition at the University of California, Los Angeles UCLA, the location of his first academic appointment. In the 1960s, UCLA had developed a healthy tradition of tolerance for non-mainstream ideas and, as the beneficiary of that same atmosphere of tolerance, it is a privilege to be able to use this occasion to acknowledge the debt that I owe to Axel as both a mentor and a friend.

In the following paragraphs, I will describe a plan to embed a version of search theory into a general equilibrium model in a way that provides a microfoundation to the economics of the *General Theory*. Since UCLA has some claim to be the birthplace of search theory (with the work of Armen Alchian, 1970 and John McCall, 1970), this project is the continuation of a rich UCLA tradition in more ways than one.

Whereas Keynes argued that the general level of economic activity is determined in equilibrium by aggregate demand, this idea is not present in new-Keynesian economics which views unemployment as a short-run phenomenon that arises when prices are temporarily away from their

long-run equilibrium levels. Since the appearance of the work of Edmund
Phelps (1970) and Milton Friedman (1968), the concept of demand
failure as a purely temporary phenomenon has been enshrined in the
concept of the natural rate of unemployment. Although the natural rate
hypothesis has become a central part of all of modern macroeconomics
it is not a component of the theory I will develop here. As a consequence
the welfare and policy implications of old- and new-Keynesian economics are very different.

I begin, in section 2.2, by sketching a simple one-period model that captures the essence of my argument. The idea is to model the process of
moving workers from unemployment to employment with a neoclassical
search technology of the kind introduced to the literature by Phelps (1968).
I will argue that this technology cannot easily be decentralized because
moral hazard prevents the creation of markets for the search inputs.
Instead, I will introduce a market in which workers post wages in advance
and I will assume that all workers post the same wage. This leads to a model
with one less equation than unknown since the two markets for search
inputs must be cleared by a single price. This underdetermined labor
market is a perfect match for a Keynesian theory of demand determination
in which the quantity of output produced and the volume of labor
employed is determined by aggregate demand. I call this a demand constrained equilibrium. In section 2.3 I provide a sketch of how the equilibrium concept of a demand-constrained equilibrium can be extended to a
full-blown dynamic stochastic general equilibrium model.

2.2   A ONE-PERIOD MODEL

This section describes my main idea. Its purpose is to lay out a simple
environment in which one can compare the socially efficient allocation of
resources to the allocation that occurs in a decentralized equilibrium.
In more sophisticated versions of the theory, described in section 2.3, I
introduce investment as a key determinant of demand. In the current
section, all economic activity takes place in a single period. In this one-
period model, government purchases take the place of investment spending as an exogenous determinant of the level of economic activity.
Although this environment abstracts from many important elements of
the real world, it is rich enough to capture the basic idea: that a modified
search-theoretic model leads to inefficient equilibria because of a missing
market.

The Economic Environment

Consider a one-period model with a large number of workers and firms. Firms produce output using a constant-returns-to-scale technology in which labor is the sole input. Labor is transferred from households to firms using a constant-returns matching technology with unemployment and vacancies as inputs.

There is a unit measure of entrepreneurs, each of whom runs a firm. Each entrepreneur has access to a technology that produces output Y from labor input L:

$$Y = AL \qquad (2.1)$$

where $A > 0$ is the marginal product of an extra unit of labor input. Entrepreneurs are identical and, the symbols Y and L refer interchangeably to average aggregate variables and to individual variables. The utility of the entrepreneur is captured by a continuous increasing concave function $J^E(X^E)$, where:

$$X^E = C^E - V \qquad (2.2)$$

is the sum of the entrepreneur's consumption C^E, and V measures the disutility of posting vacancies. The cost of vacancies is measured in consumption units.

In addition to the mass of entrepreneurs there is a continuum of workers with preferences $J^W(C^W)$ where J^W is a concave increasing utility function and C^W is workers' consumption. Each worker supplies one unit of search effort inelastically to a constant-returns-to-scale matching technology:

$$m = BU^\theta V^{1-\theta} \qquad (2.3)$$

where m is the measure of workers that find jobs when U unemployed workers search for jobs and V vacancies are posted by entrepreneurs. B is a scaling parameter. Since $U = 1$ (all workers are initially unemployed) this reduces to the expression:

$$m = BV^{1-\theta}. \qquad (2.4)$$

In a dynamic model, employment will appear as a state variable in a programming problem since it takes time to recruit new workers. In this chapter, I abstract from this aspect of labor market dynamics by assuming that all workers must be recruited in the current period. This assumption

implies that employment, equal to the number of matches, is represented
by the equation:

$$L = m. \tag{2.5}$$

This completes a description of preferences and technology. Next I turn
to the problem solved by a benevolent social planner whose goal is to maximize a weighted sum of the utilities of the two agents.

The Social Planning Problem

The social planner faces the following problem:

$$\max \lambda J^W(C^W) + (1 - \lambda)J^E(C^E - V) \tag{2.6}$$

such that:

$$L = BV^{1-\theta} \tag{2.7}$$
$$C^E + C^W \leq AL. \tag{2.8}$$

This problem has the following solution for the optimal quantity of
employment, L^*:

$$L^* = B^{\frac{1}{\theta}}(A(1 - \theta))^{\frac{1-\theta}{\theta}}. \tag{2.9}$$

Since workers do not receive disutility from work, all unemployed
workers search all of the time. Entrepreneurs do not like to search and
optimal employment balances the disutility of search against increased
output from greater employment.

In the planning optimum, employment depends on three parameters, A, B
and θ. A measures the productivity of the production technology and B the
productivity of the search technology. If either of these parameters increases,
search effort becomes more productive and the social planner will choose
more of it. The effect of an increase in θ is ambiguous and may cause an
increase or a decrease in search effort depending on the values of the other
parameters. The allocation of output between workers and entrepreneurs is
determined by the parameter λ which is a number between 0 and 1 that represents the weight placed by the planner on the worker in social utility.

A Decentralized Solution

In order to discuss the role of government policy, in this section I will add
a government to the model that taxes output with a proportional tax τ and

purchases commodities G. I will assume that commodities purchased by government do not directly yield utility, in order to make the point that apparently socially inefficient government expenditure can be Pareto improving.

Since the environment I have described satisfies all the desiderata of the welfare theorems, standard results from general equilibrium theory imply that the social planning solution could be decentralized by a complete set of competitive markets. To achieve this decentralization one would need to treat the matching technology in the same way as the production function and to assume the existence of a set of profit-maximizing employment agencies. Each agency would purchase, from workers, the exclusive right to be matched with an entrepreneur and it would purchase, from entrepreneurs, the exclusive right to be matched with a worker. There are moral hazard reasons why competitive markets for these trades do not exist since it is difficult to monitor the exclusivity of the contract. In the presence of such markets one might expect an unemployed worker to cheat and sign employment contracts with multiple agencies. On being matched, the worker would have an incentive to claim incompatibility with the employer and to continue to be paid for further search activity.

Consider instead the following decentralized environment which is based on the idea of a competitive search equilibrium due to Espen Moen (1997). In this environment, firms post wages in advance and, in equilibrium, all firms post the same wage. Firms and workers meet randomly and on meeting, the entrepreneur and worker form a matched pair and produce output using the technology described by equation (2.1). The worker receives wage income from the match and the entrepreneur receives profit Π where:

$$\Pi = AL - \omega L. \tag{2.10}$$

The worker and the firm take the numbers p^u and p^v as given. p^u is the probability a worker receives a job and p^v is the measure of workers hired by an entrepreneur that posts one vacancy. Later, I will describe how these variables are determined in equilibrium. Each worker secures a job with probability p^u. The worker is paid an after-tax wage which he spends on consumption C^W. Each entrepreneur posts V vacancies and hires a measure of workers of size Vp^v. Each vacancy posted yields one unit of disutility.

The worker's problem is trivial since he needs only to search for a job and to spend his after-tax income on consumption. The utility-maximizing entrepreneur will choose V, L and C^E to solve the problem:

$$\max J^E(C^E - V) \tag{2.11}$$

such that:

$$C^E \leq \Pi(1 - \tau) \tag{2.12}$$

$$\Pi = AL - \omega L \tag{2.13}$$

$$L = p^v V \tag{2.14}$$

where the rate of tax on profit is the same as the rate on labor income. The solution to the entrepreneur's problem is given by the correspondence:

$$V = \begin{cases} \infty & \text{if} \quad (A - \omega)p^v(1 - \tau) > 1 \\ [0,\infty] & \text{if} \quad (A - \omega)p^v(1 - \tau) = 1 \\ 0 & \text{if} \quad (A - \omega)p^v(1 - \tau) < 1. \end{cases} \tag{2.15}$$

Government chooses a tax rate τ and a level of purchases G.

The Equilibrium Concept

This section introduces my equilibrium concept. To describe it, I have appropriated a term, 'demand constrained equilibrium', that was used in a literature on general equilibrium with fixed prices that evolved in the 1970s from the work of Jean Pascal Benassy (1975), Jacques Dreze (1975) and Edmond Malinvaud (1977). Although fixed-price models with rationing of the kind studied by these authors are sometimes called demand constrained equilibria, that is not what I mean here. Instead I will use the term to refer to a competitive search model that is closed with a materials balance condition. The common heritage of both usages of demand constrained equilibrium is the idea of effective demand from Keynes's *General Theory*.

Definition 1 (Demand constrained equilibrium). For any given τ and G a demand constrained equilibrium (DCE) is a real wage ω, an allocation $\{C^W, C^E, V, L\}$ and a pair of matching probabilities, p^u and p^v, with the following properties:

1. Feasibility:

$$C^E + C^W \leq (1 - \tau)AL \tag{2.16}$$

$$L \leq BV^{1-\theta} \tag{2.17}$$

$$G \leq \tau AL. \tag{2.18}$$

2. Consistency with optimal choice:

$$V = \begin{cases} \infty & \text{if} & (A - \omega)p^v(1 - \tau) > 1 \\ [0,\infty] & \text{if} & (A - \omega)p^v(1 - \tau) = 1 \\ 0 & \text{if} & (A - \omega)p^v(1 - \tau) < 1. \end{cases} \qquad (2.19)$$

3. Consistency of matching probabilities:

$$p^u = L \qquad (2.20)$$

$$p^v = \frac{L}{V}. \qquad (2.21)$$

Property 3 needs some explanation. The probability of contacting a partner is determined by how many others are searching. Let $\overline{V}$ represent the average number of vacancies posted by entrepreneurs and let $\overline{L}$ represent the aggregate number of successful matches (equal to aggregate employment). The probability that a worker finds a job, and the measure of workers hired by an entrepreneur who posts V vacancies, are determined by the conditions:

$$p^u = \overline{L}, \qquad p^v = \frac{\overline{L}}{\overline{V}}. \qquad (2.22)$$

In a symmetric equilibrium, the search intensities must be the same across agents and hence:

$$V = \overline{V}, \; L = \overline{L}. \qquad (2.23)$$

The Keynesian Cross

In modern DSGE models the government is assumed to choose expenditure and taxes subject to a constraint. Models that incorporate a constraint of this kind were dubbed Ricardian by Robert Barro (1974). But in models with multiple equilibria there is no reason to impose a government budget constraint and Eric Leeper (1991), discussing models of monetary and fiscal policy, has argued that one should allow government to choose both taxes and expenditure and that this choice selects an equilibrium. He calls a policy in which the government choose both taxes and expenditure an 'active fiscal regime'. The modified-search model of the labor market is one with multiple equilibria and hence, one can close the model in the way advocated by Leeper.

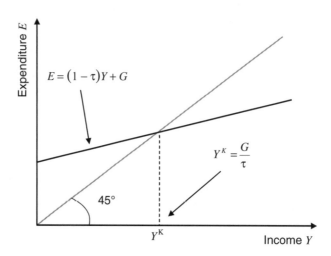

Figure 2.1   The Keynesian cross

In textbook descriptions of simple Keynesian models, equilibrium is typically described by the diagram pictured in Figure 2.1. The 45 degree line in this diagram is a supply curve, representing the assumption that whatever is demanded will be supplied. The second upward sloping line is a Keynesian demand curve obtained by combining the equations:

$$Y = C + G, \tag{2.24}$$

$$C = (1 - \tau)\, Y, \tag{2.25}$$

to yield the equilibrium condition:

$$Y = \frac{G}{\tau}. \tag{2.26}$$

It is precisely this pair of equations that determine equilibrium output in the current model.

The central difficulty faced by old-Keynesian economics was that the Keynesian model as expounded by John Hicks and Alvin Hansen had no microfoundation. They could not answer the question: Why doesn't the real wage fall to establish equilibrium in the labor market? The answer I propose to that question is that there is a missing market. A complete decentralization of the search process as a competitive equilibrium would require a market for vacancies and a separate market for the search time of entrepreneurs. In practice there is a single competitive search market in which competition forces all firms to post the same wage.

Determining the Equilibrium Wage

Standard competitive theory does not have a good explanation of the process by which an equilibrium is established. Nor do I. Instead, I will argue that equilibrium in the labor market is determined by the aggregate demand for commodities and that the equilibrium wage will adjust to the point where neither firms nor workers have an incentive to vary their search intensities.

Replacing the equilibrium values of the probabilities from equations (2.20) and (2.21) into the first-order condition, Equation (2.19), leads to the following equation:

$$(A - \omega) \frac{L}{V} (1 - \tau) = 1. \tag{2.27}$$

Combining equation (2.27) with the matching function leads to the expression:

$$L = B^{\frac{1}{\theta}} [(A - \omega)(1 - \tau)]^{\frac{1-\theta}{\theta}}. \tag{2.28}$$

Equation (2.28), graphed in Figure 2.2 for the case of $\theta = 1/2$, defines a relationship between the real wage and employment similar to the labor demand curve in a Walrasian model. Unlike the Walrasian case, in a demand constrained equilibrium there does not exist a corresponding labor supply curve to determine price and quantity simultaneously. Instead, equilibrium employment is determined by aggregate materials balance and equation (2.28) determines the wage at which no entrepreneur has the incentive to offer employment at a higher or a lower wage.

To summarize, the modified-search model of the labor market provides a microfoundation to the Keynesian cross that characterized textbook descriptions of Keynesian economics in the 1960s. Income, equal to output, is demand determined and is equal to a multiple of exogenous expenditure. Since I have abstracted in the one-period model from saving and investment, aggregate expenditure is determined by government purchases and output is determined as a multiple of government purchases where the multiplier is the inverse of the tax rate.

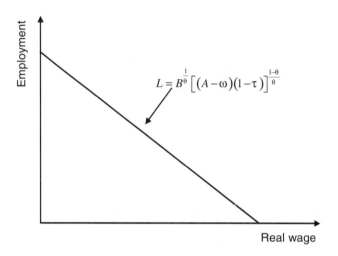

Figure 2.2   The wage function

Fiscal Policy and Social Welfare

Contrast the DCE allocation with the socially efficient level of employment, given by the expression:

$$L^* = B^{\frac{1}{\theta}}(A(1-\theta))^{\frac{1-\theta}{\theta}}. \tag{2.29}$$

Since the welfare of an entrepreneur is linear in the sum of consumption
and vacancies, the social planner operates by first maximizing the sum:

$$\Omega = AL - V \tag{2.30}$$

which I will refer to as social utility. By replacing V with the expression
$V = (\frac{L}{B})^{\frac{1}{1-\theta}}$ from the matching function, this expression can be written as a
function of L:

$$\Omega = AL - \left(\frac{L}{B}\right)^{\frac{1}{1-\theta}}. \tag{2.31}$$

Given the maximal value of Ω, the social planner distributes consumption across entrepreneurs and workers to maximize a weighted sum of
individual utilities. Notice that the maximization of social utility leads to
the expression given in equation (2.29).

   In a demand constrained equilibrium, employment (the superscript K is
for Keynes) is given by the expression:

$$L^K = \frac{G}{A\tau} \tag{2.32}$$

and social utility by:

$$\Omega = (1 - \tau)AL - \left(\frac{L}{B}\right)^{\frac{1}{1-\theta}} \equiv f(\tau). \tag{2.33}$$

Comparing equation (2.33) with (2.31) it follows that for any positive tax rate, social utility, given L, will be lower in any demand constrained equilibrium with positive taxes, reflecting the fact that government purchases are assumed to yield no utility. The set of possible demand constrained equilibria is depicted in Figure 2.3. The curves $f(\tau_1)$ and $f(\tau_2)$ represent attainable levels of adjusted social utility (the right side of equation 2.33) for different tax rates. The curve $f(0)$ is the limit of these curves as $\tau \to 0$.

For a given tax rate, employment increases as government purchases increase or as the tax rate decreases. For example, holding government purchases fixed at G_1 the vertical lines at L_1^K and L_2^K represent the equilibrium values of employment for tax rates τ_1 and τ_2 where $\tau_2 > \tau_1$. Lowering taxes unambiguously increases employment as the locus $f(\tau)$ shifts up and to the right and the vertical line $G/A\tau$ shifts right. The Keynesian equilibrium is at the intersection of these two loci.

But although lowering taxes and increasing government purchases increases employment these policies do not unambiguously increase welfare. If G/τ is too large, the Keynesian equilibrium will occur to the right of the maximum of the locus $f(\tau)$. At a point like this there is overemployment as the economy devotes too many resources to the activity of job search.

The maximum of the locus $f(0)$ represents the planning optimum. This value of welfare can be approached but never reached in a Keynesian equilibrium. Consider sequences of policies, indexed by s, in which $\tau(s) \to 0$, $G(s) \to 0$ and $G/A\tau = L^*$. Policies in this class will converge to a point where welfare is equal to the optimal value Ω^*, although in practice they may be hard to attain since small mistakes in correctly setting G or τ will lead to large mistakes in Ω. This argument suggests that there is a trade-off between distortions and stability. Reducing taxes lowers distortions but when τ and G are very small, small fluctuations in G will cause large fluctuations in equilibrium welfare.

2.3   AN INTERTEMPORAL MODEL

My purpose in this section is to provide a brief sketch of how one might develop the static model, described above, into a full-blown dynamic

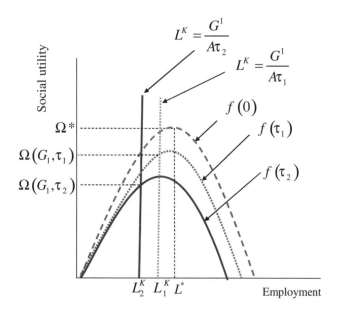

Figure 2.3   Welfare properties of Keynesian equilibrium

stochastic general equilibrium model. The work I will describe is in progress and will be reported in more detail elsewhere. There are neverthe-less several important details of the generalization that are worth describing and also some preliminary results that may be of interest.

The equilibrium I will use is a generalization of the static concept of demand constrained equilibrium. Since the factor markets are incomplete, I will close the model by assuming that investment expenditure depends on the self-fulfilling beliefs of entrepreneurs. The result is a model with multiple stationary equilibria, indexed by beliefs.

Recursive Utility and the Real Interest Rate

The conventional approach to dynamic general equilibrium posits the existence of a representative agent with time additively separable preferences. This approach restricts the long-run real interest rate to equal a parametrically determined rate of time preference and it is too restrictive for my purposes. Since I will be concerned with the role of fiscal policy I will need to describe a model in which aggregate expenditure is a function of the real

interest rate. If this is fixed by the time preference rate, government purchases will 'crowd out' private consumption and have no effect on equilibrium employment in the long run. For this reason, I chose to model
preferences with a recursive utility function of the kind studied by Uzawa
(1968), Lucas and Stokey and Epstein and Hynes (1983) and adapted by
Farmer and Lahiri (2005) to allow for balanced growth.

Recursive utility functions allow the long-run real rate of interest to
depend on consumption sequences. An alternative model with this property is a version of the overlapping generations model with long-lived
agents. I will not follow this approach here since empirically plausible versions of the overlapping generations model are more complicated than the
recursive representative agent approach.

Utility is defined by the equation:

$$J_t = A_t \sum_{k=t}^{\infty} E_1 \left[-\rho_t^k \left(\frac{A_k}{C_k} \right)^{\eta} \right] \tag{2.34}$$

Where:

$$\rho_t^t = 1 \tag{2.35}$$

$$\rho_t^k = \beta^{k-t} \prod_{s=t+1}^{k} \left(\frac{A_s}{A_{s-1}} \right) \left(\frac{A_{s-1}}{C_{s-1}} \right)^{\eta}, k > t. \tag{2.36}$$

The term A_t is an exogenous trend that grows at the rate of growth of the
economy and β and η are parameters. These preferences allow the representative agent's discount rate to depend on consumption relative to a
growing trend. The inclusion of a trend in preferences is necessary for this
representation to be consistent with balanced growth and it could potentially arise from a more fundamental assumption in which one assumes a
home production sector (as in Benhabib, et al., 1991) where home productivity grows at the same rate as productivity in the market sector.

Some Details of the Model

The representative agent is situated in a relatively standard one-sector
growth model with the additional twist that there is a matching technology
for moving labor from households to firms. This technology implies that
labor in place at firms in period t is given by the expression:

$$L_t = L_{t-1}(1 - s) + B(1 - L_t)^{\theta} V_t^{1-\theta} \tag{2.37}$$

where s represents exogenous separations, the second expression on the right-
hand side of equation (2.37) represents matches at date t and $1 - L_t$ is the
fraction of the labor force unemployed. The timing of the matching function

is chosen to enable demand shocks to influence output contemporaneously – that is, workers can produce in the period in which they are employed.

Output is produced with the technology:

$$Y_t = K_t^\alpha (A_t X_t)^{1-\alpha} \tag{2.38}$$

where X_t is labor used in productive activity, and it is related to L_t (total labor in place at the firm) and V_t (labor used in recruiting) by the expression:

$$V_t + X_t = L_t. \tag{2.39}$$

Other elements of the model are standard. The representative agent inelastically supplies a unit measure of labor to the market and at any given date U_t units of labor are unemployed and L_t are employed where $U_t = 1 - L_t$.

I will assume that agents are able to trade a complete set of contingent claims and that fundamental uncertainty is indexed by histories of events that I will denote σ^t. Thus, σ^t is a list of everything relevant to the economy that occurred up to and including date t. The agent faces a sequence of real wages and interest rates and chooses consumption sequences to maximize expected utility subject to a sequence of budget constraints:

$$K_{t+1} = K_t(1 - \delta) + \omega_t L_t + \Pi_t - C_t \tag{2.40}$$

$$\lim_{T \to \infty} Q_1^T(\sigma^T) K_{T+1}(\sigma^T) \geq 0 \tag{2.41}$$

where Π_t is profit, ω_t is the real wage and $Q_1^T(\sigma^T)$ is the present value price of capital at date T in event history σ^T.

A Definition of Equilibrium

The following definition is a sketch of how the DCE concept can be extended to a DSGE model. Let $I_t \equiv Y_t - C_t$.

Definition 2 For a given sequence $\{I_t\}$ a demand constrained equilibrium (DCE) is a 4-tuple of quantity sequences $\{C_t(\sigma^t), V_t(\sigma^t), L_t(\sigma_t), K_{t+1}(\sigma^t)\}$ (as functions of event histories), a sequence of matching probabilities $\{p^v(\sigma^t)\}$, a sequence of rental rates and wage rates $\{q_t(\sigma^t), \omega(\sigma^t)\}$, and a sequence of utility levels and profits $\{J(\sigma^t), \Pi(\sigma^t)\}$, with the following properties:

1. Taking as given the sequences of rental rates, wage rates and matching probabilities the quantity sequences maximize the expected net present value of the firm.

2. Taking as given the sequences of rental rates and wage rates and the profit sequence the quantity sequences maximize the expected utility of the households.

3. The matching probabilities are determined in equilibrium by equality of average and agent specific unemployment and vacancy rates and the demands and supplies for all commodities are equal.

Comparing an Equilibrium with a Planning Optimum

Given the model outline sketched above one can show that, given certain bounds on investment sequences, there exists a different demand constrained equilibrium for every stationary investment sequence. One can also establish the existence of a unique balanced growth path that characterizes a stationary planning optimum. Both concepts are characterized by the following set of seven equations in the eight variables j_t, c_t, k_t, y_t, i_t, L_t, X_t and V_t. Lower-case letters represent the ratio of variables to the trend growth path and $\gamma = \frac{A_t}{A_{t-1}}$ is the trend growth factor:

$$j_t = E_t \left\{ (-1 + \beta \gamma j_{t+1}) \frac{1}{c_t^\eta} \right\} \tag{2.42}$$

$$k_{t+1} = \frac{1-\delta}{\gamma} k_t + \frac{1}{\gamma} y_t - \frac{1}{\gamma} c_t \tag{2.43}$$

$$y_t = k_t^\alpha (X_t)^{1-\alpha} \tag{2.44}$$

$$y_t = i_t + c_t \tag{2.45}$$

$$X_t = L_t - V_t \tag{2.46}$$

$$L_t = (1-s)L_{t-1} + B(1-L_t)^\theta V_t^{1-\theta} \tag{2.47}$$

$$\frac{1}{c_t} = E_t \left\{ \left(\frac{1}{c_t} \right)^\eta \left(\frac{j_{t+1}}{j_t} \right) \frac{\beta}{c_{t+1}} \left(1 - \delta + \frac{y_{t+1}}{k_{t+1}} \right) \right\}. \tag{2.48}$$

A social planning optimum is defined by the previous seven equations and the additional condition:

$$\frac{1}{c_t} \left[\frac{(1-\alpha)y_t}{X_t} g_1 \left(L_t, L_{t-1} \right) + \right. \tag{2.49}$$

$$\left. E_t \left\{ \left(\frac{1}{c_t} \right)^\eta \left(\frac{j_{t+1}}{j_t} \right) \frac{\gamma \beta}{c_{t+1}} \frac{(1-\alpha)y_{t+1}}{X_{t+1}} g_2 \left(L_{t+1}, L_t \right) \right\} \right] = 0.$$

where $g(L_t, L_{t-1})$ is a function that describes the relationship between X_t (labor used to produce output) and the stocks of labor at the firm at dates

t and $t - 1$. One can show that a demand constrained equilibrium is determined by the same seven equations (2.42)–(2.48) but the system is closed by the assumption that investment follows the following exogenous stochastic process:

$$i_t = i_{t-1}^{\chi} e_t \qquad (2.50)$$

where χ is the parameter that measures persistence of the exogenous investment sequence and e_t is a stochastic innovation to beliefs.

It is worth pausing at this point to draw attention to equation (2.50) since it is the main feature that makes this a model of old-Keynesian economics. The term i_t is defined as the ratio of investment to a growing trend and this equation states that investment evolves exogenously with no regard for expected future profits. It is precisely this idea which I take to be central to the *General Theory* and which has disappeared from much of modern macroeconomics. Although my own previous work with Jess Benhabib (Benhabib and Farmer 1994) and Jang-Ting Guo (Farmer and Guo, 1994) went part way to rehabilitating the Keynesian idea that investment is driven by the 'animal spirits' of market participants in that work we only considered a model with a unique steady state. The current proposal goes far beyond the previous literature since I am proposing to allow the steady state of the economy itself to be influenced by beliefs. As in my previous work, all of these belief-driven equilibria are fully rational and leave no room for arbitrage opportunities or for mistaken expectations.

To explain the behavior of prices and matching probabilities in a belief-driven equilibrium one can derive a separate set of equations that describes how the rental rate q_t, the real wage rate ω_t and the match probability p_t^y depend on the state. The real wage, for example, follows the process:

$$\omega_t = (1 - \alpha)\frac{y_t}{X_t}\left(1 - \frac{1}{p_t^y}\right) + E_t\left\{\gamma Q_t^{t+1}(1 - \alpha)\frac{y_{t+1}}{X_{t+1}}\frac{(1-s)}{p_{t+1}^y}\right\} = 0 \quad (2.51)$$

Where

$$p_t^y = \frac{L_t - (1-s)L_{t-1}}{L_t - X_t}. \qquad (2.52)$$

Some Preliminary Results

As a preliminary check on the chances of this model to fit data I simulated a demand constrained equilibrium for an investment sequence calibrated fit to the properties of time series data; for this purpose I chose the shock to have a standard deviation of 0.04 and the autocorrelation parameter to equal 0.5. Figure 2.4 compares the properties of a single simulated data

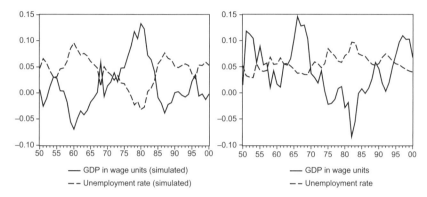

Figure 2.4   GDP and unemployment

series (left panel) with the US data (right panel) for GDP and unemployment and Figure 2.5 does the same for GDP, investment and consumption. In all cases the data were detrended in the manner described in section 2.4.

The exercise that I carried out to simulate these data series was similar to that which characterizes many real business cycle papers. But the shock that is driving the model is entirely driven by demand. Of course there are many features of this explanation still to be ironed out. I have not provided data on productivity or real wages although my preliminary investigations suggest that these series too will have approximately the right properties. Although the model does not have a total factor productivity (TFP) shock, an econometrician who estimates a standard Cobb–Douglas production function has a mis-specified model since the variable X_t that enters the production function differs from total employment L_t by the labor V_t used in recruiting. Since V_t is procyclical, it will appear in these data that output is driven by TFP.

An important question to which this model provides a very different answer from standard models concerns the welfare cost of business cycles. Figure 2.6 plots the consumption series against the social planning optimum. Since all uncertainty (in this simulation) arises from the animal spirits of investors, the social planner can, and will, choose a constant (detrended) consumption sequence. The figure illustrates that consumption in the simulation is always below the optimum and deviations from the first-best can be as high as 2.5 percent of steady-state consumption. Overemployment is as bad in this model as underemployment since it results from diverting too many resources to recruiting and away from productive activity.

With an investment sequence similar to that which occurred during the 1930s, the welfare loss from this model could be substantially higher than

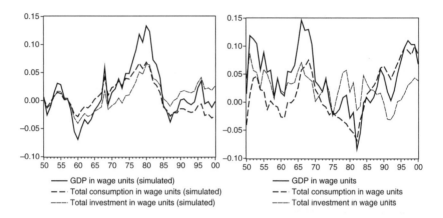

Figure 2.5　GDP, consumption and investment

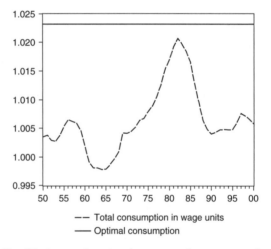

Figure 2.6　Equilibrium and optimal consumption compared

that which I have reported. This simulation no doubt overstates the importance of belief-driven cycles since it is unlikely that all business cycle fluctuations arise as a consequence of belief shocks. It does make the point however that models in this class are likely to lead to much larger welfare costs of business cycles than the fraction of a percentage point described in Robert Lucas's (1987) work. One should consider this example to be the opposite extreme to the real business cycle assumption that all shocks arise as a consequence of aggregate disturbances to TFP.

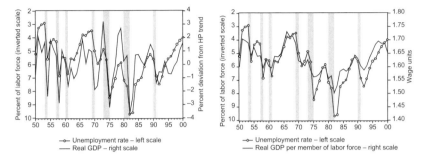

Figure 2.7   Two ways of detrending data

2.4   A NOTE ON MEASUREMENT

I want to raise one further issue in this chapter that relates to the way that macroeconomists report data. Since the work of Hodrick and Prescott (1997), macroeconomic data have typically been detrended with a two-sided filter. Since the models I am interested in may contain important low frequency relationships between series; detrending each individual series by a separate low-frequency component is not very sensible since it removes relevant information from the data that could potentially discriminate between theories. I will be concerned with the question: Is the long-run rate of unemployment a function of fiscal policy? To answer a question of this kind I need a way of detrending data that does not remove a different low-frequency component from each series.

The data reported in this paper were detrended by a method suggested by Keynes in the *General Theory*. This involves deflating nominal series by a measure of the nominal wage to arrive at series measured in 'wage units'. Figure 2.7 compares unemployment with GDP detrended using the Hodrick-Prescott (HP) filter (left panel) with this alternative method. Notice that when GDP is measured this way, it moves much more closely with unemployment (measured on the left axis using an inverse scale).

2.5   CONCLUSION

It is a dangerous business to claim to have uncovered the meaning of Keynes and although it has become fashionable recently to assert that the *General Theory* was a misstep in the history of thought, I do not take that view. I am old enough (just) to have learned Keynesian economics at graduate school, and as an undergraduate, and foolish enough to have believed at least part of what I was taught.

In distilling a complex book like the *General Theory* into a logically coherent argument one necessarily makes compromises since the pieces of the jigsaw come from different puzzles. The task is infinitely more complicated when one is required to fit them together with modern ideas that adopt the fiction of the representative agent, the aggregate production function, complete contingent claims markets and so on. But it is equally distressing when the accepted interpretation of the Keynesian heritage in the form of new-Keynesian economics distorts the central message of the *General Theory* into a form in which the message is so diluted that it becomes unrecognizable. That message is that unregulated capitalist economies sometimes go very wrong and the cure, when this happens, is deficit spending. I hope, in this chapter, to have provided a framework in which this Keynesian theory of public finance, at least conceptually, makes sense. Whether this is a good description of the world is a different question, but surely it is one worth asking.

NOTE

* This paper was prepared for a Conference in honor of Axel Leijonhufvud held at UCLA on 30–31 August 2006. Although I am certain that Axel will not agree with everything that I say in this chapter, I hope that he will recognize a trace of the Leijonhufvud influence creeping through the pages. I would like to thank Masanori Kashiwagi who read and corrected the entire manuscript – I alone remain responsible for any remaining errors. The research was supported by NSF award SES 0418074.

REFERENCES

Alchian, A.A. (1970), 'Information costs, pricing, and resource unemployment', in E.S. Phelps, (ed.), *Microeconomic Foundations of Employment and Inflation Theory*, New York: Norton, pp. 27–52.
Barro, R.J. (1974), 'Are government bonds net wealth?' *Journal of Political Economy*, **82** (6), 1095–1117.
Benassy, J.P. (1975), 'Neo-Keynesian disequilibrium theory in a monetary economy', *Review of Economic Studies*, **42**, 503–23.
Benhabib, J. and R.E.A. Farmer (1994), 'Indeterminacy and increasing returns', *JET*, **63**, 19–46.
Benhabib, J., R. Rogerson and R. Wright (1991), 'Homework in macroeconomics: household production and aggregate fluctuations', *Journal of Political Economy*, **99**, 1166–87.
Dreze, J.H. (1975), 'Existence of an exchange economy with price rigidities', *International Economic Review*, **16**, 310–20.
Epstein, L.G. and J.A. Hynes (1983), 'The rate of time preference and dynamic economic analysis', *Journal of Political Economy*, **91**, 611–35.
Farmer, R.E.A. and J.T. Guo (1994), 'Real business cycles and the animal spirits hypothesis', *JET*, **63**, 42–73.

Farmer, R.E.A. and A. Lahiri (2005), 'Recursive preferences and balanced growth', *Journal of Economic Theory*, **125**, 61–77.

Friedman, M. (1968): 'The role of monetary policy', *American Economic Review*, **58** (March), 1–17.

Hodrick, R.J. and E.C. Prescott (1997), 'Post-war US business cycles: a descriptive empirical investigation', *Journal of Money Credit and Banking*, **29**, 1–16.

Keynes, J.M. (1936), *The General Theory of Employment, Interest and Money*, London: Macmillan & Co.

Leeper, E.M. (1991), 'Equilibria under "Active"and "Passive"Monetary and Fiscal Policies', *Journal of Monetary Economics*, **27** (1), 129–47.

Leijonhufvud, A. (1968), *On Keynesian Economics and the Economics of Keynes*, London: Oxford University Press.

Lucas, Jr., R.E. (1987), *Models of Business Cycles*, Oxford: Basil Blackwell.

Lucas, R.E.J. and N.L. Stokey (1984), 'Optimal growth with many consumers', *Journal of Economic Theory*, **32**, 139–71.

Malinvaud, E. (1977), *The Theory of Unemployment Reconsidered*, Oxford: Basil Blackwell.

McCall, J.J. (1970), 'Economics of Information and Job Search', *Quarterly Journal of Economics*, **84** (1), pp. 113–126.

Moen, E. (1997), 'Competitive search equilibrium', *Journal of Political Economy*, **105** (2), 385–411.

Phelps, E.S. (1968), 'Money wage dynamics and labor market equilibrium', *Journal of Political Economy*, **76**, 678–711.

Phelps, E.S. (1970), 'The new microeconomics in inflation and employment theory', in E.S. Phelps. (ed.) *Introduction: The New Microeconomics in Employment and Inflation Theory*, New York: Norton. pp. 1–23.

Uzawa, H. (1968), 'Time preference, the consumption function, and optimal asset holdings', in *Value, Capital and Growth: Papers in Honor of Sir John Hicks*, J.N. Wolfe, (ed.) Edinburgh: Edinburgh University Press. pp. 485–504.

3. Interest rate setting in the presence of investment prospects and Knightian uncertainty

Edmund S. Phelps*

The subject of this chapter is monetary policy. Wicksell around 1900 and Keynes in the 1930s were seminal figures. Wicksell argued that a central bank setting the interest rate below the 'natural' interest rate would cause rising inflation; Keynes that setting it above the natural rate would drive employment below what today we would call the 'natural' level. The splendid 1968 book of our honoree, Axel Leijonhufvud, was devoted to bringing out and supporting Keynes's penetrating insights on the challenges the Bank of England and the Federal Reserve face in seeking to prevent or combat depression. The book showed that Keynes had in mind a two-sector model, which 'Keynesians' drew back from. Keynes also had in mind a capitalist economy, thus one whose structure and future were not completely known – owing in part to drift in the structure and novelty in the future. My work too, as in *Structural Slumps* (1994), has given a central role to the varying real price of the business asset in its models. The 1970 conference volume *Microeconomic Foundations* (Phelps et al., 1970) was tacitly about an economy with an evolving and thus imperfectly known structure. So I have long had an affinity for Keynes and Leijonhufvud, even if in some ways I have departed from them. And the two main points of the present chapter take up in the context of policy rules these same two themes.

The key additions since then have been: (1) suppliers' expectations of prices and wages, thus expected inflation; (2) non-synchronous price or wage adjustments; and (3) the 'rational expectations' premise in modeling inflation expectations, thus the banishment of all Knightian uncertainty over the economy's current structure and future development. A hallmark of this new literature is that the behavior of the economy's actors, called 'agents' (as if they were hired to do the maximizing of the 'utility' of unseen 'principals'), is generally reducible to stationary rules of behavior. In this spirit, central banks came to be modeled as carrying out their stabilization mandate by practicing one or another sort of feedback-type rule (Fair,

1978; Taylor, 1979). Later, John Taylor studied the stabilizing properties of a simple interest rate rule for setting short rates, now known as the Taylor rule (Taylor, 1993).

As much as most state agencies, central banks have long been drawn to explicit rules or unstated rules of thumb. At central banks adhering to the gold standard, the operative monetary policy took the form of explicit rules. Another regime started up with the Bretton Woods agreement establishing fixed exchange rates vis-à-vis the US dollar and, in the US, the 1951 Treasury Accord restoring Federal Reserve Bank autonomy over short-term interest rates.[1] Just before its pivotal Volcker period, estimates by Ray Fair (1978) suggested that the Federal Reserve had followed a single interest rate rule over the entire era from 1951 to 1978.[2] During the Volcker period, the 'operating procedure' of the Federal Reserve changed from controlling the money supply to controlling short-term interest rates, more precisely, the Federal funds rate – with the aim of guiding inflation and nudging unemployment as before. Estimates in 1993 by Taylor convinced him that in the post-Volcker era the Federal Reserve was again following a rule (though, in Taylor's view, a rule different from the prior one).[3]

This chapter raises questions about the formulation and the application of interest rate rules and arrives at some proposals for change. Is there in principle any interest rate rule that it would make sense for a central bank to follow for a whole decade or whole era despite a sense that the structure of the economy has been evolving in myriad ways? What factors had better be added to the 'Taylor rule' if it is to be safe for normal use? And when should the rule be suspended in favor of considerations and tacit insights not in the formal rule? I am particularly interested in arguing that a good interest rate rule will make a place for one or more business asset prices, but that notwithstanding the broad usefulness of such asset prices, a good rule must have a good escape clause.

3.1 WHY A RULE AT ALL – EVER?

It might reasonably be wondered why a rule of any kind should be practiced and supposed by scholars to be practiced, in normal circumstances at any rate. To discuss the question it is necessary to specify what the term 'rule' means. By a rule I will mean a standard practice understood to be subject to change only under extraordinary circumstances or when a consensus forms for adopting some other rule in its place. A rule, then, is stable as long as it is in force and it is retained as long as developments do not arise that are quite novel, thus qualitatively different from the past, and conditions stay tolerably close to foreseen bounds. It is like an incomplete contract in that the rule applies only to envisioned conditions and minor deviations from what is envisioned.

Historically, the most compelling advantages of a policy rule are those that arise in an economy that normally experiences an appreciable amount of change and uncertainty, so that there is less than perfect transparency. When an agency, such as the central bank, follows a rule, the benefit felt right away by the public is that the rule initially removes the uncertainty over what the agency's responses to data are going to be. Yet as the world evolves there is apt to emerge uncertainty over the continued practice of the rule that eventually becomes worse than the uncertainty initially removed by the adoption of the rule. A succession of small events might at some point trigger a huge response in the form of a change in the rule itself. An example is the rule of a pegged exchange rate in conditions where the rate could be reset at a new peg. For some experts, the ground for a pegged exchange rate is simply that it provides a unit of account – a metric useful to calibrate prices whether or not the metric is sometimes changed (like the change from yard to meter).

The bureaucratic and political benefits of a rule are unambiguous and mostly decisive. Having a rule enables the agency to say to the public: 'These are our rules, we go by the book, and experience has shown the results to be satisfactory.'[4] As a result, the agency does not have to incur the administrative costs of frequently rehearsing its grounds for its action as it would if it were responding on a case-by-case basis. Furthermore, the rule, once it has gained enough political acceptance to be adopted, may save the agency from having to give grounds for an action that it would rather not make explicit to one or more interest groups; and it may save the agency from having to try to give an in-depth justification for its action when the agency knows it does not understand the situation well enough to be able to do that. Another benefit is that interested parties will see that while application of the rule may hurt them when the economy is doing one thing, the rule will help them when the economy is reversing course. Finally, it will be understood that the agency cannot break its rule for one interest group at the present time and yet be steadfast about its rule for all other interest groups at all future times.

The apparent propensity of central banks to respond to data in a stable, routine manner, as if following a rule of thumb, and the apparent potential of the rule being practiced to survive with little change for a long time, do suggest that there has been calculation – even a sort of 'maximization' – within these banks. They are not responding randomly. But what is best for a central bank is not necessarily best for the country. They may have bureaucratic reasons for passing up some changes to the rule that the bank itself would view as likely improvements. (Explaining the merits, negotiating with opponents, and containing the changes to the ones sought might be too challenging.) Also, they may suffer limitations in their understanding of how the economy works (as all of us do) that have left them blind to ways to improve on the rule. Studies have found evidence that the central bank in the US has succeeded in erasing much of the destabilizing effects of 'monetary' shocks, which operate and manifest themselves through the inflation rate. But has anyone tested over the three or four major swings in the US economy in the past 35 years whether the Fed could have done better through one or two innovations to its rule? The time is ripe for a hard look at the design and use of the existing sort of interest rate rule that appears to be practiced by central banks over much of the world. In particular, one wonders whether the central banks are taking account as much as they could of the episodes of structural change and intensified uncertainty that the economy from time to time experiences.

3.2   WHAT IS THE THEORY OF THE TAYLOR RULE?

The earliest rule is suggested by Knut Wicksell and later Friedrich Hayek. It is the rule of 'neutral money' – a central bank policy of maintaining the expected short-term real interest rate equal to the natural short-term real interest rate. For a time in the 1930s just such a neutral monetary policy rule was championed at the Netherlands Central Bank by B.O. Koopmans. It never became actual policy, though, to my knowledge.

The earliest explicit formulation of the interest rate rule regarded as in practice at some central banks, at least tacitly, is the rule associated with John Taylor. In essence, it is a 'feedback rule' that calls for the expected short-term real interest rate to react to any deviation of the inflation rate from the target rate. The exposition here will draw on what may be the most common textbook formulation. In that formulation, the current period short-term real interest rate set by the central bank deviates from its natural level according to: (1) the latest deviation of the inflation rate from its fixed target; and (2) the latest deviation of output from its natural level – the level corresponding to the natural unemployment rate.[5] The equation for the rule in textbook form is:

$$r_t = r^N + \alpha \left(f_t - \pi \right) + \beta \left(z_t - z^N \right), \tag{3.1}$$

where r is the expected real interest rate, f is the inflation rate and z is the level of employment or, equivalently if we abstract from changing technological and capital inputs, output. The coefficients α and β are positive constants. Taylor later assigned the value 0.5 to both coefficients for illustrative purposes. The constant r^N is the natural real interest rate, the constant z^N is the natural level of employment, and π is the constant target inflation rate.

The intent of the rule is to establish a sort of random, or 'stochastic', steady state in which the rule serves to aim the inflation rate (each period, that is, all the time) at the target level while the market economy (all the time) reliably aims output at its natural level. If we imbed the rule in the standard textbook model of the economy, the mean value (or 'expected value') of the inflation rate jumps immediately to the target rate, whatever path it may have taken recently; and the mean (or expected value) of the output level jumps immediately to its natural level, wherever it may have been previously. These implied properties of the textbook model hinge on its premise of 'rational expectations' – perfect foresight up to the 'random disturbances' – and its premise that all prices and wages are continuously free to jump without restrictions. The two properties mean, respectively, that the mean value around which f_t fluctuates randomly each period is always equal to π and the mean value around which z_t fluctuates randomly is always equal to z^N. Those two conditions imply in view of the rule that the real expected interest rate set by the bank is required to be fluctuating randomly around its natural level, r^N. We need not go into the workings of the underlying model in order to grasp this central feature of the simplified Taylor rule.

It might be asked why the rule calls for the central bank to raise the real expected interest rate when current random disturbances cause the inflation rate to exceed the target. After all, the rational expectations model and the rule combine to imply that the public understands that the inflation rate is all the time fluctuating around the target inflation rate, so there seems to be no point in punishing the economy with an above-average real interest rate whenever by chance the inflation rate is above average.[6] The answer is that if there were no such systematic punishment or reward there might be insufficient reason for the public to have confidence that the central bank was still there, steadfastly aiming to keep the inflation rate on average at the announced target level.

It might also be asked why, in the context of the textbook model in which the Taylor rule is usually set, the rule requires the central bank to respond to the random occurrence of an above-average (below-average) output level with an above-average (below-average) real interest rate. Once the output deviation from its natural level is observed, it is too late to do anything about it, so why respond with a near-contemporaneous hike in the real interest rate? But the same question might have been raised about the rule's response to the inflation rate. The answer would appear to be the same in either instance: it serves to moderate fluctuations in the inflation rate and in aggregate demand to have 'agents' who know that the rule will 'punish' a blip in the inflation rate and, likewise, 'punish' a blip in the output rate. The anticipation of such responses serves to warn setters of prices and demanders of output that the greater the general inflation pressure sensed in the marketplace and, likewise, the greater the output pressure sensed in the marketplace, the greater will be the increase in the real interest rate that the central bank will routinely implement in response; and the latter thinking will serve to moderate the consequent blip in the inflation rate and in the output rate. Therefore, in the event of a momentary dip in oil supplies and resulting dip in output alongside a blip in the inflation rate, the rule would on that account require a corresponding dip in the short-term real interest rate. In responding with an interest rate decrease to the output dip, the rule serves to temper or possibly offset or outweigh its calculated real interest rate increase on account of the blip of the inflation rate.[7]

What if we change the theoretical setting in which the rule is imbedded from the simplest textbook model, in which all prices and output are free to jump, to the standard new-Keynesian model, developed primarily at Columbia in the 1970s and early 1980s, where prices or wages are staggered, so hardly any prices or wages would jump at any one time? This is, in fact, the setting Taylor always had in mind. In that standard new-Keynesian model, a fall of output would then justify a cut of the real expected interest rate for another reason: if output has fallen to a below-natural level, it will take time to recover and it is not too late for therapy: the recovery will be speeded up by setting a lower real interest rate (though at the expense of greater – though fading – inflation ahead). The main suggestions to be made in this chapter do not stand or fall on which of these two models of price and wage setting we use in making this or that point.

So the Taylor rule is, in its way, highly sophisticated. And so is the underlying model if the new-Keynesian model is used, even the standard one. Yet even the standard new-Keynesian model is over-simple for purposes of addressing the questions arising in stabilization policy. It has earned its place as the starting point for analyses of normal, or routine, stabilization. Yet there are omissions in the Taylor rule stemming from the narrowness of the model in which the rule is imbedded. We have already encountered the problem that price shocks are analyzed as if supply shocks generally left the natural employment level (or even the natural output level) invariant to the supply shock; but that particular problem is not the focus here. In short, the Taylor rule is an important dimension of the starting point for formulating an optimum stabilization policy – it is a 'breakthrough', as some have said – but it is not going to be the end point. (Undoubtedly Taylor is not unhappy that the research he started is ongoing, especially in recent years.)

Yet as a practical matter the rule is in some ways quite problematic. It is often commented that the rule is beset with non-operational elements – so much so that it may come across as almost unworldly (much as the Nash model of bargaining might strike professional negotiators as unworldly). One such element is the expected inflation rate, which the bank needs to subtract from the nominal interest rate it sets to obtain the expected real rate that its decision would constitute. (Alternatively, the bank needs to add the expected inflation rate to the natural real rate.)[8] The focus here is on the two other non-operational elements: the natural real rate of interest and excess demand (or supply) – in other versions of the rule, the gap between the unemployment rate and the natural unemployment rate. Yet the difficulty goes deeper.

There appear to be two sorts of problems. First of all, in analyses where an interest rate rule is imbedded in the textbook model or, equally, the standard new-Keynesian model, it sufficed for the interest rate to react to (fluctuations in) the current inflation rate and the level of output or employment, since disturbances in these two variables were, essentially, the only moving parts of the system. The natural real interest rate and the natural unemployment rate are treated as if they were constants; so if they can be taken as constants, it does not matter that they are 'non-operational' or 'unobservable'. In reality, and in various models that recognize the point, variables such as the capital stock, the stock of customers, the stock of job-ready employees, and so forth constitute the state of the economy. These 'state variables', when driven off their home base, or resting point, in turn drive the natural real interest rate and the natural unemployment rate off their normal levels, if such exist. Accordingly, the Taylor rule has to be formulated to recognize that in a setting of economic change the two natural rates are variable rather than constant:

$$r_t = r_t^N + \alpha \, (f_t - \pi) + \beta \, (z_t - z_t^N), \qquad (3.1')$$

Hence the more general Taylor rule would require the central bank to adjust the expected real interest rate that the bank establishes in the marketplace to the jumps and swings that the natural real interest rate and natural unemployment rate may take: in short, to take account of structural change, such as the arrival of technological or commercial breakthroughs opening up new opportunities for gains in productivity. But that task lands the central bank into the problem that the movements of these two natural rates are not observable. The way out of this problem, to the extent that there is a way out, is to find formulae for the natural real rate and the natural unemployment rate in terms of causal variables that are observable and hence part of the central bank's data.[9]

The second problem facing the Taylor rule, which to an important degree grows out of structural change, is that the models in which the rule has been imbedded omit the presence of 'unmeasurable' uncertainty about the future (as well, possibly, as the present) – now generally called 'Knightian uncertainty' or, especially in other contexts, ambiguity. The Taylor rule is conceived as the optimal stabilization policy for all time in a theoretical economy in which the natural interest rate and the natural unemployment rate, if not observable, are at least calculable by the market and by the central bank – as if these variables were known quantities deriving from complete knowledge of the economy's future prospects. In any enterprising economy and certainly an economy operating in a global environment subject to innovations (not to mention political change), markets cannot really know the mean future course of asset returns and asset prices on which the term structure of the 'rational expectations' real interest rates depends. Unless the central bank is unaware of the market's uncertainty and oblivious of its own uncertainty, it has to figure out how to take this uncertainty into account.[10]

This chapter first addresses the former problem, the non-fixity of the natural real rate and the natural unemployment rate, by advocating the use of a 'structuralist' model of the economy (into which the Taylor rule is to be imbedded) to endogenize the natural interest rate and natural unemployment rate. To this end, section 3.3 draws upon the open-economy version of one of the models in *Structural Slumps* in order to have a model-theoretic basis for examining how the interest rate rule might be expanded to contain additional variables serving as estimates of the unknown natural rates. Then section 3.4 grapples with practicalities. One is the question of whether the values of the assets on which the natural rates theoretically depend can be satisfactorily proxied by observable share prices. Section 3.5 considers the possibility that it would be repeating the mistake of antecedents who like to mechanize their models if one were to portray even the shadow prices attached to projects by CEOs, let alone the share prices, as a good representation of future business prospects, since the CEOs are to some extent flying blind; few of them could be said to have made a stab at identifying the contingencies to hedge against, their seriousness and their likelihood. When the world is especially uncertain, what should the bank do with its rule?

3.3   A ROLE FOR BUSINESS ASSET VALUES – WITH RATIONAL EXPECTATIONS

As touched on above, a glaring problem with the interest rate rule is that the bank does not observe the jumps and swings in the natural rate of interest implied by household behavior in their saving/disssaving decisions and business behavior in their expansion decisions. Even if we imagine that the private sector has rational expectations, hence has made no systematic errors, it is even less plausible to suppose that the central bank can sense from its observations of the economy the current 'natural' interest rate. This natural rate is a great deal more than just the Fisher–Ramsey parameter known as the rate of 'pure time preference', or rate of 'utility discount'. If the natural rate fell, unbeknownst to the central bank, or fell far more than the bank guessed, the bank would be left overestimating the natural interest rate that the private sector compares with the expected real rate of interest set by the bank; in that case it would set the real interest rate too high – higher than it would have with a correct estimate of the natural real rate.

The implied consequences of using a mistaken natural rate are worth spelling out. In the more general situation, in which the central bank does not know the natural rate, it is natural to modify the model so that the interest rate rule now determines the excess of the expected real interest rate over the estimated natural rate (as estimated by the bank). Then, absent any difference between the expected inflation rate and the target or any algebraic excess demand, such as might be the case in the starting conditions, the drop in the natural rate unaccompanied by a drop in the estimated natural rate would create an incipient excess of the expected real interest rate set by the bank over the new natural rate – in the amount of the overestimate. The modified rational expectations model, however, still implies that in the steady state equilibrium the expected real interest rate will equal the natural rate that households use in deciding their consumption demand. This implies that, in that steady state, if and when attained, the inflation rate must have dropped to a level below the target by just enough to induce the bank to reduce the expected real interest rate to the (new and lower) natural rate of interest. The bank is driven to lower and to keep appropriately low the expected real rate despite its belief that the natural rate is as high as before, because it constantly heeds the new chronic shortfall of the expected inflation rate from its target.[11]

At the practical level, though, such a scenario brushes plenty of dirt under the carpet. For one thing, a point-and-a-half drop, say, in the natural real rate would require a three-point drop of the expected inflation if the coefficient on the inflation rate gap is one-half; a two-and-a-half-point drop would require a five-point drop of the expected inflation rate. Another consideration is that the only path – whether an equilibrium path or one strewn with mistakes – leading to the much lower expected inflation rate would take a few years to reach its destination. The model does not imply that the expected inflation rate and the other variables can snap into the new steady-state values in place of the old ones they had before the fall of the natural rate. During the transition period, the expected real rate of interest will not have been pushed down to its former relation to the natural rate; and if the bank's estimates of the market's expected inflation rate lags behind, the expected real interest rate may actually rise before it begins to fall. The third consideration is that, absent the good luck of a boom alongside the disinflation, a firm (when ready to reset its price) will not raise its price all the way to the price of the front-runner, the firm with the highest price. Thus the disinflation can be expected to be quite protracted and the salutary negative gap between expected inflation rate and the target rate can be quite slow in growing to the desired size.

At another level, such shifts in the inflation rate would raise concern about the information and the knowledge possessed within the central bank and maybe even the competence and the wisdom of the leaders in the bank. If the globalized economy into which so many nations have now entered will be one of more rapid structural shifts and greater dynamism than central banks and the rest of us were accustomed to in decades gone by, it will be important for the confidence in which the central bank is held that it be able to do well in containing the inflation rate – no matter how employment and growth rates are behaving.

There is no reason to despair, though. In the interest of having an operational rule it might be an acceptable solution to use existing economic models to endogenize the natural interest rate rather than allow it to be a 'free parameter' set at some level thought to be its 'historical' level. The bank could draw upon a model with the structure appropriate to capture most or at any rate some of the major variations in the natural rate, and could proceed to estimate econometrically the model's ultimate, boiled-down implications for the determination of the natural interest rate – the reduced-form equation. Then the bank could periodically insert the appropriate current market data on the determinants of the natural rate into this equation to calculate the 'fitted value' of the current natural rate.[12] This is a reasonable step, though not the only move toward a more reasonable procedure.

What exactly is the concept of the natural interest rate to be used here? In simpler times, the pioneering theorists of the concept, such as Wicksell, could invoke a stationary state and define the natural interest rate as the steady interest rate that would equate steady consumer demand to steady consumption supply. In any general intertemporal model, such as the one to be used here, a variant is required. In the view here, the current (short-term) natural real interest rate is the real interest rate that is required – the real interest rate that the current expected real interest rate is required to equal – for a match between the rate of change of (consumer) demand and the rate of change of consumer supply. Furthermore, in the model used here (and a much wider class of models), an increase of the expected real interest rate cuts the level of consumption demand and increases the rate of change of consumption demand; and it boosts the level of consumption supply and decreases the rate of change of consumption supply – thus cutting excess demand while increasing its rate of change. In the notation to be used below, the expected real interest rate, r, and the natural interest rate, r^N, enter oppositely as determinants of the rate of change in excess demand implied by consumer and business plans:

$$dc^d/dt - dc^s/dt = (r - r^N)\, c. \tag{3.2}$$

So the current natural real interest rate is the level of the real rate required for excess demand (supply) to be unchanging – just high enough to pull up dc^d/dt and pull down dc^s/dt into equality.

In general, this natural real interest rate is not going to be constant. (Neither is the companion natural unemployment rate nor, in terms of the equations here, equilibrium consumption.) A suitable model, however, will provide a theoretical formula for the current natural real rate. With such a model, what would the theoretical formula for the current r^N_t look like?

In a model that has turned out to be rather convenient for analyzing various macro questions about the small open economy, namely the macro-economic extension in Phelps et al. (2005) of the Phelps–Winter customer market model, the formula for the natural rate is straightforward to derive, though a little complicated. To begin: the model takes the planned growth rate of consumer demand to be that given by the Yaari–Blanchard formula, which is the expression in square brackets in (3.3):

$$dc^d/dt = [(r - \rho) - \theta(\theta + \rho)(W/c^d)]\, c^d, \tag{3.3}$$

Here ρ is the rate of pure time preference, θ is the force of mortality, and W is private wealth of nationals. In the simplest of cases, if x is the stock of domestic customers and if firms owned by nationals have all of them and no other, then W is given by qx, where q is the value of firms per asset, the asset being their stock of customers, x. If the change of consumer demand were the only component of the change in excess demand, as would be the case if the supply of the consumer good were fixed, the term $\rho + \theta(\theta + \rho)(W/c^d)$ would be the natural interest rate in its entirety, in view of the definition in (3.1).[13] Excess demand would be increasing if this natural rate were less than the expected real interest rate, to be denoted r; and decreasing if the inequality were reversed.

In the customer market model, though, consumption supply per customer is not fixed. Its current level, c^s, is implicitly determined by:

$$1+[\eta(1)/\eta'(1)]-\zeta(c^s x) = -(q/c^s)[1/\eta'(1)][g_1(1, e) + eg_2(1,e)], \eta(1) = 1, \tag{3.4}$$

where q is the shadow price at which an additional customer is valued; $\eta(p^i/p)$ is the ith firm's demand, $\eta(1) = 1$; ζ is unit cost, which is a function of $c^s x$; and $g(1,e)$ is the growth rate of domestic firms' stock of customers. The algebraic growth rate of c^s is therefore some function, denoted J, of the rates of change dq/dt, de/dt, dx/dt and the levels q, e, x and c. Now subtract (3.4) from (3.2) and, as an approximation, equate c^d to c^s, letting c denote the common value to which they are approximately equal:

$$dc^d/dt - dc^s/dt = \{r - [\rho + \theta(\theta + \rho)(W/c^d) + J(dq/dt, de/dt, dx/dt, q, e, x)]\}c. \tag{3.5}$$

The expression in square brackets gives the natural rate of interest. Thus $J(dq/dt, de/dt, dx/dt, q, e, x)$ is the supply-side term in the formula for r^N. We may use Fisher's familiar arbitrage condition to substitute for the planned rates of change dq/dt and de/dt and use the model's customer growth rate function $g(1, e)$ to substitute for dx/dt:

$$r^N = \rho + \theta(\theta + \rho)(W/c^d) + J(r^Nq - R(q), r^*e - r^Ne, g(1, e)x; q, e, x) \tag{3.6}$$

Recall the announced theme of this section. Theoretical formulae for the not-directly-observable natural real interest rate such as that in equation (3.6) offer some hope of being usable as a means to circumvent the problem that the natural real rate is both varying and unobservable. So we are interested in what lessons the formula from our illustrative model has to teach.

A key lesson is that r^N is impacted by the value put on the business asset, to be denoted q. Specifically, r^N is increasing in q.[14] Thus, if the bank observes a recent major increase in q or, at any rate, observes an increase in some proxy for q, the bank can reasonably assume that r^N has increased concomitantly and ought to act on that assumption (by adjusting r to match) rather than carry out the rule as if r^N were a constant and therefore had not changed.[15] To grasp why r^N is increasing in q consider first the second term in equation (3.6). The ratio W/c in that term is nationals' wealth relative to their consumption, where an element (if not the whole) of W is the total value of the customer stock that nationals indirectly 'own' through their shares in domestic firms, essentially qx. In the model it is assured that when q increases, thus increasing wealth, consumption increases proportionally less, so the wealth-consumption ratio also increases on balance. On this account, then, (3.6) implies that the natural interest rate increases with q, just as it would increase with ρ.

(Interpretation: an increase in either instantly boosts the initial level of the planned consumption path over the future but slows the initial growth rate of that path; so the expected real interest rate must be increased to keep that growth rate from being below the growth rate of consumption supply.) Consider now the third and last term. To understand it, recall its origin, equation (3.3), which determines firms' consumption supply to their customers. Other things equal, an increase in q increases c^s in the same proportion, although the resulting increase of output increases unit cost, which increases the left-hand side of (3.3), forcing c^s to fall back somewhat. (Note that if the increase of q did not increase c^s at all, unit cost would not change either, an outcome that could not satisfy the equation.) What is the effect on the planned growth rate of c^s, however? At any given interest rate, a higher q would mean a lower yield and hence require a higher expected growth rate of q. Hence faster expected growth of q would mean a higher planned growth rate of consumption supply. On the account, too, the natural interest rate must increase with q. (Interpretation: if planned supply grows faster than demand, then for intertemporal equilibrium demand must grow faster; so the expected real interest rate must be increased some more to prevent the growth rate of demand from being below the growth rate of supply.)

An example worth examining is the sudden expectation (at $t0$) of a temporary slowing of productivity in upcoming years (between $t1$ and $t2$). Immediately q drops by a quantum amount. This decrease in the value put on the business asset immediately decreases the current natural level of employment (and associated real wage) through its contractionary impact on the amount of consumption supplied. Yet knowing that would not induce the bank to adjust its interest rate, since the rule does not have the bank reaction to the natural employment level itself but only to the gap between actual and natural employment, that is, between consumer demand and consumption supply. The natural real interest rate is also decreased: as we have learned from (3.6) and (3.4), the drop of q produces a drop of the natural rate of interest, owing to decreases in both the demand-side and the supply-side terms in (3.6).[16] The Taylor rule, however, calls for a cut in the expected real rate of interest by the amount of the estimated drop of the natural rate in order to prevent an excess of the expected real interest rate over the natural interest rate. That serves to moderate, or cushion, the initial drop of q and prevent output and employment from dropping even below their reduced natural levels.

A question addressed earlier was what would happen in the economy if the central bank did not know that the natural rate had fallen and the private sector had to wait for the bank to be induced to lower the expected real rate by the decline of the inflation rate below its target level. Now, using our structuralist model and persevering with the premise of rational expectations, we can address the rather different question of what would happen if – for a short and pre-specified period of time – the central bank knowingly disregarded the drop and gradual recovery of the natural real rate and of the natural employment level and adopted, say, an unchanging expected real interest rate. Absent a cut of the expected real rate of interest in response to the reduced natural rate, there would then be an extra drop of q and thus an extra drop of consumption; and from that extra-reduced level planned consumption demand would then be growing (relative to what its growth rate would have been on the equilibrium path) faster than consumption supply would have been growing (relative to the consumption growth on the equilibrium path). The 'underconsumption' disequilibrium is fed, so to speak, by false expectations of consumption growth over the future that exceeds what businesses will be willing to meet. If instead the central bank heeds the dictate of the rule to lower the expected real rate to match the fallen natural real rate, that serves to prevent the emergence of an ongoing over-saving disequilibrium in which households wrongly expect that the extra cutback of consumption in the present will be rewarded at a false market interest rate with extra increases of consumption in the future. In short, keeping the expected real interest rate for a time above its natural level would not only exact the welfare cost of creating an artificially depressed pseudo-natural level (with reduced consumption demand to match the reduced consumption supply); it would also exact the welfare cost of causing households to miscalculate (in the up direction) the reward to an additional unit of saving. (Hayek would have been grateful for this point.)

A more extreme case illustrates clearly another welfare cost. Suppose that market participants, following the new prospects of slowed productivity growth for some years ahead, foresee that the central bank will not ever implement a cut of the expected real rate; the bank prefers to wait for the time when the productivity slowdown will be over and the natural real rate is back up to the unchanged level of the expected real interest rate. Let the mountain come to Mohamed. Then q will initially drop much more than would have been caused by a mere delay in cutting the expected real rate. Further, q may very well be lower every day over the future than it otherwise would have been right up to the day when the productivity slowdown is over. In that case, the country's firms would be underinvesting in keeping customers throughout the slowdown and the country would bleed more of its 'capital' – its stock of customers – to competing overseas firms than it would have done had the bank allowed the real interest rate to drop down to the path of the natural real rate. Similarly, new prospects of some future acceleration of productivity accompanied by the same policy of fixity in the expected real interest rate would generate an overelevation of q throughout the period of faster productivity growth and thus result in firms overinvesting in new customers. (Obviously the openness of the economy is crucial to this reasoning.)

Another cost in this latter case of a permanent expected real interest rate in the face of swings in the natural real rate is that disinflation would emerge, with the inflation rate possibly going negative, until the time when the productivity slowdown is over. Similarly, when prospects develop for a shift of productivity onto a higher trend path, the resulting rise of the natural real rate leads to rising inflation until the faster productivity growth ends.[17]

From the present point of view, with its maintained hypothesis of 'rational' expectations in the private sector, the bank's job is to enable the economy to take its 'natural' way. The bank's interest rate cut is motivated by what would emerge if it did not accommodate the fall in the natural rate of interest. Monetary policies that fix the expected real interest rate would cause productivity slowdowns that would be exacerbated by underinvestment and disinflation, and accelerations would be followed by overinvestment and rising inflation.

It should be noted that the theoretical formula for the natural real interest rate derivable from the structuralist model used here contains the real exchange rate alongside the real prices of the business asset(s).

It should also be noted that the real value, or price, of business assets also impacts on the current natural unemployment rate or, in the terminology of the model used here, the current natural consumption level – not simply on the natural real rate of interest. This observation could be of some significance. A rise of q, in pulling up the natural consumption level and thus reducing the algebraic excess of actual consumption over natural consumption, taken alone operates to decrease the required value of the expected real interest rate, according to the rule. This second effect of q in the rule would have to be taken into account. Conceivably it would offset or at any rate importantly temper the effect on the expected real rate coming from the effect of q on the natural real rate of interest.

Two more comments are appropriate before closing this section. One is that if the economy were not only free of unmeasurable uncertainty, as I have been supposing, but also free of parametric shifts, such as the (so-to-speak) technical slowdowns and speed-ups just discussed, then the economy could always be describable in terms of 'transitional dynamics' that make q and e a derivable function of x. In that case q would have no information value not already deducible from observations of x. The discussion of the past few pages rests on the strong possibility that any real-life economy is subject to the occasional parametric shift and thus also the subjective expectation of such shifts. In the previous discussion, it was such a (prospective) parameteric shift that sparked the jump of q onto a new path (and, if the central bank did not accommodate, onto an 'unnatural' one).

The other comment is that even if there never were parametric shifts, present or future, for the economy to exploit or contend with, the 'vibrations' of x may be unobservable while, notwithstanding, q is relatively observable. In such a case, q may have information value in estimating the path of x. When q goes up, that is evidence, taken alone, that firms are trying to expand their customer base. But this is a procedure in which it would be good to use information about e alongside information about q.

3.4 DIFFICULTIES AND PITFALLS IN USING BUSINESS ASSET VALUES

The previous section envisions that central banks can improve the sort of interest rate rule now practiced, however loosely, by endogenizing the natural real rate; they are to accomplish this through the use of some existing macro models that make the natural interest rate (and the natural unemployment rate) functions of the real prices of the main business assets. But how well would that work out?

One set of difficulties with the idea of using asset values, particularly the value of each principal kind of business asset, arises from the measurement of these values and with the estimation of their effects. It is one thing to pay attention to changes in asset values; it is another thing to estimate their effects on the underlying structure of the economy. Even if we could observe business asset values and could construct some reasonably comprehensive index of them, estimating the size of economic effects on the natural real rate and the natural employment level of a given change in such an index would raise all sorts of questions. The big and difficult task of central banks is to respond to the big swings in economic activity in such a way as to damp or prevent big shifts or swings in the rate of inflation from resulting. So one wants annual or quinquennial observations, and lots of them, since there are not so many big swings in activity over a century. Yet most countries do not have time series over asset values and other macroeconomic times series stretching back to 1830 or 1900 or even 1940. And even if the country is fortunate enough to have time series of such generous length – think of the US and the UK – there would be issues about the reliability of estimates obtained over a span in which there must have been considerable structural change.

The worst difficulty, though, is apt to be the problem that the business asset values are not observable. So readers might conclude that the idea of using business asset values is doomed to be 'theory' with no possibility of 'practice'. However, there exists a next-best thing. Probably the best single proxy for the 'average' of these asset values is the value of shares in the stock market per basket of business assets in use.[18] In any case, there have been statistical investigations of the effect of such a stock market variable alongside the real prices of other 'assets', notably the real exchange rate and oil. Three important studies are Fitoussi et al. (2000), Phelps and Zoega (2001) and Phelps et al. (2005). In the last of these, all the various asset prices are inserted into a single regression: the index of normalized real stock market value, normalized by gross domestic product (GDP), the strength of the country's real exchange rate, and the real price per barrel of oil. Every one was highly successful, even with the world real interest rate entered along with the other explanatory variables. The impact of a rise in the normalized stock market value on the unemployment rate was economically important and had a high level of statistical significance. The impact of a strengthening of the currency was also positive for employment in keeping with the structuralist theory (and not with Keynesian theory).

The great lesson from these empirical studies was that the message of 'structuralist' theory was basically right: the big swings are typically driven largely by moves in business asset values. In particular, the investment boom of the late 1990s drove down the structural, or natural, path of the unemployment rate through its stimulating effect on share prices, which presumably proxied for business asset values, and to some small extent through its stimulating effect on the strength of the real exchange rate, that is, real exchange rate appreciation. There was no rise in inflation in those Organisation for Economic Co-operation and Development (OECD) countries that enjoyed a boom, so a rise in the inflation rate could not have been the channel through which the investment boom drove up employment in the economies that boomed. What is missing in these studies from the point of view of the present chapter is an investigation of the effect of these 'asset prices' on the natural real interest rate. But to demonstrate such effects econometrically may prove challenging, since the natural rate is unobservable – indeed, it is that unobservability of the natural rate of interest that led to the idea that the asset prices could proxy for that theoretical interest rate. One could as a fallback estimate the effects of those underlying variables on the (expected or actual) real interest rate, rather than a construct purported to represent the natural real interest rate. That would not be totally useless. Yet more ingenuity would surely be welcome.

There are also dangers – pitfalls – in relying on asset prices to obtain an estimate of the natural interest rate rather than simply regarding it as some conventional constant. Some may think it would be dangerous to venture into that territory. It might be commented that central banks have long debated the wisdom of pricking 'bubbles' in asset markets so as to pull prices and quantities back to a range believed to be 'sustainable' – and the jury is still out. Evidently there is fear of involvement with asset prices, particularly stock market prices. Those who argue against doing so (the cons) explain that it is difficult to know when prices are inflated and quantities distended – and when they are not. But there is no trace of bubbles and sustainability in the argument in this chapter's section 3.2. The intent of section 3.2 was to suggest a way that might further the effectiveness of the interest rate rule in its objective of stabilizing the inflation rate – and, with luck, the fluctuations around the economy's natural path. The argument had to take up the question of how an extension of the rule to business asset prices (values) would work in situations where new prospects for the future operated to drive asset values temporarily away from their normalized trend paths – speculative booms, such as the Internet boom of the late 1990s, and speculative depression, such as the contraction in some continental European economies in the run-up to World War II. But the idea was not to try to stabilize the economy, only to stabilize what might reasonably be stabilized, such as deviations around the equilibrium detour-path that changing future prospects may induce.

Many economists nevertheless maintain that business asset values and, likewise, real exchange rates are entirely speculative and therefore provide no information of value to central bankers in carrying out their mission: If those business asset values were the 'natural' ones, it would be one thing; but since they have only the most 'flimsy' basis, as Keynes (1947) once famously put it, they are not fit inputs for an interest rule. Those taking this view would no doubt oppose the idea of raising interest rates when share prices rise, lowering rates when share prices fall.

It might be said in reply that there is a sense in which the right index of the values that chief executive officers (CEOs) place on increased holding of the various business assets cannot be wrong – as long as the CEOs are rational enough to respond to this important calculation of theirs. If they are 'down' on the value of investing, no matter what the basis for their thinking, they will invest less. However that may be, that does not mean that the stock market, in the sense of retail investors who are not generally in close touch with the true thinking of the CEOs, cannot be wrong. As Paul Samuelson famously quipped, the stock market has predicted '9 of the last 5 recessions' (Samuelson, 1966).

The natural instinct is to reply that one should not prematurely foreclose a plausible, even promising proposal merely because of some preconceptions or prejudices about stock markets. Let the econometricians review again whether share prices have predictive values for investments of all kinds (plant, employees, customers), for economic activity and for the natural interest rate. It is merely an empirical question to be decided by straightforward econometric methods.

But, while it would be tempting to leave it at that, it might not be so straightforward. It has to be acknowledged that there is uncertainty about the reliability of the statistical inferences that are drawn. It could be that we have just lived through a stretch of decades in which a suitably normalized stock market variable indeed does very well in predicting those macroeconomic variables. In principle, though, we cannot be at all sure that this stock market variable would perform as well in another era. What we have learned is that the stock market variable appears to be rather powerful since World War II. But there is evidence that the stock market did not do as well in long spans before that war – though why we do not know. In addition, it is a fact that that the stock market variable performs much less well – if it performs well at all – in some countries than in others.

3.5   OVERRIDING A HERETOFORE SATISFACTORY RULE

Situations have arisen in which an interest rate policy rule that has behaved tolerably well for a decade or more is simply put aside in favor of a radically different sort of arrangement. In wartime, monetary policy often looks different. Markets are reined in as the government deploys rationing, the draft and appeals to social responsibility. There are times when a country gives priority to stabilizing short-term interest rates, at others to stabilizing the currency.

What is it about those times that the rule judged should be judged unsuitable or inadequate to them? It is possible that current conditions are so extreme that there is a loss of confidence that the quantitative features of the interest rate rule would be applicable. If, with a target inflation rate of 2 percent per annum, the actual inflation rate is running at, say, 102 percent, it might be judged wildly unlikely that the right thing to do is to apply a coefficient (the α in equations 3.1 and 3.2) with the usual value, say 0.5 (the assumed value in most illustrative calculations), so that the expected real rate would be set at 50 percent. It might be thought that to bring down the inflation rate quickly it would be enough to raise the expected real rate to, say, 25 percent. Nothing would be served by postponing the last dollar of new planned investment expenditure (new construction starts, and so on). The point is that the interest rate rule is to be understood as a linear approximation that is valid enough in the neighborhood of the economy's natural path. When the economy is in some respects far from that neighborhood, the appropriate reaction to the size of the inflation rate and consumption, or employment, is not generally the same as when the economy is in the zone for which the rule was designed. The appropriate reaction is apt to be smaller. The appropriate general rule may well be strictly concave rather than linear.

It is also possible that the times are marked by much greater Knightian uncertainty than is normally present in the economy. Frank Knight brought to the attention of economists in his 1922 book the concept of 'unmeasurable' uncertainty – where the decision makers do not even know the probabilities of the different possible outcomes and may not even know what all the possible outcomes are. He argued that a market economy with predominantly private enterprise confronts the manager of virtually every business, not just Schumpeter's start-up entrepreneur, with such unmeasurable uncertainty about the future business climate and the firm's own costs and demand. (Had market socialism come under discussion a little sooner, Knight could have added that even socialist managers have to wonder about future developments among their suppliers and buyers.) A market economy that is rather stagnant could face considerable Knightian uncertainty stemming from overseas forces operating in the global economy, not to mention potential outbreaks of war and disease. In the present age, there is the specter of a possible stoppage of the capital flows that have been coming from Germany, China and the Middle East to the United States, and a possible reverse flow back to those countries and others. There is the specter of an enormous demographic overhang and the prospect of increasing public indebtedness when, seemingly, sound finance requires large budgetary surpluses. There are the uncertainties posed by the Middle East and the nuclear ambitions of Iran. Perhaps CEOs' valuations of each of the various kinds of business assets have consciously 'priced in' each of these risks. So may retail investors in the shares of these companies. But these are Knightian uncertainties, so there is no right price.

Since Knightian uncertainty is an everyday feature of business, central banks are also accustomed to living with it. Suppose, however, that it surges to a very high level. What then? The work of Keynes on probability theory and the post-war work of William Fellner portrayed this radical uncertainty as causing the known probabilities of the known contingencies to add up to a sum that is less than one. The gap between one and the sum is a measure of this uncertainty. In the spirit of that view, I would suggest that a central bank usually acts as if the model of the economy on which its rule (or rule of thumb) rests is true – or true enough – with a probability of something like 99 percent. When this probability drops down to, say, 70 percent, the bank decides to respond to inflation and employment (and its estimate of the natural real rate and natural employment level) by scaling back the responses called for by its rule. When this probability drops to something on the small side, such as a number below 50 percent, the bank decides to suspend its rule for the time being. When there is very little 'visibility' it is time to over-ride the interest rate rule. The fact that the rule was well rooted in the way the economy operated for quite awhile, so it was right to go on adhering to the rule, does not justify using it when the environment has become – at least for a time – different in unknown ways.

What would it mean to suspend the rule? There is no general way of characterizing what would follow such a suspension. Every situation is *sui generis*. But, in a way, this is a hopeful line of argument. For it means that there is some commonsense merit in a central bank's hewing to a rule in what may be called normal, or low-uncertainty, times. At the same time it is commonsense to acknowledge that there will be situations in which the rule can no longer be applied with any confidence. Then ad hoc intuitions will be brought into play to deal with the unique uncertainties of the time.

3.6 CONCLUDING REMARKS

This chapter has addressed two seeming drawbacks to explicit adoption of a Taylor-type interest rate rule. One drawback to literal application of the Taylor rule at central banks is that the rule as it now stands is afflicted with non-operational elements – so much so that it comes across as almost unworldly. And this aspect of the Taylor rule would make it embarrassing for a central bank to make adoption of such a rule explicit. This chapter has focused on two such weak points: the unobservability of the current natural real rate of interest, and the unobservability of the current natural employment level – thus the excess of actual employment over natural employment or, in an alternate formulation, the excess of consumer demand over consumer supply. The former unobservability is a problem because the natural real rate is not a constant nor even a slow-moving variable; it may dart from one level to another. Thus, some Keynesian and monetarist critics of monetary policy in the interwar depressions, for example, believed that the central banks in the US and the UK had grievously erred in not inferring that the natural real rate had sunk to very low levels by the 1930s. The latter is problematic in an economy in which the market at any time might fail to close the excess demand, since in such a model the excess demand would also be variable. Thus, some supply-siders complained that the Federal Reserve in the latter half of the 1990s was inferring from the historically high employment that employment exceeded its natural level – an inference that might be wrong much of the time – when they presumed that the structure of the economy was changing in such a way that the natural employment level itself was in an upswing.

In response to this drawback, I have explored in this chapter some implications and consequent costs and benefits of imbedding, or submerging, a Taylor rule in a model in which the natural real rate and natural employment (as well as natural output and natural consumption) are variables but they are theoretically determinable from conditions that are – theoretically, at any rate – observable. Taylor's old constants representing the natural real rate and the natural employment level are to be replaced by the model's formula for the natural real interest rate and for excess demand (or for the excess of employment over the natural employment level). The chapter acknowledges that there may be qualms over whether the values of the assets on which the natural rates theoretically depend can be satisfactorily proxied by share prices. It is recognized too that it would repeat the mistake of antecedents who like to mechanize their models if one were to portray even the shadow prices attached to projects by CEOs, let alone the share prices, as a good representation of future investment activity, since the CEOs are to some extent flying blind; few of them could be said to have made a stab at identifying the contingencies to hedge against, their seriousness and their likelihood. On the other hand, who are better situated to judge future investment prospects than the CEOs? At least their assessments ought to be important in interest rate setting.

The second drawback of an explicit interest rate rule, including the rule expanded in section 3.3 to encompass business asset values, is that to acknowledge openly the practice of an interest rate rule would risk embarrassment for the central bank should conditions arise that cause the bank to change its policy or to wish it could be changed. The central bankers might look unwise to be practicing a rule to begin with.

I suggested that the bank might find it satisfactory to practice a rule that it believes will work satisfactorily, at least in normal conditions, if the public understands that occasions may arise in which it is best to limit or even suspend the rule. When conditions become so extreme as to be outside past experience, it makes sense for the bank to curb, or limit, the interest rate response to those conditions. When there is greatly heightened uncertainty of the Knightian type, it is sensible for the central bank to suspend the interest rate rule and follow instead its intuitions about the best response to the new uncertainties. Such actions do not create a presumption that the bank made a mistake in adopting and practicing its past rule; any curbing or suspending of the rule is without prejudice, as the bank may very well go back to the old rule once the temporary emergency has passed.

It might seem that the upshot of this lengthy discussion is a strong endorsement of what central bankers actually do: practice a rule of thumb, which evolves slowly if at all, and stand ready to limit its responses or put it aside in abnormal times. But such a characterization does not get it quite right. Actual practice is perhaps best described as the unacknowledged use of some undisclosed Taylor-type rule as a first-round approximation to the upcoming interest rate decision – with ad hoc adjustments added, based on other data and unmeasurable impressions. Taylor rules may have performed well to date. Yet, if central banks were pressured into making known their Taylor-type rules, that would force them to discuss, analyze and try improvements of their first-round rule. As matters now stand, we on the outside have little chance to identify what may be weaknesses in the prevailing rule of thumb and we have little sense of how much room for improvement the prevailing rule of thumb may leave. As I hope this chapter suggests, it is very likely feasible now to build a second-generation Taylor rule that gives hope of performing distinctly better – at least in what were the normal conditions of the past – than has the original rule.

APPENDIX: EQUATIONS OF THE STABILIZATION MODEL

This Appendix sets out the rational expectations model with Taylor rule that is the subject of section 3.3 of the text. The exposition is hoped to be enough to convey the logic of the reduced-form system of equations. Most of these equations appeared in Phelps (1994) and Phelps et al. (2005). The basic features of the 'customer market' and some features of the customer market equations come from Phelps and Winter (1970).

The setting is a small open economy. The domestic firms have customers to whom to sell and use domestic labor to produce. They compete to regain national customers or to take foreign customers from overseas firms. The net acquisition of customers constitutes the country's net national investment. Nationals, all in the labor force, earn wages from employment and save by accumulating shares in home firms or overseas assets paying the world real interest rate. In the asset markets one witnesses the movement of share prices and the exchange rate.

One block of equations, taking the asset prices as given, treats firms' supply decisions and the concomitant determination of wages and employment. A firm setting a price, p^i, with some expectation about the general, or industry, price level, p^e, and informed about the current real exchange rate, e, can expect that its stock of customers, x^i, will show a growth rate $g(p^i/p, e)$, where $g_1 < 0$; $g_{11} \leq 0$; $g_2 < 0$; $g_{22} \leq 0$; $g(1,1) = 0$. The firm's corresponding per-customer supply c^s_i is a sort of inverse of the supply price. It is a function of p, e, as well as the value, or shadow price, that it puts on having an added customer, q^i. More precisely, what matters is the 'Q ratio', q/c^s, in which the denominator is the output volume to which any price cut or hike would be applied.

Here attention is restricted at all times to atemporal equilibrium, in which case beliefs about the price level among domestic competitors are all correct. For simplicity of exposition it is also supposed that all firms are alike. Then, setting, $p^e = p = 1$, we have for the representative firm:

$$(dx/dt)/x = g(1, e), \tag{3A.1}$$

It is supposed that as we look in on the economy, it is at its rest point, with the corresponding steady-state real exchange rate, $e = 1$. Moreover, at this rest point the country is neither a net creditor nor a net debtor. Furthermore, all nationals are domestic customers and all domestic customers are nationals, that is, residents. Later the analysis is confined to the short run in which the growth rate may be positive or negative (following a structural shift) but x is treated as always close to its (ultimately unchanged) rest point value.

The maximization at each firm of the firm's value leads to an equation implicitly determining (at price $p = 1$) the consumption supply per customer:

$$1+[\eta(1)/\eta'(1) - \zeta = -(q/c^s)[1/\eta'(1)][g_1(1, e)+eg_2(1, e)]; \eta(1) = 1. \tag{3A.2}$$

The left-hand side is the algebraic excess of marginal revenue over marginal cost, a negative value in customer market models as the firm supplies more than called for by the static monopolist's formula for maximum current profit, giving up some of the maximum current profit for the sake of its longer-term interests. An increase in

q means that profits from future customers are high so that each firm reduces its price (equivalently its markup) in order to increase its customer base. The real exchange rate, e, also matters. An increase in e makes domestic firms increase their output even further beyond the point where current marginal revenue equals marginal cost as dictated by a static monopolist. This channel is present if either $g_{12}(1,e) < 0$ or $g_{22}(1, e) < 0$. In two specifications of the labor market unit cost, ζ, is rising with output, $c^s x/\Lambda$. One specification posits a (rising) 'wage curve' based on a shirking view of the labor market; a quitting or turnover view would complicate the story. Another posits a neoclassical labor supply that is positively sloped in the (employment, real wage) plane.

From (3A.2), then, one can express consumer-good supply per customer relative to productivity, c^s/Λ, in terms of q/Λ, e, and x, that is:

$$c^s/\Lambda = \Omega(q/\Lambda, e, x); = \Omega_1(\ ) > 0, \Omega_2(\ ) > 0, = \Omega(\ ). \qquad (3A.3)$$

One can show that $0 < \varepsilon_{q/\Lambda} = d\ln(c^s/\Lambda)/d\ln(q/\Lambda) < 1$; $\varepsilon_e = d\ln(c^s/\Lambda)/d\ln e > 0$; and $-1 < \varepsilon_x = d\ln(c^s/\Lambda)/d\ln x < 0$, where ε_j denotes the partial elasticity of c^s/Λ with respect to the variable j. Again, higher q encourages investing in new customers at a faster rate through a reduced markup, which expands output supply and employment. An increase in e, that is, a real exchange rate appreciation, causes markups to decrease as domestic firms face stiffer competition from foreign suppliers and consequently leads to increases in output and employment. Noting that the markup, say, μ, can be expressed as $1/\zeta$, we can say that our theory implies that, for given x, the markup is inversely related to q/Λ and to e so we write $\mu = m\,(q/\Lambda, e)$. Given x, there is a monotonically negative relationship between the natural rate of employment and the markup. So output supply and the employment level it entails are both positively related to q/Λ, the normalized shadow price, and to e, the real exchange rate – thus increased by real exchange rate appreciation. In a diagram with q/Λ and e on the axes, the iso $(1 - u)$ contours are downward sloping; a northeast move corresponds to an increase in $1 - u$.

A second block of equations deal with saving and consumer demand, investment, and ultimately domestic interest rates and asset prices. Households have to plan their wealth and consumption in the future, putting their savings in domestic shares; any excess is placed overseas and any deficiency implies the placement of shares overseas. Firms have to plan their accumulation of customers, issuing (retiring) a share for each customer gained (lost); any excess of customers over the domestic population implies some customers are overseas and any deficiency means that foreign firms have a share of the market. With the stock of customers, hence shares, sluggish, the general level of share prices is left to clear the asset market.

Consumer demand growth derives from the Blanchard–Yaari setting with its exponential mortality and corresponding wealth accumulation. The growth rate of demand per customer, c^d, is governed by an equation involving the excess of the interest rate over the rate of pure time preference, ρ, and the ratio of (non-human) wealth, W, to consumption, c^d:

$$d\,c^d/dt = (r - \rho)\,c^d - \theta(\theta + \rho\,)W, \qquad (3A.4)$$

where θ denotes the instantaneous probability of death and $W = qx$ here.

The instantaneous rate of return per unit of the customer stock depends on the current price put on a customer (equivalently the price put on a share), the markup, level of consumption, rate of capital gain, and rate at which the customer stock is multiplying or eroding as a result of the real exchange rate, thus competitiveness with overseas firms:

$$[1-\zeta]\, c^s /q + (dq/dt)/q + g(1, e) = r. \tag{3A.5}$$

For international capital market equilibrium with perfect capital mobility, the real interest parity condition must be satisfied, which states that any excess of domestic real interest rate, r, over the exogenously given world real rate of interest, r^*, must be met by an exact amount of expected rate of real exchange depreciation. This equation is:

$$r = r^* - (de/dt)/e. \tag{3A.6}$$

The last point is that the labor market determines a product wage, here also the real wage in terms of consumption, at the intersection (in the familiar Marshallian plane) of an upward sloping 'wage curve' with the sort of demand curve derivable from (3A.2). At this intersection point, where firms employ the amount they require to produce what they want to supply, consumer supply is equal to consumer demand – or, better, *ex ante* consumer demand, which is the expected value of consumer demand. (The firms would have no reason to supply more or to supply less.) This gives us:

$$c^s = c^d \tag{3A.7}$$

Equations (3A.1), (3A.3'), (3A.4), (3A.5), (3A.6) and (3A.7) constitute six equations in the six variables c^s/Λ, c^d/Λ, q/Λ, e, r and x. If we use (3A.7) to replace both c^s/Λ and c^d/Λ by c/Λ we are down to five variables; and by using the relation $c/\Lambda = \Omega(q/\Lambda, e, x)$ in (3A.3') and substituting for r one can reduce the system to the three dynamic equations in the three variables: q/Λ, e and x, the last being a slow-moving variable. The dynamics of the system can be described by the behavior of the endogenous variables q/Λ, e and x after substituting out for c^s/Λ using $c^s/\Lambda =\Omega(q/\Lambda, e, x)$:

$$(dq/dt)/q = [(1+\varepsilon_e)/(1-\varepsilon_{q/\Lambda}+\varepsilon_e)]f(q/\Lambda, e, x)+ [\varepsilon_e/(1-\varepsilon_{q/\Lambda}+\varepsilon_e)]h(q/\Lambda, e, x), \tag{3A.8}$$

$$(de/dt)/e = [(1-\varepsilon_{q/\Lambda})/(1-\varepsilon_{q/\Lambda}+\varepsilon_e)]h(q/\Lambda, e, x)- [\varepsilon_{q/\Lambda}/(1-\varepsilon_{q/\Lambda}+\varepsilon_e)]f(q/\Lambda, e, x), \tag{3.A9}$$

$$(dx/dt)/x = g(1,e), \tag{3.A10}$$

where

$$f(q/\Lambda, e, x) = -[1-Y(\Omega(q/\Lambda, e, x)x)][\,\Omega(q/\Lambda, e, x)/(q/\Lambda)]+\rho+ [\theta(\theta+\rho)qx/(\Lambda\,\Omega(q/\Lambda, e, x))] - [1+\varepsilon_x]g(1, e),$$

$$h(q/\Lambda, e, x) = r^* - \rho - [\theta(\theta + \rho)qx/(\Lambda \Omega(q/\Lambda, e, x))] + \varepsilon_{xs}g(1, e).$$

An analysis may be found in Phelps et al. (2005).

Introducing inflation and the central bank.

The problem of inflation stabilization through the institution of a central bank introduces a new dimension to the system. 'Money will not manage itself', as Bagehot said, so a monetary policy is required for 'stabilization', or 'inflation targeting'. Obviously these considerations introduce new equations. The weightier point, however, is that the bank's freedom to establish arbitrary real expected interest rates – leaving aside the limits to that freedom – raises the need to capture the possibility that the bank could (inadvertently or not) inject an element of intertemporal disequilibrium into an economy that otherwise, thanks to the blessings of rational expectations, would unfailing have avoided such a course.

A basic departure from the above model is that, even though the current wage has equated supply to *ex ante* demand in the customer market, the bank, which intervenes like a *deus ex machina*, could cause an expected real interest rate that is, say, above the natural real interest rate generated by the earlier system of equations. And, as the original model implies, that would cause households to drop the level of their consumption demand with the expectation of saving more and seeing faster growth of their consumption in return:

$$dc^d_t/dt - dc^s_t/dt = \varepsilon (r_t - r^N_t) \tag{3.A11}$$

The fundamental point is that the economy would be in disequilibrium if households were planning to increase their consumption demand faster (or more slowly) than firms are planning to increase their supply. The excess demand equation states that such a disequilibrium occurs if and only if the real expected short-term interest rate exceeds the current natural real interest rate.

An abbreviated Taylor rule has the interest rate respond (in theory) to the natural real interest rate and to any gap between the inflation rate, f, and the target rate:

$$r_t = r^N_t + \alpha (f_t - \pi) \tag{3A.12}$$

It is immediately clear that the bank, by causing the expected real rate to 'track' the natural real rate of the earlier system – before the bank entered the stage – can support and discipline preservation of the inflation rate at the target level. Simultaneously, in this Taylor scenario, the market can clear the goods market and equilibrate the labor market by paying the wage that firms expected was the ruling wage. In theoretical terms, the interest rate of the previous system is actually r^N and the bank is adding a new variable, r, whose behavior is governed by a new equation, (3A.8). Since the two rates are equal, it is explicit that the path taken does not imply an emerging imbalance between the intended path of consumption demand and the intended path of consumption supply – an intertemporal disequilibrium. Equation (3A.11) is a new equation but in the Taylor scenario it does not clash with the previous system; it was already implied by the previous system, though it was redundant in that context.

Much of the text is preoccupied with central bank errors. What if, in terms of actual behavior, the central bank were to make an error, so that:

$$r_t = r_t^N + \delta + \alpha \, (f_t - \pi) \tag{3A.13}$$

When we substitute this errant behavioral rule into the enlarged system, the error, δ, is non-neutral for the system. The only way by which (3A.13) can avoid contradicting the rest of the system is through the last two terms on the right-hand side offsetting each other.

NOTES

*   McVickar Professor of Political Economy and Director, Center on Capitalism and Society, Earth Institute, Columbia University. I am grateful to Roman Frydman and Hian Teck Hoon for numerous conversations.
1.   According to Fair (2006), the earliest study that conceives of the Federal Reserve as following a rule is a paper about the first decade or so after the Treasury Accord by William Dewald and Harry Johnson (1963).
2.   It is at first hard to believe that the monetary authorities in that span had nothing to learn, since it was in 1968 that the Friedman–Phelps thesis of a natural unemployment rate came along and transformed employment theory. However, the Federal Reserve never lacked economists who believed with Wicksell that if the real interest rate were held below the 'natural' real rate there would sooner or later result an explosive rise in the rate of inflation. Many of those economists never believed that the Fed could stabilize employment, no matter what its Congressional mandate said. So the natural unemployment rate concept did not require them to depart significantly from their accustomed reactions to events.
3.   In contrast, Fair (2006) estimates that the form of the interest rate rule he estimated in 1978 also described well the interest-rate setting practiced at the Fed since 1982 and that even the quantitative coefficients are not significantly different between the two periods. We need not enter into this controversy.
4.   If an agency has to have written rules yet monitoring its adherence to them is problematic, it may like best a pseudo-rule that allows it to change the rule through devious means, such as changing the definitions, while it also offers them some of the cover that a genuine rule offers. However, the central bank does not have to have a written rule and, whether it did so or not, outsiders could use their estimates of the bank's actual behavior to forecast the bank's decisions, paying no attention to the way the bank may describe its practices.
5.   Fair's rule, which has what might be called 'learning' in it, makes the short rate depend not only on the inflation rate and the unemployment rate but also the change in the unemployment rate and its own lagged value and the lagged changes in it before that. To facilitate analysis this chapter will exclude the sorts of gradualism present in Fair's rule and start instead with the conveniently static Taylor rule.
6.   If the economy is 'punished' with an above-average r whenever there is an above-average f the market will reduce the current z in response.
7.   A fuller discussion would be required to do justice to the issues. Analyses in the 1970s such as Phelps argued at a time when monetary policy was often described in terms of money supply reactions by the central bank rather than interest rate reactions that a temporary oil shock might require a temporary increase of the money supply to 'accommodate' the shock – to enable the increase in the demand price of output to match the hike in the supply price (both prices calculated at a given employment level). That prescription might be translated to mean that a temporary drop of the real interest rate is required. Note also Phelps (1994) examines at length how the natural employment level may be disturbed by an increase in the real price of overseas oil.

8. In many advanced economies there is at least one inflation-indexed bond such as the Tips in the US. The difference between its interest yield and that on a comparator bond of the unindexed type is widely used as a crude measure of the expected inflation rate, but this difference in yields may reflect market factors other than expectations of the inflation rate. There are opinion surveys of inflation expectations but the average expectation of the inflation rate among respondents may fail to represent closely the average expectation in the market – among households making saving decisions and financiers making investment decisions.

9. New Keynesian modelers generally identify the natural interest rate as the known mean interest rate and they identify the natural unemployment rate and the known unemployment rate; but the former are not best defined as the means of stationary stochastic processes. Below I define them in economic terms.

10. I would comment that, in this respect, the 'stabilization' addressed in my early work (Phelps, 1967, 1972) was the one-time problem of wringing inflation expectations out of the economy by disappointing them to the optimum extent; as a consequence there was not a big premium to knowing precisely the current values of the natural real interest rate and the natural employment level for the next couple of years; and certainly no need to know these natural rates over a long future. It seems to me that the knowledge requirements were much less.

11. A piece of mine opposing rigid adherence to a pre-specified interest rate rule saw only the extra unemployment during the falling inflation and not the implied return to the natural unemployment rate. I had not thought through the adjustment process, which in driving the inflation to farther and farther below the target rate would lead the bank to keep lowering the expected real interest rate, no matter that it was overestimating the natural rate. Gregory Mankiw and Michael Woodford independently brought this point to my attention. I argue in the next paragraph, though, that this scenario is not as benign as they saw it to be.

12. The bank could also compare these estimates with what might be inferred from the actual behavior of consumption, although such an observation is clouded by the possibility that a decrease of consumption is the result of a decrease of consumption supply by firms rather than of consumption demand by households.

13. One way to see this is to rewrite (3.2) in the form $r^N = r - [\,dc^d/dt - dc^s/dt\,]\,(1/c)$ and then substitute (3.3) for $dc^d/dt\,(1/c)$, which cancels out r. It is then clear that the natural rate is higher the faster consumption demand is planned to increase and is lower the faster consumption supply is planned to increase.

14. I hope no one will say this is obvious. I do not recall becoming aware of that relationship over decades of occasional study of models with the customer or the employee as the business asset. It was only in Phelps et al. (2005) that we found this result and began to understand it.

15. This may be the time to comment with regard to the formula in (3.6) that the natural real rate is a function of the expected real rate. Imaginably that would wreak havoc: if r^N were to increase and if r were to be pushed up by the same amount, might r^N then be pushed up as much, so that r would have to be increased again, ad infinitum? The model is such that the derivative of r^N with respect to r is less than 1, so such divergence does not arise.

16. The drop in q, in increasing computed yields, would imply an increase in the expected rate of return on assets were it not for the expectation that there will be a further gradual decline of q over a subsequent period.

17. It would appear to be quite impossible for the nation's central bank to set and maintain indefinitely an expected real rate of interest that exceeds (always by a constant or at any rate non-vanishing amount) the world real interest rate (r^* in the notation of the Appendix). However, no such heroic effort is being imagined here. In keeping the (domestic) expected real interest rate unchanging in spite of the sag in the natural real interest rate, the central bank is thus keeping that rate equal to the world rate. In effect, the exercise in the text is an exploration of the consequence of the bank's maintaining a fixed real exchange rate.

18. Published data on 'market capitalization' appear to calculate for a country the value of the shares in its organized stock exchange or exchanges and then calculate that value per unit of output originating in the companies traded on the exchange. This ratio is commonly taken to be representative of the ratio in the business sector as a whole, although that is unlikely to be true, especially in countries, such as Austria and Italy, where the stock market is severely underdeveloped as compared with other economies having the same high productivity.

REFERENCES

Dewald, William G. and Harry G. Johnson (1963). 'An objective analysis of the objectives of American monetary policy, 1952–61', in Deane Carson (ed.), *Banking and Monetary Studies*, Homewood, IL: Richard D. Irwin, pp. 171–89.

Fair, Ray (1978), 'The sensitivity of fiscal policy effects to assumptions about the behavior of the Federal Reserve', *Econometrica*, **46**, 1165–79.

Fair, Ray (2006), 'Evaluating inflation targeting using a macroeconometric model', Cowles Foundation Discussion Paper 1570, June.

Fitoussi, Jean-Paul, David Jestaz, Edmund Phelps and Gylfi Zoega (2000), 'Roots of the recent recoveries: labor market reforms or private sector forces?' *Brookings Papers on Economic Activity*, Spring, 237–311.

Keynes, J.M. (1947), 'The General Theory of Unemployment', in S.E. Harris (ed.), The New Economics: Keynes' Influence on *The New Economics: Keynes Influence on Theory and Public Policy*, New York: Alfred A. Knopf, p. 145.

Leijonhufvud, Axel (1968), *Keynesian Economics and the Economics of Keynes*, Oxford: Oxford University Press.

Phelps, Edmund S. (1967), 'Phillips curves, expectations of inflation and optimal unemployment over time: reply (to J.W. Williamson)', *Economica*, **34** (135) (August), 254–81.

Phelps, Edmund S. (1972), *Inflation Policy and Unemployment* Theory, New York: W.W. Norton.

Phelps, Edmund S. (1994), *Structural Slumps: The Modern-Equilibrium Theory of Unemployment, Interest and Assets*, Cambridge, MA: Harvard University Press.

Phelps, Edmund S. et al. (1970), *Microeconomic Foundations of Employment and Inflation Theory*, New York: W.W. Norton.

Phelps, Edmund, Hian Teck Hoon and Gylfi Zoega (2005), 'The structuralist perspective on real exchange rate, share price level and employment path', in Willi Semmler (ed.), *Monetary Policy and Unemployment: the US, Euro-Area and Japan*, London: Routledge, pp. 107–32.

Phelps, Edmund S. and Sidney G. Winter, Jr. (1970), 'Optimal price policy under atomistic competition', in E.S. Phelps et al., *Microeconomic Foundations of Employment and Inflation Theory,* New York, W.W. Norton, pp. 309–337.

Phelps, Edmund and Gylfi Zoega (2001), 'Structural booms: productivity expectations and asset valuations', *Economic Policy*, **32** (April), 85–126.

Samuelson, Paul A. (1966), 'Science and Stocks', *Newsweek*, September.

Taylor, John B. (1979), 'Estimation and control of a macroeconomic model with rational expectations', *Econometrica*, **47** (September), 1267–86.

Taylor, John B. (1993), 'Discretion versus policy rules in practice', *Carnegie Rochester Conference Series on Public Policy*, **39**, 195–214.

4. Macroeconomics of broken promises

Daniel Heymann*

4.1 INTRODUCTION

The study of macroeconomic disorders has analytical and practical relevance. The work of Axel Leijonhufvud has been marked by a concern about the scope and limitations of the self-adjustment potential of economic (and social) systems. Hence his maintained interest in the mechanisms and the effects of macroeconomic disruptions, such as the 'two types of crises' (Leijonhufvud, 1998b) that put to the test the ability of economies to deal with stresses. High inflations shorten decision horizons and restrict financial transactions and, in the limit, even the realization of everyday trades (Heymann and Leijonhufvud, 1995). In credit crashes, economies and policies must process the consequences of large-scale 'broken promises' (Leijonhufvud, 2003). This chapter focuses mainly on this second kind of disturbance.

Episodes of recession linked to currency and credit crises have been recently observed in several 'emerging economies' (Kaminsky and Reinhart, 1999). The abruptness of some transitions, and the difficulty of finding statistical associations between the emergence of crises and the past history of 'fundamental variables' (Calvo, 1998; Kaminsky, 1999) have oriented the quest for explanations to 'sudden deaths' associated with multiplicities of rational expectations equilibriums (for example Sachs et al., 1996), or to phenomena of herd behavior (Chari and Kehoe, 2003).

Effects of contagion and imitation seem relevant in critical junctures, when agents perceive that the system may be approaching a sharp turning point, and are prepared to respond with speed and intensity to what others around them are doing. However, agents should already be in a state of alert to the possibility of a discontinuity. This does not look likely to happen without fundamental reasons for people to presume that the economic environment may change quickly and substantially.

Macroeconomic configurations and histories may be interpreted differently. Often, in countries with current account deficits of some size, or

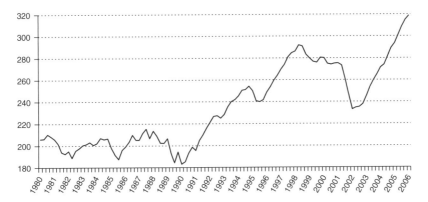

Figure 4.1   GDP at constant prices (billions of pesos of 1993)

where the volume of debts is increasing rapidly, opinions are divided between those that consider the willingness to borrow and to lend as rational responses that correctly contemplate future repayment capacities, and those that anticipate difficulties in the fulfillment of obligations (Heymann, 1994). The assessments of sustainability, in fact, depend on conjectures about future income levels, and thus about the growth potential. By their intricate nature, growth processes are liable to generate heterogeneous and changing beliefs, especially in economies which appear to be undergoing transitions.

The macroeconomic experience of Argentina may offer an illustration of interactions between large-amplitude cycles and the actual and anticipated growth performance. The aggregate output of that economy has clearly not cycled around a fixed linear trend (Figure 4.1). The changes in the medium-term outlook and the wide fluctuations were part of a history characterized by an eventful evolution of private behaviors and public policies. In various instances, the performance of the economy differed considerably from what would have resulted from extrapolating past observations This was noticeable in recent years, marked by a deep crisis in 2001–02.

Trying to make sense of a history of this sort probably requires paying attention to the mechanisms of a general sort that shape behavior, and also to the real-time evolution of beliefs and decisions. The next section discusses some analytical points that seem relevant to large credit crises, especially the role of wealth perceptions, the denomination of financial contracts, and potential effects that may dampen or amplify disturbances. This discussion highlights themes which appear in the context of Argentine fluctuations, an account of which is presented in section 4.3.

4.2   INFORMATION, COORDINATION AND MACROECONOMIC CRISES

Small Fluctuations and Large Crashes

Most normal business cycles are relatively mild ups and downs around more or less well-defined trends. For the average individual, consumption may fall somewhat in a recession, but lifetime living standards are not much changed. Some segments of the population are more exposed to macro-economic movements than others, but an episode of standard magnitude will not alter the income distribution much. If certain agents are interconnected through a network of transactions, most links could be expected to remain in existence after a small recession. The economy keeps its main organizational features even as aggregate real variables oscillate.

Macroeconomic crashes appear as phenomena of another type, in their intensity and in the nature of the processes at work. Given the sizes of the falls in real activity and consumption, working and living patterns of large parts of a population undergo considerable changes (for example during the 1998–2002 Argentine recession, aggregate private consumption declined by more than 20 percent). Such events have major welfare consequences. They can have sizable and lasting implications for the economic prospects of individuals, and may modify substantially the anticipated paths of income and spending.

A precise definition of what constitutes a promise, or the breaking of a promise, would imply non-trivial problems when it is observed (for example, through the values of risk premiums built into interest rates) that the parties have recognized that explicit commitments are not literally unconditional, but at the same time the set of events that would lead to default remains undetermined, and even *ex post* agents may express different opinions as to what circumstances would qualify as 'legitimate' contingencies. However, even without such a sharp definition, it is an observed characteristic of some macroeconomic crises that large numbers of contractual agreements throughout the economy are not fulfilled. In one way or another, those agreements are subject to renegotiation, and the absence of objectively stated contingency clauses complicates the process. While the rearrangement of rights and obligations goes on, production and exchange are hindered by tight credit constraints, and by uncertainties or legal restraints on the command and use of resources. Many firms are closed or reorganized. Trading relationships get broken or disturbed, which complicates the coordination of market exchanges (Howitt, 2006). The economic disorder associated with a crisis may operate like a strong shock on measured aggregate productivity.

Even among major crashes there may be different degrees of intensity, according to the extension of the set of defaulting agents. In an episode of the historical significance of the Great Depression itself, the solvency of public sectors was not put into question everywhere, and thus governments retained some leeway to use the credit available to them in order to alleviate constraints on private spending (Leijonhufvud, 1973). In other cases, the state of default may reach the government, as well as important segments of the private sector. Then, it is practically the whole set of economic obligations which has to be redefined. The system goes through an overall recalculation of asset values, as old estimates (or, at least, old 'face values') have been made irrelevant. But those recalculations themselves and, in general, the potential estimates of future incomes of agents across the economy, are highly uncertain in the midst of a crisis.

In the limit, it is conceivable that a very large shock causes bankruptcies throughout the private sector and default on the public debt, and that desperate monetary expansions or the public's mistrust induce a flight from the national currency. Such a combination of depression and hyperinflation can thoroughly disorganize the economy. It is hard to say how close Argentina came to this outcome in its 2002 crisis. It was prevented, probably through a coincidence of some useful inertia in the behavior of agents, who acted 'in normal mode' in aspects of their everyday economic activity, and a policy response driven by the fearful image of a perfect storm.

Leveraged Growth, Defaults and Renegotiations

Revisions of beliefs about income prospects may generate phenomena typically associated with large credit fluctuations.[1] In contracts subject to default risk, the contractually determined interest rate increases with the size of the debt. There can be a ceiling on the supply of credit, given by the volume of debt that would induce future default even in 'good' states of the world. If some news lowers the ceiling, a sudden adjustment of spending by the debtors may be called for. This effect can induce corridor-type effects. If debtors suffer a small negative income shock with both permanent and transitory components, unrestricted access to credit allows them to smooth the current impact on consumption. By contrast, a large shock that triggers credit rationing can force a large adjustment in the present period, so that the effect of the shock is initially amplified.

In the event of a contraction in the supply of credit, debtors can 'accept' it, or else choose to default. The incentive to default is limited by the costs associated with the breakdown of contracts; however, if the credit 'stop' would induce a too sharp fall in consumption, the shock may cause a suspension of contractual payments. In this sense, credit contractions would be motivated by potential default but, at the same time, they actually occur when their anticipated impact is not so severe as to induce an actual default. When default takes place, there may be circumstances where a restructuring occurs at once; however, sometimes the parties may have incentives to delay an agreement (Ghosal and Miller, 2005). This possibility could arise because of flexibility preference, if future information about the repayment capacity is sufficiently valuable; when the expectations about the future incomes are very diffuse at the time of default, but may become more precise later on, waiting may generate large savings on expected default costs.

Those effects would depend on the values of parameters which are not easy to determine precisely, like the distribution of future output, and the size of the 'penalties' in the case of default. The evolution of views and perceptions about such parameters as new information arrives and gets to be processed, and the decisions taken in consequence, may produce quite eventful histories, as suggested by the Argentine experience.

Wealth Perceptions

Large macroeconomic movements induce changes in wealth perceptions. Reciprocally, widespread defaults on debts and dramatic drops in consumption are naturally interpreted as indications that agents made mistaken forecasts of their own incomes and those of their debtors. Such events disappoint expectations under which agents planned their consumption and asset holdings or, at least, they reveal a 'bad draw' of the lottery that determines income sequences. As a matter of observation, both calculated risk-taking and actual disappointments seem at work in crises. Indicators like interest rate spreads show awareness of the possibility of defaults. However, market behavior sometimes also suggests large differences of beliefs between agents, with some of them taking precautionary measures (for example, by building up liquidity in 'safe' assets) before the crisis became imminent, while many others appear to have been surprised by the event. The Argentine crisis of the first years of this decade provides indications of that heterogeneity.

Everywhere, some agents make mistakes or have bad luck, and the outcomes are somehow processed. Technological innovations by themselves generate irreversible and hardly predictable changes. 'Normal' economies show much volatility at the micro level (Fanelli, 2006). Aggregate wealth is not easy to estimate even there (Haussmann and Sturzenegger, 2005). However, overall, those economies have reasonably well-established trends. Episodes of exuberance may happen in perhaps sizable segments of the economy. Problems of fiscal sustainability may emerge on the horizon. But, typically, the historical experience allows for a certain confidence in extra-polating stylized features of economic growth. In most likely scenarios, broad categories of agents, including the public sector, will face opportu-nities roughly in line with expectations, and service their debts. Everyday problems in coordinating intertemporal decisions (Leijonhufvud, 1981, 1998a) surface in adjustments in the level of consumption of individual households, in low returns for particular firms, or in bankruptcies which are handled routinely. Despite the existence, in principle, of much deep uncer-tainty those results may be seen, on the whole, as unlucky outcomes in rea-sonable gambles.

In entrenched very high inflation, transactions are disturbed, but there are few formal promises to be broken: agents recognize the macroeconomic uncertainty and, therefore, they are reluctant to enter into contracts. Planning and decision horizons are very short; economic behavior shows strong flexibility preference. By contrast, debt crises require agents to have been confident enough to borrow and lend, or to consume beyond their 'permanent' capacity. They must have foreseen a sufficiently good, and probable enough, state of the world to overcome high perceived risks (or have perceived that such risks were not that large). These are features of economies which at a certain moment can appear likely to move up on the international income scales. Crises may mark the uncertainty of the catch-up process.

Uses of the Past

Crises are relatively rare events in a single economy, and they may have dis-tinctive features that limit the information resulting from pooling observa-tions of various episodes (Kaminsky, 2003) The tension between the potential usefulness of analogies with events in other times and places and the arguments for 'differentiation' between cases is observed in practice in the opinions and attitudes of analysts and agents (Leijonhufvud, 2006).

Recommendations of 'structural reforms' have been abundant in policy discussions of recent decades. Whether because of such reforms or for other reasons, some economies appear at times to be undergoing rapid changes in their configuration and behavior. The 'emerging' or 'transition' tags refer to economies which seem in the process of modifying their per-formance in permanent ways; the evidence suggests that these economies experience relatively more intense shifts in measured growth trends (Aguiar and Gopinath, 2004b). In such processes, agents must learn about their future opportunities and constraints. The problem of intertemporal coor-dination appears in concrete terms: whether the actions of other agents in the future will validate the anticipations and actions of an individual.

Different types of behavior may or may not be sustainable, depending on future realizations. A configuration with lower savings rates, real appreciations and investments concentrated in the production of non-tradable goods may, with reasonable motives, generate concerns about the sustainability of dollar debts, but it may turn out to be part of a well-coordinated path if the economy happens to generate enough increases in the supply of tradable goods. In a growth transition, forward-looking behaviors are likely to be based on the anticipation of future changes. A shock to expectations may be immediately identifiable by an outside observer, but it may also consist of 'something that does not happen', such as, in the case just mentioned, less-than-anticipated rises in productivity.

During growth transitions agents are engaged in predicting ongoing development processes. Those can have general features and patterns, but they also appear to contain historical, non-repetitive elements. 'Objective' probabilities of future trends are hard to establish. Decisions are based on conjectures, about expected outcomes, and about the confidence that should be assigned to those expectations. Both type I and type II errors are possible. On occasions, individuals may focus on the existence of strong uncertainties, or on a history of false starts, suggesting caution and skepticism; in others, they may react strongly in an upswing to the prospects of future improvements. A naive form of the rational expectations assumptions ('market variables are generally the result of correct expectations') would lend the appearance of sustainability to current patterns of behavior (as if most collective prophecies were to be fulfilled). In any case, economies subject to crises may have features that could provide rationalization for widely different levels of average income. The sharply changing views about the trends of real and dollar incomes in Argentina illustrate these effects.

The Denomination of Financial Contracts

Incomes measured in terms of foreign currencies are relevant variables when financial contracts are dollarized. The diffusion across countries of the practice of denominating obligations in international currencies, and the consequent potential for debt deflations in the event of real devaluations, have received much attention in recent literature (Jeanne, 2003; Ize and Levy Yeyati, 2003; Cespedes et al., 2000; Chang and Velasco, 2001). Contractual dollarization probably reveals the persistence of doubts about macroeconomic and, particularly, monetary policies. In an economy that has stabilized after a high inflation, the practice of writing dollar contracts may respond to residual fears of a collapse of stabilization in which domestic prices rise abruptly, which offset the perceived risks of shocks on the real exchange rate (Heymann and Kawamura, 2005). An economy which experiences a large expansion of dollarized credits would then correspond with a special configuration of beliefs, with optimism about its real opportunities (so that, in particular, a sustained internal demand would imply high levels of prices and incomes in dollar terms) while, at the same time, agents are suspicious about policy surprises varying the real value of nominal (or indexed) contracts. At the same time, financial dollarization causes 'fear of floating' (Calvo and Reinhart, 2000), and increases the exit costs of fixed-exchange regimes. In the Argentine case, this lock-in effect was particularly important, perhaps much more so than the legal status of the convertibility regime in effect between 1991 and 2001.

Dollarized contracts make the fulfillment of obligations contingent on the stability of real incomes and the real exchange rate. Various types of shocks or expectation changes can shift – considerably – the sustainable real exchange rate, and the perceptions about its value. Irrespective of whether it happens through deflation or nominal depreciation, large relative price movements can then result in insolvencies.

Stabilizers and Multipliers

Even if financial dollarization is a source of vulnerability, not every shock will generate a crisis. If, on average, the shock calls for a relatively small reduction of incomes in terms of the unit of account, the size and diffusion of defaults on debts can also remain limited. A moderate adjustment in aggregate real spending may then restore budget constraints to positions perceived as sustainable, without generating big secondary effects. Large shocks, by contrast, can induce additional rounds of impulses. The crisis that ended the convertibility system in Argentina provides indications of such feedback reactions, where doubts about the solvency of debtors and fears about the future state of the economy led to capital flight and credit contraction, and depressed internal spending, which interrupted trading relationships, in turn reinforcing the spiral. In a state of panic, it would appear that prices of goods and assets must fall considerably to induce 'stabilizing speculation'.

The Argentine crisis illustrates the deep disruptions provoked by the expectation and the realization of a contractual breakdown. At the same time, the recovery after the crash points to the existence of endogenous mechanisms that likely contributed to reverse the decline of real activity. Here, the initial impulse was not a fiscal expansion, which a bankrupt government could hardly attempt (although emergency transfers to low-income households may have helped to maintain demand). A significant effect probably resulted from a reaction of spending (and a moderation of capital flight) by agents who had profited from the massive impact of a large devaluation on the real value of dollar assets (many of which were held in liquid form) and incomes generated in tradable sectors. In a situation of depressed aggregate incomes and tight liquidity constraints, these beneficiaries of a massive redistribution of purchasing power had the resources to initiate a demand injection.

Policies and Institutions

Economic policies are the result of objectives and perceptions of policy-makers. Their incentives, and the special principal–agent problems associated with them, can certainly affect economic performance. However, pure incentive misalignments do not seem capable of generating crises (in the sense of widespread contractual breakdowns) without the intervention of errors in expectations. Policy decisions, as well as the actions of private agents, are predicated upon conjectures about future conditions. The estimation of permanent or normal levels of incomes is an issue for the government, and its prospective creditors, as well as for private parties. Apart from politically induced myopia, policies that appear *ex post* procyclical may also be the result of confusion about macroeconomic trends.

Tightly defined rules may be used to deal with incentive biases in the negotiation, design and implementation of economic policies. Macroeconomic shocks or inconsistencies typically call for policy flexibility. Countries where the political process has tended to produce socially undesirable outcomes (such as a history of high inflation) and which are also potentially subject to large real disturbances will have difficulties in establishing durable and well-functioning macroeconomic institutions. Unbounded discretion may lead to a short-sighted maximization of narrow interests, or to volatile policies responsive to the pressures of the groups that wield the stronger influence at a particular moment. Policy regimes based on rigid rules make seemingly unconditional promises irrespective of contingencies, and may end up breaking down when those commitments become untenable. The Argentine experience of the last decades offers examples of both types.

A monetary rule can only provide an imperfect substitute for a set of stable policies and institutions. The Argentine convertibility regime was instrumental in stopping an endemic inflation; over time it became a central reference for a public who mistrusted political and economic institutions. Eventually, the monetary system was seen as supplying not only a (rigid) nominal anchor, but perhaps also an implicit promise of stability of aggregate income. The fixed exchange rate did serve as an 'external scaffold' (Clark, 1998) to organize economic behavior, but its promised permanence was contingent on the real performance of the economy. The system seemed designed to maximize credibility in order to take advantage of opportunities in a potential 'good state', characterized by high sustainable income levels and a historically appreciated real exchange rate. Almost by construction, neither monetary policies nor the financial sector nor the political system were prepared to handle a situation where a substantial real depreciation was required.

The choice of institutions and policies depends on the political game (interests, power), and also on how the public and policy-makers process past experiences (Sargent, 2001). The choice of the convertibility regime in Argentina in the early 1990s was influenced by the particular inflationary history of the country. Traces of the past experience of the economy can also be found in features of the economic and policy behavior after the breakdown of convertibility.

Crises typically motivate intensive learning (or, at least, changes of beliefs and opinions) on the part of private and public agents. At the same time, they manifest or induce problems in policy-making. Ultimately, high inflation reflects a failure of societies and political systems to agree on systematic ways to deal with the pressures on the government budget. Credit crises in open economies may involve an overspending by the public sector that does not elicit a 'Ricardian' response of spending restraint in the public. In any case, crises like that of Argentina throw into an already disturbed political arena the question of whether, and how, to intervene to revise broken contracts when 'the rules on the ways to deal with the violation of rules have been violated' (Leijonhufvud, 2003; Vaz, 1999). And, even in a post-crisis recovery, rebuilding institutions after a big shock is certainly a non-trivial matter.

4.3   CRISIS AND RECOVERY IN ARGENTINA[2]

After Hyperinflation: Large-Scale Reforms, Tight Constraints on Monetary Policies

By the end of the 1980s, Argentina had an eventful history of high inflation. But even for a population with that experience, the hyperinflationary episodes of 1989 and 1990 represented truly traumatic events. These reinforced the public demand for price stabilization, and the view that dealing effectively with inflation required tight constraints on the central bank. The prominent problem was to restrict discretion and to stabilize price expectations; maintaining flexibility to manage shocks or inconsistencies was not perceived as a salient concern. At the same time, the widespread use of the dollar as a store of value and unit of denomination had made the exchange

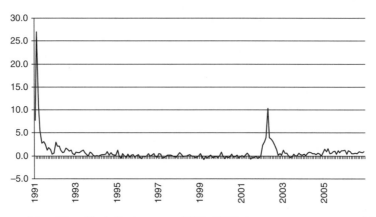

Figure 4.2   Monthly inflation rates 1991, 2006 (percentages per month)

rate a highly visible reference for everyday decisions. Thus, the public was predisposed to receive favorably the establishment of a monetary system close to a currency board. This was part of a set of comprehensive policy changes (see Heymann and Kosacoff, 2000; Stallings and Peres, 2000), with the introduction of new tax legislation and procedures, the privatization of most public enterprises and the liberalization of foreign trade. Such measures were meant, and understood, as actions designed to induce discrete changes in economic incentives and behaviors, and to produce a break in the growth trend.

Redefining Expectations

After the fixing of the exchange rate, although prices continued to drift upwards, they did so at a much slower (and decelerating) rate (Figure 4.2). The drop in interest rates indicated strong immediate impacts on expectations. The drastic fall in the heavy inflation tax and the reduced short-term macroeconomic uncertainty induced spending. Lower risk perceptions reversed incentives for capital flight and stimulated a revival of the internal supply of credit, also favored by the predisposition of international lenders to finance 'emerging economies'. After a period of bleak economic prospects, and tight liquidity constraints, aggregate consumption led a strong expansion of domestic spending and real activity.

Discriminating trends from transitory effects was not an easy task. Policy reforms lacking credibility as to their persistence or transitory disinflations can in principle stimulate consumption through intertemporal substitution effects. The permanence of the convertibility regime (which lasted ten years, until its eventual collapse) was not firmly established, and doubts

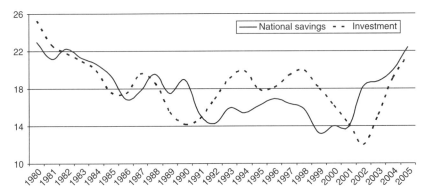

Figure 4.3   National savings and investment at current prices (percentages of GDP)

remained about the effects of the reforms. This was reflected in indicators such as the absence of a large market for assets in domestic currency except for short maturities. However, many decisions taken during the period seemed to reflect the expectation of sustained increases in incomes, in real and in dollar terms, inducing stronger propensities to consume, to invest in production for local use, and to supply and demand credit in order to finance those activities. A fluid repayment of the newly contracted debts was contingent on the realization of high enough future incomes in dollar terms, and consequently, on sufficient growth in the supply (or in the world prices) of tradable goods.

Changes in Behavior, Re-evaluations of Permanent Incomes

The expansion showed, as a characteristic feature, a decline in the savings rate (and particularly in private savings), along with a recovery in investment[3] (Figure 4.3), much of which went to activities that mainly served the domestic market. Employment increased, especially in service sectors, although labor-saving decisions, especially in manufacturing and now privatized utilities, tended to reduce the demand for segments of workers, mainly in unskilled categories (Damill et al., 2003). Manufacturing firms faced stronger import competition, while they had access to cheaper and more varied inputs and capital goods. The response was heterogeneous, with visible increases in productivity in some enterprises, and difficulties for others, resulting in a high mortality of firms (Kosacoff and Ramos, 1999). In the export-oriented agriculture, the use of improved methods of cultivation of grains became increasingly widespread. However, the aggregate size of exports did not show any significant growth until 1994.

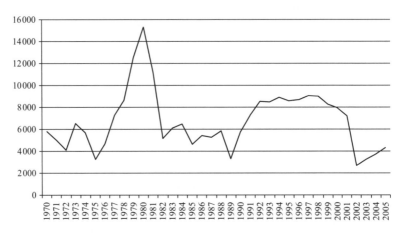

Figure 4.4   Argentina GDP per capita at constant dollars of 2000

Build-up of Dollar Liabilities

The surge in domestic demand was associated with a considerable real appreciation: although the inflation rate eventually converged to very low values, in the meantime, the level of domestic price increased substantially, as did wages. With rising gross domestic product (GDP) and a lower real exchange rate, the purchasing power of domestic output in terms of foreign currencies was greatly revalued (Figure 4.4).

Most new loans were denominated in dollars. The government did not treat this as problematic or risky: the expansion of credit and the rising capital inflows were interpreted as signs of confidence, and as precursors of more growth. Much higher tax revenues and proceeds from privatizations reduced the government's borrowing requirements (Figure 4.5). The public sector restructured its debt within the Brady Plan, which reduced the interest burden. However, the value of liabilities of the public sector increased, mainly because of the recognition of previously undocumented obligations. In 1994, the primary balance of the government was reduced by the pension reform, which transferred revenues from social security taxes to private funds.

Conflicting Signals and Credit Crunch

By 1994 the economy was in a strong expansion, although the macro performance allowed different interpretations about its sustainability. The rise in domestic demand slowed down after the increase in US interest rates; later, the Mexican devaluation at the end of the year was followed by a strong financial shock.

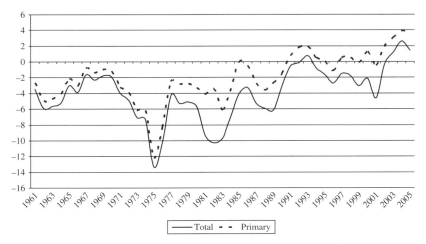

Figure 4.5   Primary and total budget balances, national public sector (percentage of GDP)

The analogy with the case of Mexico had been used in the past as a positive indication of the effect of reforms. Now the comparison seemed to operate in the opposite direction, and to suggest the existence of fragilities which had gone undetected or underemphasized. The suspicion that there may be 'something fundamentally wrong', and imitation effects, appeared to combine to generate a run on deposits. The pressure fell on the central bank, which extended rediscounts. Foreign exchange reserves declined, while bank credit contracted sharply. Aggregate demand and output fell considerably. Unemployment jumped by around six percentage points (to more than 18 percent) in the first half of 1995.

Surviving the Crunch

However, even in recession, the strongest fear of the majority of the public seemed that of a depreciation that would increase the real value of dollar debts and perhaps trigger high inflation. A package of international loans backed the government's insistence that it did not contemplate devaluation, and the definite results of the vote that re-elected the President supported that position. Funds flowed back to the banks, and real activity recovered in the last part of the year. Eventually, the episode was widely interpreted as a successful test of the resilience of the policy scheme. In the government's view, the shock did not reveal weaknesses in the macroeconomic framework, but rather the subsistence of mistaken doubts about its commitment to the monetary system.

Long-Lasting Growth?

The new expansion showed strong growth of exports (the value of which doubled in five years), propelled by improvements in external markets and, on the supply side, by productivity increases, in agriculture particularly. Investment reached peaks of about 22 percent of GDP, while savings rose above the levels of the initial years of convertibility. The current account deficit remained considerable, however, in connection with a high demand for imports and increasing interest on foreign debts. A rising proportion of external financing took the form of foreign direct investment (FDI). The broad and growing presence of international companies (in sectors like banks, manufacturing and utilities) suggested that macroeconomic concerns were not prominent in their decisions at the time.

Sustainability Issues

In 1998, seven years after the fixing of the exchange rate, real GDP had accumulated a growth of around 50 percent (5.5 percent annual average) since the start of the decade. The aggregate increase in incomes had been substantial, although distribution had become more uneven. Warnings about exchange rate misalignment had not been validated so far. The dollar value of GDP showed relatively steady levels, reaching about $9000 per capita.

However, the current account deficit had widened, while the government was generating only small primary surpluses. The public and foreign debts, and the corresponding interest flows, had been rising, in a period of rapid increases in real activity and the value of exports. Sustainability critically depended on a continuation of strong export growth. Otherwise, the alternative to a persistent use of large amounts of external credit (the availability of which a country like Argentina could hardly take for granted without visible signs of export potential) was a perhaps sharp deceleration of domestic demand. But slowdowns in government revenues would raise financing requirements while eroding perceptions about fiscal solvency. Such effects were visible in the period that led to the crisis of the convertibility system.

Trade, Financial Shocks; Recession

Exports and real activity fell in absolute terms in 1999, influenced by higher interest rates after the outbreak of the Russian crisis, lower commodity prices, and the Brazilian devaluation. Weaker revenues and pre-electoral spending, in both the national and provincial jurisdictions, pushed the deficit upwards; the government obtained exceptional financing through the sale of its remaining shares in the national oil company (YPF). Lower investment, higher levels of 'country risk' and the accumulation of foreign assets showed that segments of the private sector were starting to seek shelter. However, these behaviors were comparatively mild at first, and did not indicate a panic, or general fears of rapid collapse. The widespread discussion of the possibility of full dollarization indicated the influence of the view that the main open question was not the capability of sustaining aggregate income at the current levels, but the existence of a potential exit clause from the fixed exchange rate. The 1999 presidential election (won by a coalition of opposition parties) showed public concern about social issues but not a demand for major economic changes, particularly regarding the monetary system.

Hoping for Recovery

In any case, economic agents were alert to signals of economic strength or weakness. Attitudes and behaviors reflected the tension between the prospects of two polar scenarios. In one, real activity and exports recovered, and allowed simultaneous adjustments in the current account and fiscal deficits, and their financing at moderate costs. At the other extreme was a process of spiraling difficulties, with the likelihood that a debt deflation might trigger a financial crisis. Although the new government managed to reduce the fiscal deficit through tax increases and spending cuts, financing requirements remained high, and adjustment measures were generally interpreted as recessionary indications. With stagnant aggregate output in 2000, the lack of definite good news gradually intensified the doubts of the public, and the sensitivity to short-term signs, like the daily movements of the prices of government bonds. Nevertheless, the demand for deposits did not yet show fears for the solidity of banks.

Disappointment: Categorical Shift?

At the end of 2000, the government negotiated a package of loans from the International Monetary Fund (IMF). The announcement effect on interest rates did not last long, as real activity did not react and tax revenues were lower than anticipated. In a state of great political tension, the post of Economy Minister changed hands twice in a few days. Although the reappointment of the minister who had introduced the convertibility system tried to remove concerns about a possible devaluation, attitudes and behavior showed a sharp worsening of expectations. It seemed as if many agents went from a waiting mood to presuming that a crisis was in the making, and switched to that scenario as a basis for decisions (in a manner reminiscent of the 'thinking through categories' modeled by Mullainathan, 2002). This showed, particularly, in large-scale portfolio shifts from local assets (including bank deposits) into foreign currencies, and in a drastic fall in the demand for goods and services.

Outside the Corridor

In the last three quarters of 2001, real GDP contracted by more than 10 percent and investment collapsed. Lower realized incomes and fears of further declines combined to induce an abrupt fall in consumption. Smaller tax revenues, without hints of a recovery in sight, aggravated fiscal difficulties, while the demand for public debt kept shrinking. Cut from access to 'voluntary' credit, the government delayed payments and pressured banks and pension funds for loans. A large swap operation was organized, through which the government tried to extend the maturity of its debt. However, the very high yields of the newly issued bonds meant that repayment would be, and was expected to be, very problematic.

The perception that a hard-pressed government was using the banks as lenders of last resort, and that firms were experiencing a vertical decrease in sales, discouraged the holding of deposits and reinforced the demand for foreign exchange. The crowding-out effect and the drop in deposits induced a sharp decline in credit to the private sector. Liquidity constraints tightened throughout the economy. The central bank granted large volumes of rediscounts, while provincial governments tried to make ends meet by issuing quasi-monies; the monetary expansion was sterilized by falling reserves. Although the public generally still seemed to regard with much fear the possibility of devaluation, the spiral of falling activity, fiscal hardship and runs on deposits and foreign reserves made the end of the system of convertibility an imminent prospect.

Economic Crash, Institutional Disruption

The last part of 2001 was a period of hectic policy activity. The ongoing crisis was the subject of much discussion, domestically and abroad. However, no concrete, practical scheme emerged to stop the downward spiral, or to organize a mechanism to moderate the costs of an exit from the convertibility system and a restructuring of debts. The final months were marked by extreme political tension, culminating in demonstrations that led to the resignation of the government. After a period of much turbulence, Congress appointed a provisional President who remained in office until the elections held in 2003.

Contractual Breakdown

In December 2001, when the run was accelerating, the authorities limited cash withdrawals from banks, and restricted sales of foreign exchange. This meant suspending the convertibility of deposits into currency and domestic money into dollars. Depositors loudly protested. In an economy where many transactions were carried out with cash, those restrictions caused strong constraints on trade; their unpopularity contributed to the downfall of the government.

In the midst of a great turmoil, new authorities announced that the public sector would stop making payments on its bonds, and the termination of the convertibility system. A jump in the exchange rate immediately posed the problem of dealing with the large volume of dollar-denominated debts, and with the trade-offs between a massive intervention and a hands-off approach that would rely on arrangements between parties. The government chose not to legislate on obligations which did not involve financial intermediaries, while it decided an 'asymmetric pessification' of bank deposit and loans: dollar loans were converted into pesos at a one-to-one rate, while a 1.4 rate was used for deposits.

Although in principle the scheme increased the domestic purchasing power of deposits, public demonstrations and numerous legal demands manifested the strong reaction against pessification and the reprogramming of maturities. In part because of judicial decisions, the fall in deposits continued even while strong restrictions on withdrawals were in effect. Those restrictions and the disappearance of credit tightened liquidity constraints faced by consumers and by many firms, when the prices of imported inputs had risen sharply. Agents with available resources were unwilling to spend, and showed a strong preference for foreign assets. In 2002, in the midst of a very deep recession, the savings rate increased noticeably, and private capital outflows exceeded 10 percent of GDP (Figure 4.6). Lower tax collection resulted in a sizable primary budget deficit. Central bank credits to the government and to the financial sector fueled monetary expansion, while the issue of quasi-monies continued at a rapid pace.

Avoiding Hyperinflation

The exchange rate with the dollar multiplied by a factor of around four in the first half of 2002. However, in everyday transactions the population did not repudiate the national currency, which remained in general use as mean of payment and price denominator. Together with the depression in demand, the perception by the public that the pre-devaluation values were

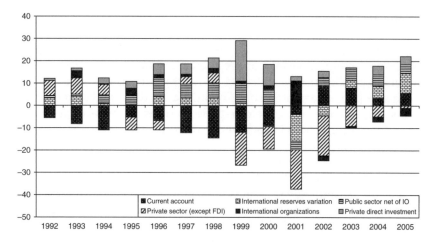

Figure 4.6   Current account and capital flows (percentage of GDP)

still pertinent to evaluate current prices probably deterred price increases. It seemed as if the collective behavior of agents invalidated their previous expectations of a monetary collapse if convertibility was abandoned, which had likely contributed to the spread of dollar contracting.

The initial response of the consumer price index (CPI) was quite slow. Although this outcome was fragile (the monthly rate of price growth reached a peak of 10 percent in April), it gave fiscal and monetary policies some time to react. The fear of hyperinflation, and its predictable political consequences, operated as a strong incentive on policy-making, even if the end of the convertibility regime had removed both the nominal anchor and the set of constraints which had ruled monetary management for more than ten years, and no clearly defined alternative system had been established in replacement.

Relative prices changed abruptly after the devaluation, with a jump in the real exchange rate. While other tax bases were at depressed levels, the imposition of export duties made a considerable contribution to revenues. The lack of adjustment in government salaries and pensions contained spending. The primary balance of the public sector turned positive which, along with a deceleration of the fall in deposits, removed pressures on monetary policies. The value of the domestic monetary aggregates had been reduced relative to that of central bank reserves, increasing the effectiveness of interventions in the foreign exchange market. Thus, the fiscal and monetary difficulties were alleviated, which represented significant news when seen against the recent prospects of total collapse.

Spending by Liquid Agents

Aggregate spending and output, in real and in dollar terms, had dropped to historically very low levels (Figures 4.1 and 4.4). While the economic and social climate encouraged capital flight, the low dollar prices of local goods and assets opened profitable opportunities for agents with liquid positions, exporters and holders of disposable dollar balances in particular. Behind the dramatic tone of everyday news, the large values of the trade surplus and of dollar hoards meant that there was a ready and sizable source of foreign exchange supply, and of domestic demand, once the fears of an imminent debacle somehow moderated.

In the second half of 2002 the capital outflow slowed down. The currency appreciated, which dissipated inflationary expectations. The central bank intervened to prevent a large fall in the price of the dollar (a policy that continued in the following years), and purchased considerable amounts of foreign exchange. Restrictions to cash withdrawals from banks were removed without consequence. The issue of quasi-monies stopped, as tax collection grew well above current government spending. Industrial output initiated a recovery, first through some substitution of imports, later mainly to supply a rising domestic absorption. Firms had benefited from the drastic pessification of their bank debts, and many had started to renegotiate other obligations, including those with foreign creditors. Wages had lagged considerably behind industrial prices; the rise in unit margins facilitated self-financing. The level of activity could start to reverse its fall despite the almost complete absence of credit.

Residues of the Crisis

The crisis left visible marks, in social conditions and in delayed repercussions of contractual breakdowns. The unemployment rate reached highs of near 25 percent, while real wages fell sharply. The drastic decline in living standards of lower-income groups, only partially alleviated by emergency social programs, was reflected in a jump in the proportion of households below the poverty line. Meanwhile, the real incomes of some sectors, producers of tradable goods, in particular, rose significantly. The revaluation of dollar assets caused a sizable wealth effect, mostly favoring groups in the upper scales of the distribution, and those who had participated in the capital outflow.

The contractual breakdown remained the source of legal and political controversy. The redefinition of the regulatory framework for public utilities implied long and problematic discussions. The public debt to be restructured had grown sharply relative to GDP and to tax revenues. In the complicated process of renegotiation, finalized more than three years after the declaration of default, the government stressed that it had no urgency to close a deal in order to access new credits. Eventually, three-quarters of the creditors participated in a bond swap based on the projection of primary surpluses in the order of 3 percent of GDP along a path with moderate growth and a gradual real revaluation, and which implied a sizable debt reduction.

Another Recovery: In Search of a Trend

Despite the remaining doubts, the economy showed a rapid revival. By the end of 2005, real GDP had regained the levels of the previous peak (with an average annual increase of about 9 percent from the trough of the recession). Savings rates, in the aggregate, and for the public sector, were higher than in the previous decade. This was reflected in the current account and budget surpluses. The rebound in real activity was labor-intensive, so that the unemployment rate declined considerably, approaching 10 percent.

A self-financed recovery appeared less vulnerable than past instances where a rising domestic demand had as counterpart the use of large amounts of foreign credit. The systemic disruption seemed to have had less permanent effects than once feared. However, there were still uncertainties about the system of policy rules and criteria that might guide longer-run decisions and govern inflationary expectations. The more favorable terms of trade depended on variable international circumstances. Planning horizons, much extended in the recovery, remained relatively short. The political system still faced the traditional problem of reconciling multiple conflicting claims on the budget. Macroeconomic conditions had improved drastically after the crisis; the search for a sustained growth trend, and for a compatible path of spending, remained an open matter.

4.4   CONCLUDING REMARKS

Macroeconomic crises are memorable events. For many individuals, they define a temporal landmark. Crises disturb plans and motivate revisions of attitudes and beliefs. In some cases, the economic malfunction can endanger the social order (Leijonhufvud, 2003). Such disruptions generate demands for analytical and for policy lessons. The search presupposes that there is something to learn in the exercise. The activity makes sense only if there is some relevant knowledge which was previously unavailable. It seems natural to assume that economic agents, who often manifest having been surprised, and shocked, by crises, have also acted on imperfect knowledge.

The 'fundamental' estimation of long-run rates of return and repayment capacities relies on uncertain, and variable, conjectures and models of behavior. Fundamentals that determine the development of economies where structures and institutions are undergoing possibly irreversible changes are not readily identified, measured and projected. Near 'bifurcations', when crises erupt or precipitate, agents visibly watch the immediate behavior of others, either to try to extract information from the particular knowledge that they may have, or to find out whether runs or panics are in the making. However, the possibility of those effects that may induce 'mass movements' seems to be conditioned by perceived fundamental processes (Burnside et al., 2000). The typical background of panics seems to be one where previous beliefs held with some confidence are seriously in doubt, and where individuals are ready to make substantial changes in their views about the future. The shift to an 'imitation mode' probably marks a situation where the procedures that agents used to form expectations by themselves are considered unreliable. In any case, crises usually alter interpretations of the economy's past, as well as anticipated prospects. Features of an economy which once could be considered major assets may come to be seen as problems or obstacles; policies or institutions which in the past served as trust-inspiring references may now be blamed for disappointments.

The Argentine economy provides vivid examples of wide economic fluctuations and large swings in opinion about growth prospects. We have suggested that both phenomena were causally related, as changing views about the trend of the economy influenced current performance, and beliefs were conditioned by the observed evolution. The predisposition of agents to vary their perceptions was probably comparatively strong in an economy with a history of 'variable trends' and where structural changes or policy shifts could motivate the expectation of discontinuities in the growth path. On several occasions it appeared that evaluations of permanent incomes experienced sharp revisions as agents gathered or reinterpreted information. The credit market seemed to generate, according to the moment, both deviation-reducing and deviation-amplifying effects of shocks, according to the shifts in the estimates of future incomes and the repayment capacity of prospective debtors. Interactions between economic performance and policy or institutional changes were frequently salient in the Argentine cycles. In some instances, these interactions probably reflected history-dependent behaviors, as in the reliance on a very tight monetary rule to stabilize in the early 1990s and the absence of a return of very high inflation when that rule was broken in dramatic circumstances.

The varied experience of this economy highlights themes which have been prominent in the work of Axel Leijonhufvud. Whatever the validity of specific arguments, a glance at experiences like that of Argentina should probably identify, in one way or another, the problems of intertemporal coordination, the counterpoint between small and large disturbances, the relevance of the sequential decision-making of agents and the interrelated dynamics of policy institutions and economic performance. The contributions of Leijonhufvud will continue to help in understanding the behavior of concrete economies.

NOTES

*   This is a shorter and revised version of a paper presented at the Conference in Honor of Axel Leijonhufvud at the University of California, Los Angeles (UCLA), 30–31 August 2006. A Spanish version was published as Heymann (2007). Thanks are due to the participants in that conference and to R. Abrutzky, G. Anllo, O. Cetrangolo, R. Farmer, L. Gorno, R. Martinez, A. Ramos, J. Reparaz, P. Sanguinetti, H. Seoane and especially to C.F. Bramuglia for their helpful comments. The usual disclaimer applies.
1. The following remarks owe much to conversations with L. Gorno. See also Heymann et al. (2001), Aguiar and Gopinath (2004a), Arellano and Mendoza (2002), Mendoza (2006).
2. The performance of the Argentina economy since the early 1990s, and especially the crisis of the convertibility system, has been analyzed in, among others, Perry and Servén (2002), Haussmann and Velasco (2002), Powell (2002), Damill and Frenkel (2003), De la Torre et al. (2002), Galiani et al. (2003), Heymann (2006) and Mussa (2002). The title of this last work: 'Argentina and the Fund: from triumph to tragedy' suggests how strong were changes in perceptions associated with the crisis.
3. Between 1990, the year of the cyclical trough, and the peak in 1994, the savings rate at current prices declined 3.5 points (from 18.9 percent to 15.4 percent), while the investment rate increased 5.8 points (from 14.1 percent to 19.9 percent). The savings rate was also lower (by 3.4 percentage points), and the investment rate higher (by 1.6 points) when comparing averages of the 1991–94 with the averages of the 1988–90 recessions.

REFERENCES

Aguiar, M. and G. Gopinath (2004a), 'Defaultable debt, interest rates and the current account', Federal Reserve Bank of Boston Working Paper 04-5.
Aguiar, M. and G. Gopinath (2004b), 'Emerging markets business cycles: the cycle is the trend', NBER Working Paper 10734.
Arellano, C. and E. Mendoza (2002), 'Credit frictions and "sudden stops" in Small open economies: an equilibrium business cycle framework for emerging market crises', NBER Working Paper 8880.
Burnside, C., M. Eichenbaum and S. Rebelo (2000), 'On the fundamentals of self-fulfilling speculative attacks', Rochester Center for Economic Research Working Paper 468.
Calvo, G. (1998), 'Capital flows and capital-market crises: the simple economics of sudden stops', *Journal of Applied Economics*, **1** (1), 35–54.
Calvo, G. and C. Reinhart (2000), 'The fear of floating', NBER Working Paper 7993.

Cespedes, L., R. Chang and A. Velasco (2000), 'Balance sheets and exchange rate policy', NBER Working Paper 7840.

Chang, R. and A. Velasco (2001), 'A model of financial crises in emerging markets', *Quarterly Journal of Economics*, **116** (May), 489–517.

Chari, V. and P. Kehoe (2003). 'Hot Money', *Journal of Political Economy*, **111** (6), 1262–92

Clark, A. (1998), *Being there*, Cambridge, MA: MIT Press.

Damill, M. and R. Frenkel (2003), 'Macroeconomic performance and crisis', New York: Initiative for Policy Dialogue, Working Paper No. 7.

Damill, M., R. Frenkel and R. Maurizio (2003), 'Políticas macroeconómicas y Vulnerabilidad Social: la Argentina de los Años Noventa', Santiago de Chile: CEPAL, Working Paper, Financiamiento del Desarrollo, 135.

De la Torre, A., E. Levy Yeyati and S. Schmuckler (2002), 'Argentina's financial crisis: floating money, sinking banking', World Bank Working Paper.

Fanelli, J. (2006), 'International financial architecture, macro volatility and institutions: an overview', CEDES Working Paper.

Galiani, S., D. Heymann and M. Tommasi (2003), 'Great expectations and hard times: the Argentine convertibility plan', *Economia* (*Latin American and the Caribbean Economic Association*), Spring, 109–47.

Ghosal, S. and M. Miller (2005), 'Bargaining with delay: growth and sustainability', University of Warwick Working Paper.

Haussmann, R. and F. Sturzenegger (2005), 'US and global imbalances: can dark matter prevent a Big Bang?' Kennedy School of Government, mimeo.

Haussmann, R. and A. Velasco (2002), 'Hard money's soft underbelly: understanding the Argentine crisis', Kennedy School of Government Working Paper.

Heymann, D. (1994), 'Sobre la Interpretación de la Cuenta Corriente', *Economia Mexicana*, **III** (1), 31–59.

Heymann, D. (2006), 'Buscando la Tendencia: Crisis Macroeconómica y Recuperación en la Argentina', Buenas Aires: CEPAL, Working Paper 31.

Heymann, D. (2007), 'Macroeconomia de las Promesas Rotas', *Revista de Economia Politica de Buenos Aires*, **1**(2), 27–54.

Heymann, D., M. Kaufman and P. Sanguinetti (2001), 'Learning about trends: spending and credit fluctuations in open economies', in A. Leijonhufvud, (ed.) *Monetary Theory as a Basis for Monetary Policy*, New York: Palgrave, 173–203.

Heymann, D. and E. Kawamura (2005), 'On liability dollarization: a simple model', CEPAL Buenos Aires Working Paper.

Heymann, D. and B. Kosacoff, (eds) (2000), *Desempeño Económico en un Contexto de Reformas: la Argentina de los Noventa*, Buenos Aires, Editorial Universitaria de Buenos Aires.

Heymann, D. and A. Leijonhufvud (1995), *High Inflation*, Oxford: Oxford University Press.

Heymann, D., R. Perazzo and A. Schuschny (2004), 'Learning and imitation in variants of the BAM', *Advances in Complex Systems*, (March), 21–38.

Howitt, P. (2006), 'The microfoundations of the Keynesian multiplier process', *Journal of Economic Interaction and Coordination*, **1**(1), 33–44.

Ize, A. and E. Levy Yeyati (2003), 'Financial dollarization', *Journal of International Economics*, **59**, 323–47

Jeanne, O. (2003), 'Why do emerging economies borrow in foreign currency', IMF Working Paper.

Kaminsky, G. (1999), 'Currency and banking crises: the early warnings of distress', Working Paper.

Kaminsky, G. (2003), 'Varieties of currency crises', NBER Working Paper 10193.

Kaminsky, G. and C. Reinhart (1999), 'The twin crises: the causes of banking and balance of payments problems', *American Economic Review*, **89** (3), 473–500.

Kosacoff, B. and A. Ramos (1999), *La Estructura Argentina Contemporánea*, 1975–2000, Buenos Aires, Universidad Nacional de Quilmes.

Leijonhufvud, A. (1973), 'Effective demand failures', *Swedish Economic Journal*, **75** (1), 27–48.

Leijonhufvud, A. (1981), 'The Wicksell connection: variations on a theme', in A. Leijonhufvud, *Information and Coordination*, Oxford: Oxford University Press, pp. 131–202.

Leijonhufvud, A. (1998a), 'Mr. Keynes and the Moderns', *European Journal of the History of Economic Thought*, **5**, 169–88.

Leijonhufvud, A. (1998b), 'Two types of crises', *Zagreb Journal of Economics*, **2** (December), 39–54.

Leijonhufvud, A. (2003), 'Macroeconomic crises and the social order', invited lecture, Universidad Nacional de la Plata.

Leijonhufvud, A. (2006), 'The uses of the past', invited lecture, The European Society for the History of Economic Thought.

Mendoza, E. (2006), 'Lessons from the debt-deflation theory of sudden stops', NBER Working Paper 11966

Mullainathan, S. (2002), 'Thinking through categories', Working Paper.

Mussa, M. (2002), 'Argentina and the Fund: from triumph to tragedy', Institute of International Economics Working Paper.

Perry, G. and M. Servén (2002), 'The anatomy of a multiple crisis: why was Argentina special and what can we learn from it?', World Bank Working Paper.

Powell, A. (2002), 'The Argentine crisis: bad luck, bad economics, bad advice', Universidad Torcuato Di Tella Working Paper.

Sachs, J., A. Tornell and A. Velasco (1996), 'The Mexican peso crisis: sudden death or death foretold?' *Journal of International Economics*, **41**, (November), 265–83.

Sargent, T. (2001), *The conquest of American inflation*, Princeton: Princeton University Press.

Stallings, B. and W. Peres (2000), *Crecimiento, Empleo y Equidad; El Impacto de las Reformas Económicas en América Latina*, Mexico: Fondo de Cultura Económica.

Vaz, D. (1999), 'Four banking crises: their causes and consequences', *Revista de Economía*, **6** (1), 29–346.

5. Bankruptcy and collateral in debt constrained markets

Timothy J. Kehoe and David K. Levine*

> The absence of private information implies that no consumer actually goes bankrupt in equilibrium: the credit agency will never lend so much to consumers that they will choose bankruptcy. This is very unlike . . . incomplete markets bankruptcy models. (Kehoe and Levine 2001)

5.1 INTRODUCTION: 'A FOOLISH CONSISTENCY IS THE HOBGOBLIN OF LITTLE MINDS'[1]

General equilibrium models of bankruptcy have generally taken the perspective that bankruptcy is observed in the world, and so general equilibrium models should attempt to account for it. This point of view is very much in the spirit of the incomplete markets models on which these models are based. The theoretical literature on equilibria with incomplete markets and bankruptcy includes Araujo et al. (2002), Dubey et al. (1995), Dubey et al. (1989), Geanakoplos and Zame (2002), Kubler and Schmedders, (2003), Orrillo (2002) and Zame (1993). Recently papers by Chatterjee et al. (2004) and Livshits et al. (2003) have constructed models with incomplete markets and bankruptcy, calibrated them to data, and used them to address policy issues. These models only partially address some fundamental questions: Why should bankruptcy be allowed? What underlying economic fundamentals lead to particular types of bankruptcy?

The enforcement constraint models of Kehoe and Levine (1993, 2001) and others attempt to answer the question of why we observe incomplete markets for insurance. The answer given is that not all profitable transactions can be carried out because some would violate the individual rationality constraint that under some circumstances it would be better to 'run away' than to pay an existing debt. This links insurance possibilities to economic fundamentals.

This chapter is an approach to bankruptcy and collateral based on these enforcement constraint models. Although, as the authors observed in the opening quotation to this chapter, no consumer actually runs away in equilibrium, we argue here that 'running away' is not the proper interpretation of bankruptcy. Rather, the Kehoe–Levine enforcement constraint model requires complete contingent claims and, in practice, these claims are implemented not through Arrow securities, but rather through a combination of non-contingent assets and bankruptcy. With this in mind, we re-examine the example of Kehoe and Levine (2001) and show how the efficient – that is, second-best – stationary equilibrium allocation can be implemented in an equilibrium without contingent claims, but with bankruptcy and collateral.

This reinterpretation brings new economic insight. If the model has consequences for unanticipated shocks, then the institution of bankruptcy and collateral that may be well suited for 'ordinary' shocks may break down when subject to unusual shocks. This is closely related to Leijonhufvud's (1973a) 'corridor of stability'. Our perspective, then, is quite different from that in the incomplete markets literature or that in the work of Kiyotaki and Moore (1997). In those models, it is hypothesized that bankruptcy and collateral are an inefficient solution to a not completely well-specified economic problem. Here we view bankruptcy and collateral as an efficient solution to the problems posed by ordinary transactions. We also recognize that solutions which may suit ordinary events well, however, may be fragile when exposed to less-ordinary events.

5.2 A MODL 'FINELY CARVED FROM THE BONES OF WALRAS'

We start by summarizing the model of Kehoe and Levine (2001). There are an infinite number of discrete time periods $t = 0, 1, \ldots$. In each period there are two types of consumers, $i = 1, 2$, and a continuum of each type of consumer. At each moment of time, one consumer has high productivity and one has low productivity. The state $\eta_t \in \{1, 2\}$ at time t is the index of the consumer who has high productivity at that time. This random variable follows a Markov process characterized by a single number, the probability of a reversal, that is, a transition from the state where type 1 has good productivity to the state where type 2 has good productivity, or vice versa.

Uncertainty evolves over an uncertainty tree. The root of the tree is determined by the fixed initial state η_0. A state history is a finite list $s = (\eta_1, \ldots, \eta_t)$ of events that have taken place through time $t(s)$, where $t(s)$ is the length of the vector s, the time at which s occurs. The history immediately prior to s is denoted $s - 1$, and if the node σ follows s on the uncertainty tree, we write $\sigma > s$. The countable set of all state histories is denoted S. The probability of a state history is computed from the Markov transition probabilities:

$$\pi_s = pr(\eta_{t(s)}|\eta_{t(s)-1})pr(\eta_{t(s)-1}|\eta_{t(s)-2})\cdots pr(\eta_1|\eta_0). \tag{5.1}$$

There is a single consumption good c; the representative consumer of type i consumes c_s^i if the state history is s. Both consumers have the common stationary additively separable expected utility function:

$$(1-\beta)\sum_{s\in S}\beta^{t(s)}\pi_s u(c_s^i). \tag{5.2}$$

The period utility function u is twice continuously differentiable with $Du(c) > 0$, satisfies the boundary condition $Du(c) \to \infty$ as $c \to 0$, and has $D^2u(c) < 0$. The common discount factor β satisfies $0 < \beta < 1$.

There are two types of capital: human capital (or labor) and physical capital (or trees). The services of the one unit of human capital held by type i consumer in state η are denoted $w^i(\eta)$. These services take on one of two values, ω^b and ω^g, with $\omega^b < \omega^g$, corresponding to low and high productivity, respectively. Moreover, if one consumer has high productivity, then the other consumer has low productivity, so if $w_t^i = \omega^b$ then $w_t^{-i} = \omega^g$, where $-i$ is the type of consumer who is not type i. Finally, the state indexes which consumer has high productivity, so $\omega^\eta(\eta) = \omega^g$, $\omega^{-\eta}(\eta) = \omega^b$.

There is one unit of physical capital in the economy. This capital is durable and returns $r > 0$ of the consumption good in every period. We can interpret this physical capital as trees, with r being the amount of consumption good produced every period by the trees. A consumer of type i holds a share θ_s^i of the capital stock contingent on the state history s. Initial physical capital holdings are θ_0^i.

The total supply of the consumption good in this economy is the sum of the individuals' productivities plus the return on the single unit of physical capital, $\omega = \omega^g + \omega^b + r$. The social feasibility conditions for this economy in each state are:

$$c_s^1 + c_s^2 \le \omega^g + \omega^b + r = \omega \tag{5.3}$$

$$\theta_s^1 + \theta_s^2 \le 1. \tag{5.4}$$

5.3 THE DEBT CONSTRAINED ECONOMY: 'VENTURING STARK NAKED OUT INTO THE CHILL WINDS OF ABSTRACTION'

Our first model of intertemporal trade is the debt constrained economy. Borrowing, lending, and the sale and purchase of insurance contracts are possible. There are, however, debt constraints. These come about because consumers have the option of opting out of intertemporal trade. If they choose to do this, they renege on all existing debts. They are excluded from all further participation in intertemporal trade, however, and their physical capital is seized. The endowment of human capital is assumed to be inalienable: it cannot be taken away, nor can consumers be prevented from consuming its returns.

Formally, this is a model in which consumers face the individual rationality constraint:

$$(1-\beta)\sum_{\sigma\geq s}\beta^{t(\sigma)-t(s)}(\pi_\sigma/\pi_s)u(c_\sigma^i) \geq$$
$$(1-\beta)\sum_{\sigma\geq s}\beta^{t(\sigma)-t(s)}(\pi_\sigma/\pi_s)u(w^i(\eta_\sigma)). \qquad (5.5)$$

This constraint says that, in every state history, the value of continuing to participate in the economy is no less than the value of dropping out.

In this debt constrained economy, since markets are complete, consumers purchase contingent consumption for the state history s for the present value price p_s and they sell the return on their capital $w^i(\eta_s)+r\theta_0^i$ at the same price. The corresponding optimization problem is:

$$\max \ (1-\beta)\sum_{t=0}^{\infty}\beta^t u(c_t^i)$$

subject to

$$\sum_{s\in S}p_s c_s^i \leq \sum_{s\in S}p_s(w^i(\eta_s)+\theta_0^i r) \qquad (5.6)$$

$$(1-\beta)\sum_{\sigma\geq s}\beta^{t(\sigma)-t(s)}(\pi_\sigma/\pi_s)u(c_\sigma^i) \geq (1-\beta)\sum_{\sigma\geq s}\beta^{t(\sigma)-t(s)}(\pi_\sigma/\pi_s)u(w^i(\eta_\sigma)).$$

Notice that we have written the budget constraint in the Arrow–Debreu form. As is usual in this sort of model, we can equally well formulate the budget constraint as a sequence of budget constraints in complete securities markets:

$$c_s^i + q_{(s,1)}\theta_{(s,1)}^i + q_{(s,2)}\theta_{(s,2)}^i \leq w^i(\eta_s)+(v_s+r)\theta_s^i \qquad (5.7)$$
$$\theta_s^i \geq -^{\text{TM}}, \ \theta_0^i \ \text{fixed},$$

where $q_{(s,\eta)}$ is the price of the Arrow security traded in state history s that promises a unit of physical capital to be delivered at state history (s,η). A standard arbitrage argument implies that $q_{(s,1)}+q_{(s,2)}=v_s$. The constraint $\theta_s^i \geq -^{\text{TM}}$ rules out Ponzi schemes, but is a positive constant chosen large enough not to otherwise constrain borrowing in equilibrium.

An equilibrium of the debt constrained economy is an infinite sequence of consumption levels and consumption prices such that consumers maximize utility given their constraints and such that the social feasibility condition for consumption is satisfied.

A symmetric stochastic steady state satisfies the equilibrium conditions for an appropriate choice of initial capital holdings $\bar{\theta}_0^1$ and $\bar{\theta}_0^2$ and is specified by consumption c^g when productivity is high, c^b when productivity is low, and the rule:

$$c_s^i = \begin{cases} c^g & \text{if } w_s^i = \omega^g \\ c^b & \text{if } w_s^i = \omega^b \end{cases}. \tag{5.8}$$

Kehoe and Levine (2001) prove that every stochastic steady state in which the individual rationality constraint binds on at least one consumer type is symmetric. They also analyze transition paths and prove that the equilibrium reaches the stochastic steady state as soon as a reversal has taken place.

5.4 SOLUTION OF THE DEBT CONSTRAINED MODEL

We find the symmetric stochastic steady state by decreasing c^g from ω^g until we either achieve the symmetric first best at $x^g = \omega^2$ or until the individual rationality constraint binds. We define a function proportional to the difference between the utility from the steady state consumption plan and consumption in autarky. A recursive calculation shows that this function is:

$$f^D(c^g) = (1 - \beta(1 - \pi))(u(c^g) - u(\omega^g)) + \beta\pi(u(\omega - c^g) - u(\omega^b)), \tag{5.9}$$

where $c^b = \omega - x^g$.

Proposition 1: A symmetric stochastic steady state c^g of the debt constrained economy is characterized by $f^D(\omega/2) \geq 0$ and $c^g = \omega/2$ or by $\omega^g > \omega/2$, $f^D(c^g) = 0$, and $c^g \in (\omega/2, \omega^g)$.

Proof: The function f^D is concave and satisfies $f^D(\omega^g) > 0$. Observe first that $\omega^g \leq \omega/2$ implies that $f^D(\omega/2) > 0$. Either $f^D(\omega/2) \geq 0$ or $f^D(\omega/2) < 0$. If $f^D(\omega/2) \geq 0$, then $f^D(\omega^g) > 0$ and the concavity of f^D imply that $f^D(c) > 0$ for all $c \in [\omega/2, \omega^g]$. Consequently, the unique steady state is characterized by $c^g = \omega/2$. If, instead, $f^D(\omega/2) < 0$, then $\omega^g > \omega/2$. In this case, $f^D(\omega^g) > 0$ and the concavity of f^D imply that $f^D(c^g) = 0$ for a unique $c^g \in (\omega/2, \omega^g)$.

Proposition 2: A symmetric stochastic steady state exists in the debt constrained economy. There is only one symmetric stochastic steady state.

An interesting question is how the steady state level of consumption depends on the parameter $1 - \pi$ measuring the persistence of the shock.

From the implicit function theorem, in the case where the debt constraint binds, we can compute:

$$\frac{dc^g}{d(1-\pi)} = \frac{\partial f^D / \partial \pi}{\partial f^D / \partial c^g}.$$

(5.10)

At an interior steady state f^D must intersect the axis from below, so $\partial f^D / \partial c^g$ is positive. We can also rewrite f^D as:

$$f^D(c^g) = (1-\beta)(u(c^g) - u(\omega^g))$$
$$+ \beta\pi(u(\omega - c^g) - u(\omega^b) + u(c^g) - u(\omega^g)).$$

(5.11)

When $f^D(c^g) = 0$, since the first term is negative, the second term is positive, and since $\partial f^D / \partial \pi$ is proportional to the second term, it is also positive. We conclude that:

$$\frac{dc^g}{d(1-\pi)} > 0,$$

(5.12)

implying that a more persistent shock results in greater consumption by the consumer with the high endowment, or, equivalently, less risk sharing between the two consumers.

5.5   A NUMERICAL EXAMPLE

To see how the equilibrium works in more detail, we examine a numerical example. We suppose that the discount factor is $\beta = 4/5$, that the probability of reversal is $\pi = 1/8$, and that the endowments are:

$$w^i_s = \begin{cases} 54 & \text{if } \eta_t = i \\ 8 & \text{if } \eta_t \neq i \end{cases}.$$

(5.13)

There is a single unit of physical capital that produces $r = 1$ unit of the good every period.

The first-order conditions for the consumer's problem are:

$$\beta^{t(s)}\pi_s \frac{1}{c^i_s} - \lambda^i_s + \beta^{t(s)}\pi_s \frac{1}{c^i_s} \sum_{s_\sigma \leq s} \mu^i_\sigma = 0$$

(5.14)

and

$$-\lambda^i_s q_{(s,\eta')} + \lambda^i_{(s,\eta')}(v_{(s,\eta')} + r) = 0,$$

(5.15)

where λ^i_s is the Lagrange multiplier for the sequential markets budget constraint (5.7) for consumer type i in state history and μ^i_s is the Lagrange multiplier for the individual rationality constraint (5.5).

If $c_{(s,\eta')}^i = c^b$, then the individual rationality constraint does not bind and $\mu_{(s,\eta')}^i = 0$. First, consider the case where $c_s^i = c^g$ and $c_{(s,\eta')}^i$ is c^b. Then, since $\mu_{(s,\eta)}^i = 0$, we can write the first-order condition for $c_{(s,\eta)}^i$ as:

$$\beta^{t(s)+1}\pi_s\pi\frac{1}{c^b} - \lambda_{(s,\eta')}^i + \beta^{t(s)+1}\pi_s\pi\frac{1}{c^b}\sum_{\sigma \leq s}\mu_\sigma^i = 0. \tag{5.16}$$

Combining this with the first-order condition for c_s^i, (5.14), we obtain:

$$\frac{u'(c^g)}{\delta\pi u'(c^b)} = \frac{v_{(s,\eta')} + r}{q_{(s,\eta')}}. \tag{5.17}$$

We construct an equilibrium assuming that capital prices are constant, $v_{(s,\eta')} = v$. Kehoe and Levine (2001) prove that this is the only possibility.
    The first-order condition (5.15) becomes:

$$q_{(s,\eta')} = q_r = \frac{\beta\pi u'(c^b)}{u'(c^g)}(v + r). \tag{5.18}$$

Here q_r is the price paid for an Arrow security to purchase one unit of physical capital in the case of reversal – where $\eta_s = 1$, for example, but $\eta' = 2$.
    Consider now the case where $c_s^i = c^b$ and $c_{(s,\eta')}^i$ is c^b. (We can think of this as the same state history s; we are just looking at the other consumer type's first-order conditions.) We obtain:

$$\frac{u'(c^b)}{\delta(1 - \pi)u'(c^b)} = \frac{v + r}{q_n}, \tag{5.19}$$

where

$$q_n = \beta(1 - \pi)(v + r). \tag{5.20}$$

Here q_n is the price paid for an Arrow security to purchase one unit of physical capital in the case of no reversal.
    Consider now that the function:

$$f^D(c^g) = (1 - \beta(1 - \pi))(\log c^g - \log 54) + \beta\pi(\log(63 - c^g) - \log 8). \tag{5.21}$$

Setting $f^D(c^g) = 0$, where $\beta = 4/5$ and $\pi = 1/8$, we obtain $c^g = 36$. We want to find values of c^b, θ^g, θ^b, q_r, q_n, and v such that these variables constitute a symmetric steady state. Obviously, $c^b = 63 - 36 = 27$. Plugging these values into the first-order conditions (5.18) and (5.20), we find that:

$$q_r = \frac{2}{15}(v + 1) \tag{5.22}$$

$$q_n = \frac{7}{10}(v + 1). \tag{5.23}$$

Notice that we can combine these two conditions to obtain:

$$q_r + q_n = v = \frac{5}{6}(v + 1),\qquad(5.24)$$

which implies that $v = 5$, $q_r = 4/5 = 0.8$, $q_n = 21/5 = 4.2$. We can plug this into the budget constraint for the consumer with the high endowment:

$$c^g + q_n\theta^g + q_r\theta^b = \omega^g + (v + r)\theta^g\qquad(5.25)$$

$$36 + \frac{21}{5}\theta^g + \frac{4}{5}(1 - \theta^g) = 54 + 60\theta^g,\qquad(5.26)$$

to solve for $\theta^g = -86/13 = -6.6154$, $\theta^b = 99/13 = 7.6154$.

To implement this steady state as an equilibrium, we can now go back and verify that all of the equilibrium conditions are satisfied for the right choice of $\bar{\theta}_0^1$ and $\bar{\theta}_0^2$.

The comparative statics of this example are of some interest. Suppose that we increase the variance of shocks by increasing (ω^g, ω^b) from $(54, 8)$ to say $(56, 6)$, and then to $(58, 4)$. A computation along the lines above shows that the equilibrium risk-sharing increases as the variance of the shocks becomes larger: (c^g, c^b) goes from $(36, 27)$ to $(32.6074, 30.3926)$ and then to $(31.5, 31.5)$, where there is complete risk-sharing. As we decrease the variance of shocks, equilibrium risk-sharing decreases: as (ω^g, ω^b) goes to $(52, 10)$ and then to $(50, 12)$, (c^g, c^b) goes to $(38.6539, 24.3461)$ and then to $(40.6209, 22.3791)$. Notice that increasing the variance of the shock reduces the attractiveness of running away and increases the desirability of trade. That is, we should not interpret this as meaning the economy as a whole has become more risky, but rather that the economy as a whole has become more specialized and interdependent. Because it is less attractive to run away, it becomes possible to enforce more efficient risk-sharing.

This negative relation between the variance of income shocks and the level of risk-sharing in equilibrium is a general feature of debt constrained models. Krueger and Perri (2006) study the empirical significance of this relation.

5.6   THE ECONOMY WITH BANKRUPTCY AND COLLATERAL: 'ENGLISH WORDS THAT HAVE CREPT INTO THEIR LANGUAGE ARE OFTEN USED IN SENSES THAT WE WOULD NOT RECOGNIZE'

In this section, we show that, when the individual rationality constraint (5.5) holds, we can support the equilibrium allocation in the debt constrained economy by a combination of bankruptcy and collateral. The possibility of bankruptcy provides a state contingency. The basic idea is that in every period each type makes a loan to the other type. Then the consumers of whichever type has low productivity in the next period default on their loans – that is, they collect the promised payment from the other type, but they do not pay back their own loan. Bankruptcy comes with a penalty: a consumer who defaults loses any holdings of physical capital and – to prevent consumers who have high productivity from defaulting – loses the returns to labor in excess of ω^b. We impose a constraint on borrowing to ensure that consumers do not borrow so much that they violate the individual rationality constraint (5.5). Notice that the imposition of this constraint makes it possible to impose the bankruptcy penalty of garnishing wages up to the level of ω^b: the choices faced by the high productivity type are: to not declare bankruptcy; to declare bankruptcy and pay the penalty; or to run away. In equilibrium, the optimum among these three choices is to not declare bankruptcy.

Let b_s^i denote borrowing by type i in state history s and let a_s^i denote lending. Because the two types have different probabilities of future default, borrowing and lending need not trade at the same price, so we let q_s^i denote the price of the asset corresponding to borrowing by type i in state history s.

Consumers of type i now face the problem:

$$(1-\beta)\sum_{s\in S}\beta^{t(s)}\pi_s u(c_s^i)$$

subject to

$$c_s^i + q_s^{i'}a_s^i - q_s^i b_s^i + v_s\theta_s^i \leq w^i(\eta_s) + \delta_s^{-i}a_{s-1}^i + \max[-b_{s-1}^i$$
$$+ (v_s+r)\theta_{s-1}^i, \omega^b - w^i(\eta_s)] \tag{5.27}$$

$$a_s^i \geq 0, \bar{b} \geq b_s^i \geq 0, \theta_s^i \geq 0, \theta_0^i \text{ fixed.}$$

There are two new market clearing conditions:

$$a_s^1 - b_s^2 = 0 \tag{5.28}$$

$$a_s^2 - b_s^1 = 0. \tag{5.29}$$

The price of a claim to one unit of the income of consumer i in state history s' is determined in $s-1$, $q_{s-1}^{i'}$. The return on this claim depends on whether or not consumer i defaults:

$$\delta_s^i = \begin{cases} 1 & \text{if } -b_s^i + (v_{(s,\eta)}+r)\theta_s^i \geq \omega^b - w^i(\eta) \\ ((v_{(s,\eta)}+r)\theta_s^i + w^i(\eta) - \omega^b)/b_s^i & \text{if } -b_s^i + (v_{(s,\eta)}+r)\theta_s^i \leq \omega^b - w^i(\eta) \end{cases}$$

$$\tag{5.30}$$

The concepts of equilibrium and of symmetric stochastic steady state for this economy with bankruptcy and collateral are defined analogously to their counterparts for the debt constrained economy.

Proposition 3: Given any symmetric stochastic steady state of the debt constrained economy, there exists a borrowing constraint $\bar{b} > 0$ such that there is a symmetric stochastic steady state of the economy with bankruptcy and collateral with the same consumption allocation.

Proof: We explicitly construct the equilibrium. In this equilibrium, consumers who have low productivity always declare bankruptcy and consumers who have high productivity never do. We use the first-order conditions for the consumer's problem (5.27) along with the budget constraints and feasibility conditions to construct an equilibrium with these properties.

We first need to determine which consumer purchases the capital. If the consumer with the high productivity purchases the capital, the first-order condition is:

$$-v + \beta(1 - \pi)(v + r) = 0, \tag{5.31}$$

which implies that:

$$v = \frac{\beta(1 - \pi)r}{1 - \beta(1 - \pi)}. \tag{5.32}$$

The first-order condition for the consumer with low productivity is:

$$-\frac{v}{c^b} + \frac{\beta\pi(v + r)}{c^g} \leq 0, \tag{5.33}$$

which holds if and only if:

$$\frac{c^g}{c^b} \leq \frac{1 - \pi}{\pi}. \tag{5.34}$$

If, on the other hand, the consumer with low productivity purchases the capital, the first-order condition in (5.33) holds with equality, which implies that:

$$v = \frac{\beta\pi c^g r}{c^b - \beta\pi c^g}. \tag{5.35}$$

In this case, the first-order condition for the consumer with high productivity is:

$$-v + \beta(1 - \pi)(v + r) \leq 0, \tag{5.36}$$

which holds if and only if the direction of the inequality (5.34) is reversed. Consequently, we can divide equilibria into two types, along with a borderline case. In the first type, condition (5.34) holds and the consumer with high productivity purchases all of the capital. In the second type, condition (5.34) is violated and the consumer with low productivity purchases all of the capital. If condition (5.34) holds with equality, it turns out that the two consumers can purchase capital in arbitrary amounts θ^g, θ^b where $\theta^i \geq 0$, $\theta^g + \theta^b = 1$, without affecting the equilibrium allocation. Notice that, in this borderline case, the two calculations of v, (5.32) and (5.35), coincide.

To keep the exposition simple, we first consider the case where condition (5.34) holds. We start by writing the budget constraints as:

$$c^g + q^b a^g - q^g b^g + v = \omega^g - b^g + (v + r) = \omega^g - b^b + \delta^g a^b \quad (5.37)$$

$$c^b + q^g a^b - q^b b^b = \omega^b + a^b = \omega^b + a^g. \quad (5.38)$$

Notice that, although consumers' consumption and asset accumulation depend only on the state in which they are, there are two ways to get to each state: either a reversal has taken place or it has not.

To construct the steady-state equilibrium, we need to compute the asset prices q^g and q^b, the lending levels a^g and a^b, and the borrowing levels b^g and b^b. Notice that $\delta^g a^b = v + r$ implies that $\delta^g = (v + r)/a^b$.

A consumer who has high productivity pays $q^b a^g$ for a return of a^g if a reversal takes place. The corresponding first-order condition is:

$$\frac{q^b}{c^g} = \frac{\beta \pi}{c^b}, \quad (5.39)$$

which implies that:

$$q^b = \frac{\beta \pi c^g}{c^b}. \quad (5.40)$$

A consumer who has low productivity lends $q^g a^b$ for a return of a^b if no reversal takes place and $\delta^g a^b = (v + r)$ if a reversal takes place. The corresponding first-order condition is:

$$\frac{q^g}{c^b} = \frac{\beta(1 - \pi)}{c^b} + \frac{\beta \pi \delta^g}{c^g}, \quad (5.41)$$

which implies that:

$$q^g = \beta(1 - \pi) + \frac{\beta \pi \delta^g c^b}{c^g}. \quad (5.42)$$

Notice that the first-order condition for borrowing becomes:

$$\frac{q^b}{c^b} - \frac{\beta\pi}{c^g} = \frac{\beta\pi c^g}{(c^b)^2} - \frac{\beta\pi}{c^g} > 0 \tag{5.43}$$

when the consumer has low productivity and:

$$\frac{q^g}{c^g} - \frac{\beta(1-\pi)}{c^g} = \frac{\beta\pi\delta^g c^b}{(c^g)^2} > 0, \tag{5.44}$$

when the consumer has high productivity. These conditions imply that the borrowing constraints $\bar{b} \geq b_s^i$ bind.

Combining the budget constraints (5.37) and (5.38) with the market clearing conditions for borrowing and lending (5.28) and (5.29), we find that:

$$a^g = b^g = a^b = b^b. \tag{5.45}$$

We can easily calculate b and set the borrowing constraint $\bar{b} = b$ so that the budget constraints (5.37) and (5.38) are satisfied:

$$(1 + q^b - q^g)b = c^b - \omega^b \tag{5.46}$$

$$\left(1 + \frac{\beta\pi c^g}{c^b} - \beta(1-\pi)\right)b - \frac{\beta\pi(v+r)c^b}{c^g} = c^b - \omega^b \tag{5.47}$$

$$b = \left(\frac{c^b}{(1 - \beta(1-\pi))c^b + \beta\pi c^g}\right)\left(c^b - \omega^b + \frac{\beta\pi r c^b}{(1 - \beta(1-\pi))c^g}\right). \tag{5.48}$$

It is straightforward, but tedious, to verify that a consumer with low productivity always chooses to default but that a consumer with high productivity never does.

The construction where condition (5.34) is reversed is similar. The budget constraints become:

$$c^g + q^b a^g - q^g b^g + v\theta^g = \omega^g - b^g + (v+r)\theta^g + \delta^b a^g = \omega^g - b^b$$
$$+ (v+r)\theta^b + \delta^g a^b \tag{5.49}$$

$$c^b + q^g a^b - q^b b^b + v\theta^b = \omega^b + a^b = \omega^b + a^g. \tag{5.50}$$

Here we treat the general case. If $\pi c^g < (1-\pi)c^b$, then $\theta^g = 1$; if $\pi c^g < (1-\pi)c^b$, then $\theta^b = 1$; and $\pi c^g = (1-\pi)c^b$, then θ^g is arbitrary. Of course, $\delta^b a^g = (v+r)\theta^b$ and $\delta^g a^b = (v+r)\theta^g$. The asset prices q^b become:

$$q^b = \frac{\beta\pi c^g}{c^b} + \beta(1-\pi)\delta^b, \tag{5.51}$$

$$q^g = \beta(1-\pi) + \frac{\beta\pi\delta^g c^b}{c^g}. \tag{5.52}$$

Once again, the first-order conditions for borrowing hold and $a^g = b^g = a^b = b^b =$. The calculation of b becomes:

$$(1 + q^b - q^g)b = c^b - \omega^b + v\theta^b \tag{5.53}$$

$$\left(1 + \frac{\beta\pi c^g}{c^b} - \beta(1 - \pi)\right)b + \frac{\beta((1 - \pi)\theta^b c^g - \pi\theta^g c^b)(v + r)}{c^g} = c^b - \omega^b + v\theta^b \tag{5.54}$$

$$b = \left(\frac{c^b}{(1 - \beta(1 - \pi))c^b + \beta\pi c^g}\right)$$

$$\left(c^b - \omega^b + v\theta^b - \frac{\beta((1 - \pi)\theta^b c^g - \pi\theta^g c^b)(v + r)}{c^g}\right), \tag{5.55}$$

where v is determined by equation (5.32) or equation (5.35) depending on the case that we are in.

When $\pi c^g = (1 - \pi)c^b$, this expression becomes:

$$b = c^b - \omega^b + \frac{\beta\pi\theta^g c^b r}{(1 - \beta(1 - \pi))c^g}. \tag{5.56}$$

Notice that, in this borderline case, the asset prices q^g and q^b, the lending levels a^g and a^b, and the borrowing levels b^g and b^b all vary with $\theta^g = 1 - \theta^b$, but the consumption levels c^g and c^b are fixed at their levels in the debt constrained equilibrium.

5.7 THE NUMERICAL EXAMPLE REVISITED: 'THE ABILITY TO SAY THE SAME THING IN SEVERAL DIFFERENT TONGUES IS A HIGHLY ESTEEMED TALENT AMONG THEM'

We now apply proposition 3 to show how the equilibrium allocation of the debt constrained economy in our numerical example can be implemented as an equilibrium allocation in the economy with bankruptcy and collateral. We first use (5.48) to calculate the levels of borrowing and lending:

$$b = \frac{1155}{26} = 44.4231. \tag{5.57}$$

Next, we use (5.32) to calculate the price of capital:

$$v = \frac{7}{3} = 2.3333. \tag{5.58}$$

Notice that this implies that:

$$\delta = \frac{v+r}{b} = \frac{52}{693} = 0.0750. \tag{5.59}$$

We can now use (5.40) and (5.42) to calculate the prices of claims on next period's income:

$$q^b = \frac{2}{15} = 0.1333 \tag{5.60}$$

$$q^g = \frac{163}{231} = 0.7056. \tag{5.61}$$

Kehoe and Levine (2001) provide a simple argument which demonstrates that the equilibrium allocation in the debt constrained model – and consequently the equilibrium allocation in this model with bankruptcy and collateral – is Pareto efficient among allocations that satisfy the individual rationality constraint. Notice how this allocation is supported by borrowing and lending assets with different returns. Proposition 3, which shows that consumers can exploit the contingencies provided by collateral to achieve an efficient allocation, is reminiscent of results in finance, like those of Duffie and Huang (1985) and Kreps (1982), which show that a small number of assets can span the uncertainty facing investors. What is important in our model is that the consumers can go long in some assets and short in others. The efficient nature of the outcome turns the advice of Polonius to Laertes in Shakespeare's *Hamlet* on its head: 'Both a borrower and a lender be.'

Now consider the comparative static experiment of increasing specialization in the sense that the variance of shocks increases by changing (ω^g, ω^b) from $(54, 8)$ to $(56, 6)$ and then to $(58, 4)$, as we did in the market with complete contingent claims. With complete contingent claims, we saw that equilibrium risk-sharing increased as the variance of income shocks increased. This cannot be the case with the model of bankruptcy and collateral: the borrowing limit is calibrated to the old equilibrium, not the new, so it is impossible for the equilibrium to adjust in the short run. In fact, equilibrium risk-sharing goes down, as (c^g, c^b) goes from $(36, 27)$ to $(37.4078, 25.5922)$ and then to $(38.7722, 24.2278)$. To achieve the same equilibrium allocation as in the debt constrained model, we would need to loosen the borrowing constraint $\bar{b}$ from 44.4231 to 60.6534 and then to 69.5833.

More surprising perhaps is what happens if we decrease specialization in the sense that the variance of the shocks decreases by changing (ω^g, ω^b) to $(52, 10)$. In this case the consumers with high productivity want to run away, and the equilibrium collapses to autarky. Even if we devise a scheme to keep consumers from running away in the Kehoe–Levine (2001) sense, we run into trouble as we decrease the variance of shocks still further by setting (ω^g, ω^b) to (50, 12). In this case, even consumers with high productivity choose to default, and the equilibrium collapses to autarky.

5.8 LEIJONHUFVUDIAN ECONOMICS AND THE ECONOMICS OF LEIJONHUFVUD

The literature on bankruptcy in general equilibrium typically takes the incomplete markets model as its point of departure. In this model, bankruptcy – like the incomplete markets themselves – is a pathology. Bankruptcy serves to solve no substantive economic problem, and serves only to hinder the proper working of the economy. The only conclusion we can sensibly reach from this literature is that the economy does not work well.

The idea that on a day-to-day basis the economy works poorly is deeply anti-Leijonhufvudian in spirit. Leijonhufvud's deepest insight is his (1973a) notion of the 'corridor of stability'. On a day-to-day basis in modern economies, things work well. It is not plausible that we could all be much better off if not for the nasty facts of market incompleteness, bankruptcy and collateral.

This chapter takes a point of view more consistent with Leijonhufvud's corridor of stability. Here borrowing limits, bankruptcy and collateral arise to solve a real economic problem, that of providing insurance in the presence of individual rationality constraints. In our account, this economy is second-best: given the underlying individual rationality constraints, the equilibrium is the best possible.

Having given a description of the corridor of stability where the economy responds efficiently to ordinary shocks, we are now free to ask the deeper Leijonhufvudian question: How robust are the institutions of bankruptcy and collateral in responding to a shock for which they are not designed? The answer is that these institutions are quite fragile. While the debt constrained complete market economy responds to changes in the variance of the shocks by adjusting the amount of risk-sharing, the collateralized economy cannot adjust the risk-sharing upwards in response to increased variance of shocks – and collapses completely in the face of decreased variance to shocks. This latter point is of some interest: our general intuition is that reducing the variance of shocks should be a good thing.

NOTES

*   This chapter was prepared for presentation at the Conference in Honor of Axel Leijonhufvud held at the University of California, Los Angeles (UCLA), 30–31 August

114   *Macroeconomics in the small and the large*

2006. The authors are grateful for financial support from the National Science Foundation. The views expressed herein are those of the authors and not necessarily those of the Federal Reserve Bank of Minneapolis or the Federal Reserve System.
1. With the exception of this opening quotation from Ralph Waldo Emerson's 'Self-reliance', the quotations at the beginning of sections are all taken from Axel Leijonhufvud's (1973b) 'Life among the Econ'.

REFERENCES

Araujo, A., M. Páscoa and J. Torres-Martínez (2002), 'Collateral avoids Ponzi schemes in incomplete markets', *Econometrica*, **70**, 1613–38.
Chatterjee, S., D. Corbae, M. Nakajima and J.-V. Ríos-Rull (2004), 'A quantitative theory of unsecured consumer credit with risk of default', University of Pennsylvania.
Dubey, P., J. Geanakoplos and M. Shubik (1989), 'Default and efficiency in a general equilibrium model with incomplete markets', Cowles Foundation Discussion Paper 900.
Dubey, P., J. Geanakoplos and W.R. Zame (1995), 'Default, collateral, and derivatives', Yale University.
Duffie, D. and C.F. Huang (1985), 'Implementing Arrow–Debreu equilibria by continuous trading of few long-lived securities', *Econometrica*, **53**, 1337–56.
Emerson, Ralph Waldo (1908), *The Essay on Self-Reliance*, East Aurora, NY: The Roycrofters.
Geanakoplos, J. and W.R. Zame (2002), 'Collateral and the enforcement of intertemporal contracts', UCLA.
Kehoe, T.J. and D.K. Levine (1993), 'Debt constrained asset markets,' *Review of Economic Studies*, **60**, 865–88.
Kehoe, T.J. and D.K. Levine (2001), 'Liquidity constrained markets versus debt constrained markets,' *Econometrica*, **69**, 575–98.
Kiyotaki, N. and J. Moore (1997), 'Credit cycles,' *Journal of Political Economy*, **105**, 211–48.
Kreps D.M. (1982), 'Multiperiod securities and the efficient allocation of risk: a comment on the Black-Scholes Option Pricing Model', in J.J. McCall (ed.), *The Economics of Information and Uncertainty*, Chicago and London. University of Chicago Press, pp. 203–32.
Krueger, D. and F. Perri (2006), 'Does income inequality lead to consumption inequality? Evidence and theory', *Review of Economic Studies*, **73**, 163–93.
Kubler, F. and K. Schmedders (2003), 'Stationary equilibria in asset-pricing models with incomplete markets and collateral', *Econometrica* **71**, 1767–93.
Leijonhufvud, A. (1973a), 'Effective demand failures', *Swedish Journal of Economics*, **75**, 27–48.
Leijonhufvud, A. (1973b), 'Life among the Econ', *Western Economic Journal*, **11**, 327–37.
Livshits, I. J. MacGee and M. Tertilt (2003), 'Consumer bankruptcy: a fresh start', Federal Reserve Bank of Minneapolis Working Paper 617.
Orrillo, J. (2002), 'Default and exogenous collateral in incomplete markets with a continuum of states', *Journal of Mathematical Economics* **35**, 151–65.
Zame, W.R. (1993), 'Efficiency and the role of default when security markets are incomplete', *American Economic Review*, **83**, 1142–64.

6. Growth patterns of two types of macro-models: limiting behavior of one- and two-parameter Poisson–Dirichlet models

Masanao Aoki*

6.1 INTRODUCTION

This chapter discusses a new class of simple stochastic multi-sector growth models composed of clusters, where a cluster is a collection of agents of the same or similar characteristics in some sense. Depending on the context, these clusters may be sectors of the macroeconomy, or firms of some sector of the economy, and so on. As time passes, the total number of agents in the model increases stochastically, either because a new agent (factors of production) joins one of existing clusters or because a new cluster is created by the new agent. We focus on the total numbers of clusters, that is, on the number of distinct types of economic agents in the model, and on the number of clusters of some specified sizes.[1]

These models are not stochastic growth models familiar to economists. They are, however, growth models because innovations occur in an existing cluster or new clusters are created by innovations which cause the size of models to grow unboundedly.

We then examine whether the coefficients of variation of some extensive variables, such as the number of sectors or number of clusters of some specified size, converge to zero or remain positive in the limit of total number of units in the model tending to infinity.[2]

If the limit of the coefficient of variation is not zero, then the model behavior is sample-dependent, that is, is influenced by history. This phenomenon is called non-self-averaging in the language of statistical physics.[3]

We show that the class of one-parameter Poisson–Dirichlet models of Kingman (1978a,1978b), also known as Ewens models in population genetics, denoted by $PD(\theta)$, $\theta > 0$ is self-averaging, but its extension to two-parameter Poisson–Dirichlet models by Pitman (1999), denoted by $PD(\theta, \alpha)$, where $0 < \alpha < 1, \alpha + \theta > 0$, is not, that is, non-self-averaging.[4]

6.2　THE MODEL

Consider an economy composed of several sectors. Different sectors are made up of different type of agents or productive units. The sectors are thus heterogeneous. Counting the sizes of sectors in some basic units, when the economy is of size n, there are K_n sectors, that is, K_n types of agents or productive units are in the model. The number K_n as well as the sizes of individual sectors, n_i, $i = 1,...,K_n$, are random variables, where $n = \Sigma_i n_i$.

We focus on the coefficients of variation of K_n and of $a_j(n), j = 1,... K_n$, where $a_j(n)$ is the number of clusters of size j, with the total n given. By definition K_n is the sum over j of $a_j(n)$ and the total number of units in the model is given by $n = \Sigma_j j a_j(n)$.

Time runs continuously. Over time, one of the existing sectors grows by one unit at rate which is proportional to $(n_i - \alpha)/(n + \theta)$, $i = 1,...K_n$, where α is a parameter between 0 and 1, and θ is another parameter, $\theta + \alpha > 0$. A new unit joins the existing clusters, increasing the number of clusters by one. Given that $K_n = k$, this creation of a new cluster occurs at the rate:

$$1 - \sum_{i=1}^{k} \frac{(n_i - \alpha)}{(n + \theta)} = 1 - \frac{n - k\alpha}{n + \theta} = \frac{\theta + k\alpha}{n + \theta}.$$

Define $q_{\alpha,\theta}(n, k) := Pr(K_n = k)$. Its recursion equation is then given by:

$$q_{\alpha,\theta}(n + 1, k) = \frac{n - k\alpha}{n + \theta} q_{\alpha,\theta}(n, k) + \frac{\theta + (k - 1)\alpha}{n + \theta} q_{\alpha,\theta}(n, k - 1), \quad (6.1)$$

where the expressions for the boundary $K_n = 1$ for all n, and that of $K_n = n$ are given by the equations:

$$q_{\alpha,\theta}(n,1) = \frac{(1 - \alpha)(2 - \alpha)\cdots(n - 1 - \alpha)}{(\theta + 1)(\theta + 2)\cdots(\theta + n - 1)},$$

and

$$q_{\alpha,\theta}(n,n) = \frac{(\theta + \alpha)(\theta + 2\alpha)\cdots(\theta + (n - 1)\alpha)}{(\theta + 1)(\theta + 2)\cdots(\theta + n - 1)}.$$

To reiterate, equation (6.1) states that the economy composed of k sectors increases in size by one unit either by one of the existing sectors growing by one unit, or by a new sector of size one emerging.

To express the above in another way, note that:

$$Pr(K_{n+1} = k + 1 \mid K_1,...,K_{n-1}, K_n = k) = \frac{\theta + k\alpha}{n + \theta}$$

and

$$\Pr(K_{n+1} = k | K_1,\ldots,K_{n-1}, K_n = k) = \frac{n - k\alpha}{n + \theta}$$

This equation shows that more new sectors are likely to emerge in the economy as the numbers of sectors grow.

Note that the rate of new sector creation is independent of the current number of clusters in one-parameter models, since $\alpha = 0$. This is the fundamental reason for different thermodynamic behavior between the one- and two-parameter models.

In the one-parameter model the number of clusters may be expressed as:

$$q_{0,\theta}(n, k) = \frac{c(n, k)\theta^k}{\theta^{[n]}}, \tag{6.2}$$

where $\theta^{[n]} = \theta(\theta + 1)\ldots(\theta + n - 1)$, where $c(n,k)$ is the unsigned (signless) Stirling number of the first kind. It satisfies the recursion:

$$c(n + 1, k) = nc(n, k) + c(n, k - 1).$$

Because $q_{0,\theta}$ sums to 1 for fixed n, we have:

$$\theta^{[n]} = \sum_{k=1}^{n} c(n, k)\theta^k.$$

See Aoki (2002, p. 208) for a combinatorial interpretation of the Stirling number of the first kind.

6.3 ASYMPTOTIC PROPERTIES OF THE NUMBER OF SECTORS

We next examine how the number of sectors behaves as the size of the model grows unboundedly. We know how it behaves when α is zero. It involves a Stirling number of first kind, see Hoppe (1994) or Aoki (2002, p. 184).

In the two-parameter version equation (6.3) is replaced by a slightly different expression:

$$q_{\alpha,\theta}(n, k) = \frac{\theta^{[k,\alpha]}}{\alpha^k \theta^{[n]}} c(n, k; \alpha), \tag{6.3}$$

where

$$\theta^{[k,\alpha]} := \theta(\theta + \alpha)\ldots(\theta + (k - 1)\alpha).$$

The expression $c(n, k; \alpha)$ generalizes $c(n, k)$, and $\theta^{[n]}$ is now expressible as:

$$\theta^{[n]} = \sum_k S_\alpha(n, k)\theta^{[k,\alpha]},$$

where

$$S_\alpha(n, k) := \frac{c(n, k; \alpha)}{\alpha^k}$$

satisfies a recursion:

$$S_\alpha(n = 1, k) = (n - k\alpha)S_\alpha(n, k) + S_\alpha(n, k - 1), \qquad (6.4)$$

where $S_\alpha(0,0) = 1$, $S_\alpha(n,0) = 0$, and $S_\alpha(0,k) = 0$, for positive k.

This function generalizes the power-series relation for $\theta^{[n]}$ in terms of the Stirling number of the first kind to that of this generalized Stirling number.

6.4 THE COEFFICIENTS OF VARIATION

The Number of Clusters of Model of Size n

Yamato and Sibuya (2000) have calculated moments of the number of clusters, $K_n^r, r = 1, 2,\dots$ recursively. For example they derive a recursion relation:

$$E(K_{n+1}) = \frac{\theta}{n + \theta} + \left(1 + \frac{\alpha}{n + \theta}\right)E(K_n)$$

from which they obtain an asymptotic relation:

$$E[\frac{K_n}{n^\alpha}] \sim \frac{\Gamma(\theta + 1)}{\alpha\Gamma(\theta + \alpha)} \qquad (6.5)$$

by applying the asymptotic expression of the Gamma function:

$$\frac{\Gamma(n + a)}{\Gamma(n)} \sim n^a. \qquad (6.6)$$

They also obtain the expression for the variance of K_n/n^α as:

$$var(K_n/n^\alpha) \sim \frac{\Gamma(\theta + 1)}{\alpha^2}\gamma(\alpha, \theta), \qquad (6.7)$$

where

$$\gamma(\alpha,\theta) := (\theta + \alpha)/(\Gamma(\theta + \alpha)) - \Gamma(\theta + 1)/[\Gamma(\theta + \alpha)]^2. \qquad (6.8)$$

Note that the expression $\gamma(\alpha,\theta)$ is zero when α is zero, and positive otherwise. This is the fundamental difference between the two classes of models discussed in this paper as we see next. The expression for the coefficient of variation of K_n normalized by n^α then is given by:

$$\lim C.V.(K_n/n^\alpha) = \Gamma(\theta + \alpha)\sqrt{\frac{\gamma(\alpha,\theta)}{\Gamma(\theta + 1)}}. \tag{6.9}$$

We state this result as:

Proposition The limit of the coefficient of varition is positive with positive α, and it is zero only with $\alpha = 0$.

In other words, models with positive α values are non-self-averaging, while those with zero α values are self-averaging.

This difference between these two classes of models is significant. In models with positive α, the mean values of macroeconomic variables do not convey as much information about the model's macroeconomic behavior as models with zero α, because the values are not clustered about the means. Almost exclusive attention paid to the behavior of the mean in macroeconomic models, such as dynamic stochastic general equilibrium models, would lose importance if gross domestic product (GDP), for example, turns out to be non-self-averaging. There are models besides the two-parameter Poisson–Dirichlet model that are non-self-averaging. For example see Aoki (2008).

The Components of the Pattern Vector *a*

Let $a_j(n)$ be the number of sectors of size j when the size of the economy is n. From the definitions, note that $K_n = \sum_j a_j(n)$, and $\sum_j j a_j(n)_n$, where j ranges from 1 to n.

The expected value of the number of clusters of size j, given the total size of model n is:

$$E(a_j) = \frac{n!}{j!(n-j)!} \frac{(\theta + \alpha)^{[n-j]}}{(1-\alpha)^{[j-1]}(\theta + 1)^{[n-1]}}.$$

The results in Yamato and Sibuya can be used to show that the limit of the coefficient of variation of $a_j(n)/n^\alpha$ as n goes to infinity has the same limiting behavior as K_n/n^α, that is, zero for $\alpha = 0$, and positive for $0 < \alpha < 1$. Yamato and Sibuya (2000) have shown that:

$$\frac{a_j(n)}{K_n} \to P_{\alpha,j}$$

a.s. (almost surely) where

$$P_{\alpha,j} = \frac{\Gamma(j-\alpha)}{\Gamma(1-\alpha)}.$$

The coefficient of variation of $a_j(n)$ remains positive with positive αs.

6.5 MITTAG–LEFFLER DISTRIBUTIONS

In this section we match the moments of the random variable K_n/n^α with those of the generalized Mittag–Leffler distribution, and deduce that K_n/n^α has what is called as the generalized Mittag–Leffler distribution. This is an example of the method of moments. See Durrett (2005) or Feller, Vol. 2 (1966).

The generalized Mittag–Leffler distribution has the density:

$$g_{\alpha,\theta}(x) := \frac{\Gamma(\theta+1)}{\Gamma(\theta/\alpha+1)} x^{\theta/\alpha} g_\alpha(x),$$

where $\theta + \alpha > 0$, and where $g_\alpha(x)$ is the Mittag–Leffler density uniquely determined by:

$$\int_0^\infty x^p g_\alpha(x) dx = \frac{\Gamma(p+1)}{\Gamma(p\alpha+1)},$$

for all $p > -1$. The explicit expression of g_α is given by Pollard (1948) who calculcated the inverse Laplace transform of $exp(-s^\alpha)$:

$$\exp(-s^\alpha) = \int_0^\infty e^{-sx} g_\alpha(x) dx.$$

Also see Podlubny (1999) who has some related expressions. See also Blumenfeld and Mandelbrot (1997) for comments on Feller's contribution, or Pitman (2004, p. 12).

We know that:

$$K_n/n^\alpha \to \mathcal{L},$$

in distribution, and in a.s (almost surely), as shown in Pitman (2004, Section 3), Feng and Hoppe (1998) and Yamato and Sibuya (2000).

The random variable $\mathcal{L}$ has the density:

$$\frac{d}{ds} P_{\alpha,\theta}(\mathcal{L} \in ds) = g_{\alpha,\theta}.$$

We have calculated above the variance of $\mathcal{L}$ and see that its variance vanishes if α is zero.

Power Laws

Pitman (2004, p. 73) has shown that:

$$Pr(K_n = k) \sim g_{\alpha,\theta}(s)n^{-\alpha},$$

as $n \to \infty$ with $k \sim sn^{\alpha}$.

Note that this is a power law relation. Pitman's formula for the probability of $K_n = k$, with $k \sim sn^{\alpha}$ indicates that the value of the power law index α in n^{α} is such that $2\alpha < 2 = 1 + \mu$ with $0 < \mu < 1$.

The moments of these one- and two-parameter models are related to those of the Mittag–Leffler distribution and its extension in a simple way. This is significant for the following reason. As the Darling–Kac theorem implies, Darling and Kac (1957), any analysis involving first passages, occupation times, waiting time distributions and the like are bound to involve the Mittag–Leffler functions. In other words, Mittag-Leffler functions are generic in examining model behaviors as the model sizes grow unboundedly.

6.6   DISCUSSIONS

What are some of the implications of economic models with non-self-averaging behavior? For one thing, it means that we cannot blindly try for larger-size samples in the hope that we obtain better estimates of whatever we are trying to estimate or model, since means and most probably values may be far apart.

With a non-zero coefficient of variation, the distribution of K_n/n^{α} has a long tail, hence the mean loses much of usefulness as a way of assessing policy actions by affecting the mean. We propose to apply the large deviation analysis such as in Feng and Hoppe (1998) to bound the probabilities of deviations from the mean in some specified regions.

The class of models discussed in this chapter may thus turn out to be important not only in finance but also in macroeconomics. For example, we may redo the analysis in Dixit (1989) or Sutton (2002) from the new point of view presented in this chapter. There is also a possible connection with Derrida (1994). In finance, there are already some applications of Mittag-Leffler functions by Mainardi and his associates: Mainardi and Gorenflo (2000) and Mainardi et al. (2000).

In traditional microeconomic foundations of macroeconomics one deals almost exclusively with well-posed optimization problems for the representative agents with well-defined peaks and valleys of the cost functions. It is also taken for granted that as the number of agents goes to infinity, any unpleasant fluctuations vanish, and well-defined deterministic macroeconomic relations prevail. In other words, non-self-averaging phenomena are not in the mental picture of macro- or microeconomists.

We know however that as we go to problems which require agents to solve some combinatorial optimization problems, this nice mental picture may not apply. In the limit, as the number of agents goes to infinity, some results remain sample-dependent and deterministic results will not follow. Some of this type of phenomena has been reported in Aoki (1996, section 7.1.7) and also in Aoki (1996, p. 225) where Derrida's random energy model was introduced to the economic audience.

The example in this chapter is just a hint of the potential of using combinatorial stochastic processes. Some economic analysis, such as by Fabritiis, et al. (2003) and Sutton (2002), may be re-examined with profit. See Aoki and Yoshikawa (2007b) for more systematic re-examination of macroeconomic foundations by means of tools and concepts of statistical physics and combinatorial stochastic processes.

NOTES

*   The author thanks M. Sibuya for useful discussions.
1.   The models in this chapter are in the spirit of a new class of stochastic processes called combinatorial stochastic processes by J. Pitman. See Pitman (2004) for an extensive exposition of this class. This new type of stochastic process deals with random partitions of agents as in Kingman (1978a, 1978b) or Ewens (1972). Economic agents are regarded as exchangeable and probability distributions on the sets of their random partitions are studied.
2.   The term of clusters of 'infinite' size refers to the ideal situation of very large economies. This type of limit is called a thermodynamic limit in physics. We adopt this terminology in order to distinguish this type of limit from those where time goes to infinity as in the question of ergodicity. See Aoki (2008) for further details.
3.   Sornette defines the square of the coefficient of variation as a measure of non-self-averaging; Sornette (2000, p. 369). Coefficients of variation of self-averaging extensive variables tend to zero in the thermodynamic limits.
4.   Feng and Hoppe (1998) have a model of similar structure. Their focus, however, is not on the limiting behavior of the coefficients of variation. The constraints on the parameters come from the requirements that the probabilities remain positive. See equation (6.1). In Feng and Hoppe $\theta = \beta - \alpha$ where β is the birth rate of the pure birth process in their model, hence $\alpha + \theta$ is positive.

REFERENCES

Aoki, M. (2002), *Modeling Aggregate Behavior and Fluctuations in Economics: Stochastic Views of Interacting Agents*, New York: Cambridge University Press.
Aoki, M. (2008), 'Thermodynamic Limits of Macroeconomic or Financial Models: One- and Two-Parameter Poisson–Dirichlet Model', *J. Econ. Dyn. Control*, **32**, 66–84.

Aoki, M. and H. Yoshikawa (2007a), *Reconstructing Macroeconomics: A Perspective from Statistical Physics and Combinatorial Stochastic Processes*, New York: Cambridge University, Press.

Aoki, M. and H. Yoshikawa (2007b), 'Non-self-averaging in macroeconomic models: A criticism of modern micro-founded macroeconomics', www.economics-ejournal.org/economics/discussionpapers/2007–49.

Blumenfeld, R. and B.B. Mandelbrot (1997), 'Levy dusts, Millag–Leffler statistics, mass fractal lacunarity, and perceived dimension', *Phy. Rev. E*, **56**, 112–18.

Breiman, L. (1992), *Probability*, Philadelphia: Siam.

Darling, D.A. and M. Kac (1957), 'On occupation-times for Markov processes', *Transactions of American Mathematical Society*, **84**, 444–58.

Derrida, B. (1994), 'Non-self-averaging effects in sums of random variables, spin glasses, random maps, and random walks', in M. Fannes, C. Maies and A. Verberre (eds), *On Three Levels Micro, Meso- and Macro-approaches in Physics*, New York: Plenum Press.

Dixit, A. (1989), 'Entry and exit decisions of firms under fluctuating real exchange rates', *J. Pol. Economy*, **97**, 620–37.

Durrett, R. (2005), *Probability: Theory and Examples*, Belmont, CA: Duxbury Press.

Ewens, W. (1972), 'The sampling theory of selectively neutral alleles', *Theor. Popul. Biology*, **3**, 87–112.

Fabritiis, G. de, F. Pammolli and M. Riccaboni (2003), 'On size and growth of business firms', *Physica A*, **324**, 38–44.

Feller, W. (1966), *An Introduction to Probability Theory and Its Applications*, Vol. 2, New York: Wiley.

Feng, S. and F.M. Hoppe (1998), 'Large deviation principles for some random combinatorial structures', *Annals of Applied Probability*, **8**, 975–94.

Hoppe, F.M. (1994), 'Polya-like urns and the Ewens sampling formula', *J. Math. Biol*, **20**, 91–4.

Kingman, J.F.C. (1978a), 'Random partitions in population genetics', *Proc. R. Soc. Lond. A*, **361**, 1–20.

Kingman, J.F.C. (1978b), 'The representation of partition structures', *J. London Math. Soc.*, **18**, 374–80.

Pitman, J. (1999), 'Characterizations of Browniqn motion, bridge, meander and excursion by sampling at independent uniform times', *Electronic J. Probability* 4, Paper 11, 1–33.

Pitman, J. (2004), *Combinatorial Stochastic Processes*, New York: Springer.

Podlubny, I. (1999) *Fractional Differential Equations*, San Diago: Academic Press.

Pollard, H. (1948), 'The completely monotone character of the Mittag–Leffler function E_α (-x)', *Bull, Am. Math. Soc.* **54**, 115–16.

Scalas, E. (2006), 'The application of continuous-time random walks in finance and economics', *Physica A*, **362**, 225–39.

Sornette, D. (2000), *Critical Phenomena in Natural Sciences; Chaos, Fractals, Self-organization and Disorder: Concepts and Tools*, Berlin, Heidelerg, Germany, New York: Springer.

Sutton, J. (2002), 'The variance of firm growth rates: the scaling puzzle', *Physica A*, **312**, 577–90.

Yamato, H. and M. Sibuya (2000), 'Moments of some statistics of Pitman Sampling formula', *Bulletin of Informatics and Cybernetics*, **32**, 1–10.

7. Time inconsistency of robust control?

Lars Peter Hansen and Thomas J. Sargent*

7.1 INTRODUCTION

This chapter responds to criticisms by Chen and Epstein (2002) and Epstein and Schneider (2003) of the decision-theoretic foundations of our work that builds on robust control theory. Epstein, Chen and Schneider focus on what they regard as an undesirable dynamic inconsistency in the preferences that robust control theorists implicitly impute to the decision-maker. This chapter describes representations of robust control theory as two-player zero-sum games, provides senses of time consistency that robust control theories do and do not satisfy, and asserts our opinion that the dynamic inconsistency that concerns Epstein and his co-authors is not particularly troublesome for economic applications.

Hansen et al. (2006) used ideas from robust control theory[1] to form a set of time-zero multiple priors for the min–max expected utility theory of Gilboa and Schmeidler (1989). They express the set of priors as a family of perturbations to a single explicitly stated benchmark model. Hansen et al. (2006) call the resulting min–max preferences the 'constraint preferences' because they are formulated directly in terms of a set of priors represented via a constraint on the magnitude of allowable perturbations from the benchmark model. In this way, Hansen et al. (2006) connected Gilboa and Schmeidler's approach to uncertainty aversion with the literature on robust control.

Hansen et al. (2006) show that the control law that solves the time-zero robust control problem can also be expressed in terms of a recursive representation of preferences that penalizes deviations from the benchmark model. These 'multiplier preferences' are distinct from the date-zero constraint preferences, but are related to them via the Lagrange Multiplier Theorem.[2] Multiplier problems are standard in the robust control theory literature, probably because they are readily computable.

The multiplier preferences used by Hansen et al. (1999), Anderson et al. (2003) and Anderson et al. (2000) are dynamically consistent (see

Maccheroni et al. 2006a) and have been given axiomatic underpinnings by Maccheroni et al. (2006b) and Wang (2003). But Chen and Epstein (2002) and Epstein and Schneider (2003) assert that the constraint preferences, which link more directly to Gilboa and Schmeidler (1989), are 'dynamically inconsistent'. We shall argue that the type of dynamic inconsistency to which they refer differs from that familiar to macroeconomists. Indeed, by using an appropriate endogenous state variable, the constraint preferences can be depicted recursively. The robust control law can then be viewed as the maximizing player's part of the Markov perfect equilibrium of a two-player, zero-sum dynamic game. As a consequence, dynamic programming methods are applicable.

The type of dynamic inconsistency of robust control that disturbs Epstein and Schneider is this: as time unfolds, the minimizing agent in robust control is not allowed freely to choose anew from among the original time-zero potential probability distortions. This set is so large that it includes probability distortions conditioned on events that can no longer be realized and probability distortions over events that have already been realized. Our recursive constraint implementation of robust control theory prevents the minimizing agent from exploring these types of perturbations. If he did, he would want to revise his earlier distortions of conditional probabilities conditioned on those events now known not to occur. In that sense, our multiplier formulation of robust control is time consistent.

This chapter uses dynamic games to shed light on the concerns raised by Epstein and Schneider (2003). The representation of preferences by Gilboa and Schmeidler (1989) makes decision problems look like games. The game-theoretic formulation has a long history in statistical decision theory (see Blackwell and Girshick, 1954). We will argue that the form of dynamic inconsistency that worries Epstein and his co-authors comes from arresting the equilibrium of a two-player dynamic game in the middle of the game. Their objection amounts to a quarrel about the types of state variables that should and should not be allowed within the dynamic game used to model behavior. We concede that the continuation entropy state variable that we used in Hansen et al. (2006) requires a form of commitment to the preference orders as they are depicted in subsequent time periods. However, that does not disturb us because robust control theory does have the type of time consistency that we need to study recursive competitive equilibria and asset pricing in dynamic economies.

The remainder of this chapter is organized as follows. Section 7.2 describes Bellman equations for robust control problems. Section 7.3 reviews economic reasons for dynamically consistent preferences. Section 7.4 describes how dynamic programming applies to robust control problems. Sections 7.5 and 7.6 describe the preference orderings induced by robust control problems and alternative senses in which they are or are not time consistent. Sections 7.7, 7.8 and 7.9 describe the amounts of commitment, endogeneity and separability of constraints on model misspecification built into robust control formulations, while section 7.10 concludes.

7.2 RECURSIVE PORTRAYAL OF ROBUST CONTROL PROBLEMS

A recursive version of a discrete time robust control problem can be cast in terms of the Bellman equation:

$$V(r, x) = \max_{c \in C} \min_{q^* \geq 0, r^* \geq 0} U(c, x) + \beta \int q^*(w) V[r^*(w), g(x, c, w)] F(dw)$$

where the extremization is subject to:

$$r = \int q^*(w)[\log q^*(w) + \beta r^*(w)] F(dw)$$

$$1 = \int q^*(w) F(dw)$$

In this specification, F is the distribution function for a shock vector w that is assumed to be independently and identically distributed, c is a control vector, and x is a state vector.

The decision-maker's approximating model asserts that next period's realized state is:

$$x^* = g(x, c, w).$$

To generate a class of perturbed models around the approximating model, the decision-maker distorts the shock distribution F by using a non-negative density q^* that serves as the Radon–Nikodym derivative of the distorted density vis-à-vis the benchmark model.

For reasons discussed in Anderson et al. (2000), we refer to the endogenous state variable r as conditional entropy. It measures the difference between two models and is related to statistical discrimination through the construction of log-likelihood ratios. The function r^* allocates next period's continuation entropy as a function of the realized shock. The pair (q^*, r^*) is constrained by the current entropy r. We assume that a discrete-time Bellman–Isaacs condition makes the order of minimization and maximization irrelevant.

This problem has a special structure. The envelope condition is:

$$V_r(x,r) = V_r(x^*, r^*),$$

which implies a time-invariant relation between x and r. As a consequence, we can depict policies that attain the right side of the Bellman equation as functions of x only: $c = \varphi_c(x)$ and $q^* = \varphi_q(\cdot, x)$. Moreover, it is convenient to parameterize the problem in terms of a multiplier:

$$\theta = V_r(x, r)$$

that is held fixed over time. Consider instead the control problem associated with the Bellman equation:

$$W(x) = \max_{c \in C} \min_{q^* \geq 0} U(c,x) + \theta \int q^*(w) \log q^*(w) F(dw)$$
$$+ \beta \int q^*(w) W[g(x, c, w)] F(dw) \qquad (7.1)$$

subject to:

$$\int q^*(w) F(dw) = 1.$$

This problem has one fewer state variable, implies the same solutions for q^* and c, and is more manageable computationally. Setting the multiplier θ corresponds to initializing the state variable r.

7.3   WHY TIME CONSISTENCY?

Johnsen and Donaldson (1985) contribute a valuable analysis of time consistency outside the context of model misspecification. They want a decision-maker to follow through with his or her initial plans as information accrues:

> Let us consider a decision maker's dynamic choice problem, as time passes and the states of the world unfold. Having carried out the current action of his chosen plan and knowing that state s obtains, he is free to choose any action in the set Y_s. Having ruled out any surprise as to what his remaining options are, if his choice deviates from the original plan, this may be taken as *prima facia* evidence of 'changing tastes'. If on the other hand, the original plan is carried through whatever state obtains, we may that the decision maker's tastes remain constant. His dynamic preferences will then be said to admit *time consistent planning*.

Johnsen and Donaldson also seek preference specifications for which there is no incentive to reopen markets at future dates provided that

Arrow–Debreu contingent claims are traded at the outset. Solutions to robust control problems fulfill the Johnsen and Donaldson desiderata and produce interpretable security market price predictions.

In what follows we describe two other time consistency issues and comment on their importance.

7.4 DYNAMIC PROGRAMMING AND MARKOV PERFECT EQUILIBRIA

One reason for imposing time consistency in preferences is that it guarantees that dynamic programming methods can be applied. As we shall see, the dynamic inconsistency that concerns Chen and Epstein (2002) and Epstein and Schneider (2003) does not impede application of dynamic programming. Before discussing the kind of time inconsistency that concerns them, we briefly discuss another time consistency issue that we view as central in robust formulations of decision problems.

Time Consistency and Timing Protocols

James (1992) and Basar and Bernhard (1995) like to emphasize the link between robust control theory and dynamic two-player, zero-sum games. A recipe for choosing robust decisions requires a maximizing agent to rank control processes and a second malevolent agent whose distortions of probabilities relative to the benchmark model induce the maximizing agent to prefer robust decisions. Thus, prescriptions for robust decisions come from solving a two-player, zero-sum dynamic game (see Basar and Bernhard, 1995; James, 1992). An equilibrium of the dynamic game produces a sequence of robust decision rules. We can study how dynamic games with different timing protocols, manifested in alternative restrictions on strategies, alter equilibrium outcomes and representations.[3]

In what follows, we use a discrete-time counterpart to the games studied by Hansen et al. (2006). Consider a two-player, zero-sum game in which one player chooses a control process $\{c_t\}$ and the other player chooses a distortion process $\{q_{t+1}\}$, where q_{t+1} is non-negative, depends on date $t+1$ information, and satisfies $E(q_{t+1}|\mathcal{F}_t) = 1$. The transition probabilities between dates t and $t+\tau$ are captured by multiplying $q_{t+1}\cdots q_{t+\tau}$ by the τ-period transition probabilities from a benchmark model. Value processes:

$$V_t = U(c_t, x_t) + \beta E(q_{t+1}V_{t+1}|\mathcal{F}_t)$$

and

$$W_t = U(c_t, x_t) + E\left[q_{t+1}(\theta \log q_{t+1} + \beta W_{t+1})|\mathcal{F}_t\right]$$

can be constructed recursively, where $E(\cdot|\mathcal{F}_t)$ is the expectation operator associated with the benchmark model and $\mathcal{F}_t$ is the sigma algebra of date t events.[4] Notice that the date t recursions depend on the pair (c_t, q_{t+1}). No symptom of time inconsistency appears in these recursions. The robustness games have one player choosing c_t by maximizing and the other choosing q_{t+1} by minimizing subject to intertemporal constraints, as in the two robust decision problems described in the previous section.

Time consistency issues are resolved by verifying a Bellman–Isaacs condition which guarantees that the outcomes in the equilibrium of the date-zero commitment game coincides with those for the Markov perfect equilibrium. The Markov perfect equilibrium can be computed recursively by backward induction. The equivalence of the equilibrium outcomes of these two-player zero-sum games having different timing protocols (for example commitment of both players to sequences at time 0 versus sequential decision-making by both players) is central to the results in James (1992), Basar and Bernhard (1995) and Hansen et al. (2006).

Epstein and Schneider's Notion of Time Consistency

The notion of time consistency satisfied by robust control problems is distinct from the notion of dynamic consistency that concerns Chen and Epstein (2002) and Epstein and Schneider (2003). To understand the source of the difference, recall that when Gilboa and Schmeidler (1989) construct preferences that accommodate uncertainty aversion, they solve a minimization problem over measures for each hypothetical consumption process, instead of computing values for decision pairs (c_t, q_{t+1}), as in the dynamic games. A dynamic counterpart to Gilboa and Schmeidler's procedure would take as a starting point a given consumption process $\{c_t\}$ and then minimize over the process $\{q_{t+1}\}$, subject to an appropriate constraint. A time consistency problem manifests itself in the solution of this problem for alternative choices of $\{c_t\}$, as we will see below. Nevertheless, the presence of this form of time consistency problem does not lead to incentives to reopen markets, nor does it subvert dynamic programming.

7.5   A RECURSIVE PORTRAYAL OF PREFERENCES

Using recursions analogous to the ones described above, we can also define preferences that minimize over the process $\{q_{t+1}\}$. For simplicity, suppose now that the control is consumption and that the utility function U

depends only on c_t.[5] To define preferences, we construct a value function for a general collection of consumption processes that are restricted by information constraints but are not restricted to be functions of an appropriately chosen Markov state.

We begin with a recursive constraint formulation of preferences that uses a convenient recursive specification of a discounted version of the entropy of a stochastic process. We display it in order to understand better the sense in which the resulting preferences are recursive and to investigate their time consistency.

Given a consumption process $\{c_t : t \geq 0\}$, define:

$$V_t^*(r) = \min_{q^*, r^*} U(c_t) + \beta E \left[q^* V_{t+1}^*(r^*) | \mathcal{F}_t \right]$$

subject to:

$$r = E \left[q^* (\log q^* + \beta r^*) | \mathcal{F}_t \right]$$
$$1 = E(q^* | \mathcal{F}_t),$$

where now q^* and r^* are non-negative $\mathcal{F}_{t+1}$ measurable random variables. Here we are building a function $V_t^*(\cdot)$ from $V_{t+1}^*(\cdot)$. The random variable q^* distorts the one-period transition probability. The adding-up constraint in (7.3) guarantees that multiplication by q^* produces a legitimate probability distribution.

As before, the constraint that entropy be r is used to limit the amount of model misspecification that is acknowledged, $q^* \log q^*$ is the current period contribution to entropy, and r^* is a continuation entropy that connotes the part of entropy to be allocated in future time periods. The functions V_t^* are constructed via backward induction. The preferences are initialized using an exogenously specified value of r_0.

Holding θ fixed across alternative consumption processes gives rise to a second preference ordering. This preference ordering can be depicted recursively, but without using entropy as an additional state variable. The alternative recursion is:

$$W_t^* = \min_{q^*} U(c_t) + \beta E(q^* W_{t+1}^* | \mathcal{F}_t) + \theta E(q^* \log q^* | \mathcal{F}_t),$$

$$(7.4)$$

which is formed as a penalty problem, where $\theta > 0$ is a penalty parameter.

Given two consumption processes, $\{c_t^1\}$ and $\{c_t^2\}$ we can construct two date-zero functions $V_{0,1}^*$ and $V_{0,2}^*$ using (7.2) for each process. We can rank consumptions by evaluating these functions at r_0. The larger function at r_0 will tell us which of the consumption processes is preferred. For instance, if $V_{0,1}^*(r_0) \geq V_{0,2}^*(r_0)$, then the first process is preferred to the second one. Holding the penalty parameter θ fixed differs from holding fixed the entropy constraint across consumption processes, however. The value θ that makes the solution of model (7.4) deliver that given value of r_0 depends on the choice of the hypothesized consumption. Nevertheless, holding fixed θ gives rise to an alternative but well-defined preference order. See Wang (2003) for axioms that justify these and other preferences.

7.6 CONDITIONAL PREFERENCE ORDERS

Any discussion of time inconsistency in preferences must take a stand on the preference ordering used in subsequent time periods. We now consider three different ways to construct preference orders in subsequent dates. We focus on the constraint preferences because the multiplier preferences are automatically time consistent in the sense of Johnsen and Donaldson (1985).

Implicit Preferences

Starting from date zero preferences, Johnsen and Donaldson (1985) construct an implied conditional preference order for other calendar dates, but conditioned on realized events. They then explore properties of the conditional preference order. As they emphasize, the resulting family of conditional preference orders is, by construction, time consistent. The question is whether these preference orders are appealing. To judge this, Johnsen and Donaldson (1985) define the properties of history dependence, conditional weak dependence and dependence on unrealized alternatives.

At date zero, we can use a common r_0 to initialize the constraint preference orders. However, different consumption processes are associated with different specifications $\{q_{t+1} : 0 \leq t \leq \tau - 1\}$ as well as different processes for continuation entropy r_τ. The different choices of q_{t+1} will cause history dependence, despite the separability over time and across states in the objective. Moreover, $V_\tau^*(r_\tau)$ in states that are known not to be realized based on date τ information will have an impact on the conditional preference order over states that can be realized. As time unfolds, the minimization used to define preferences induces the following unappealing feature of the implied consumption ranking: despite the recursive construction, all branches used to construct V_0^* remain relevant when it comes time to reassess the preferences over consumption from the vantage point of date τ.

Nevertheless, this aspect of the implied preference orders does not undermine the applicability of dynamic programming. Moreover, as we

will see below, there is another and more tractable way to specify preferences over time.

Unconstrained Reassessment of Date-Zero Models

In an analysis of a continuous-time multiple priors model, Chen and
Epstein (2002) take a different point of view about the intertemporal preference orders. Suppose that the date τ minimizing decision-maker uses the
date-zero family of models but cares only about consumption from date τ
forward conditioned on date τ information. Absence of dependence on
past consumptions is posited because, at least for the moment, U depends
only on c_t. Exploring the conditional probabilities implied by the full set of
date-zero models generates time inconsistency for the following reason.

The function $V_\tau^*(\cdot)$ is constructed via backward induction. But at date τ
the minimization suggested by Chen and Epstein (2002) includes minimiz-
ing over r_τ. To make the date τ conditional entropy r_τ large, the minimizing
agent would make the *ex ante* probability of the date τ observed information small. For instance, suppose that τ is one. Then at date one we consider
the problem:

$$\min_{q^*, r^*} V_1^*(r^*)$$

subject to:

$$r_0 = E\left[q^*(\log q^* + \beta r^*)|\mathcal{F}_0\right]$$
$$1 = E(q^*|\mathcal{F}_0)$$

where q^* and r^* are restricted to be non-negative and $\mathcal{F}_1$ measurable. The
objective is to be minimized conditioned on date-one conditioning information. Notice that when q^* is zero for the realized date-one information,
r^* can be made arbitrarily large. Thus, the date-one reoptimization becomes
degenerate and inconsistent with the recursive construction of V_0^*. The
source of the time inconsistency is the freedom given to the date τ minimization to reassign distortions to the benchmark probabilities that apply
to events that have already been realized.

To avoid this problem, Chen and Epstein (2002) argue for imposing separate restrictions on the set of admissible conditional densities across time
and states. For instance, instead of the recursive constraint (7.3) we could
require:

$$E\left[q^*(\log q^*)|\mathcal{F}_t\right] \leq \eta_t \tag{7.5}$$

$$E(q^*|\mathcal{F}_t) = 1$$

for an exogenously specified process $\{\eta_t\}$.[6]

A Better Approach

Our recursive construction of V and V_τ^* suggests a different approach than either the implicit approach or the unconstrained reassessment approach of the previous subsections. Suppose that the reoptimization from date τ forward precludes a reassessment of the distortion of probabilities of events that have already been realized as of date τ. That can be accomplished by endowing the time τ minimizing agent with a state variable r_τ that 'accounts' for probability distortions over events that have already been realized and thus have already been 'spent'. Thus, r_τ accounts for continuation entropy already allocated to distorting events that can no longer be realized given date τ information.

When evaluating alternative consumption processes, this state variable is held fixed at date τ. We use appropriately constructed valuations $V_\tau^*(r_\tau)$ to rank consumption processes from date τ forward. The common value of the state variable r_τ is held fixed across consumption processes. It was chosen earlier as a function of date τ shocks and is inherited by the date τ decision-maker(s). Conditioning on this state variable makes contributions from previous dates and from unrealized states irrelevant to the time τ ranking of the continuation path of consumption from τ on.

This approach allows the date τ decision-maker to explore distortions of the probabilities of future events that can be realized given date τ information. Reallocation of future conditional relative entropy r^* is permitted at date τ, subject to (7.3). Given our recursive construction, this more limited type of reassessment will not cause the preferences to be time inconsistent.

We see very little appeal in the idea of distorting probabilities of events that have already been realized, and thus are not bothered by limiting the scope of the re-evaluation in this way. Nevertheless, our formulation requires a form of commitment and a state variable to keep track of it.

While this approach results in a different family of preference orders than the implicit approach, the differences are inconsequential in recursive control problems. The preferences remain consistent in the following sense. Consider the re-evaluation of the process $\{c_t^1\}$. Associated with this process is a continuation entropy r_τ for date τ. Consider an alternative process $\{c_t^2\}$ that agrees with the original process up until (but excluding) time τ. If $\{c_t^1\}$ is preferred to $\{c_t^2\}$ at date τ with probability one, then this preference ordering will be preserved at date-zero.[7] The date-zero problem allows for a more flexible minimization, although this flexibility will only reduce the date-zero value of $\{c_t^2\}$ and so cannot reverse the preference ordering.[8]

7.7　COMMITMENT

Provided that the date τ decision-maker commits to using r_τ in ranking consumptions from date τ forward, the implied preferences by (7.2) are made recursive by supposing that the date τ minimizing agent can assign the continuation entropy for date $\tau + 1$ chosen as a function of tomorrow's realized state. A possible complaint about this formulation is that it requires too much commitment. In ranking consumption processes from date τ forward, why should the r_τ chosen for a particular consumption process be adhered to?

Some such form of commitment in individual decision-making does not seem implausible to us. We can debate how much commitment is reasonable, but then it would also seem appropriate to ask Epstein and Schneider what leads decision-makers to commit to an exogenously specified process $\{\eta_t\}$ of entropy distortions specified period-by-period as in (7.5). Neither our decision-making environment nor that envisioned by Chen and Epstein (2002) and Epstein and Schneider (2003) is, in our view, rich enough to address this question.

7.8　ENDOGENOUS STATE VARIABLE

Our representation requires an additional endogenous state variable to describe preferences. The fact that we have carried along that state variable as an argument in the function V_t^* distinguishes our formulation from typical specifications of preferences in single-agent decision problems. But state variables do play a role in other preference orders. For instance, preferences with intertemporal complementarities such as those with habit persistence include a state variable called a habit stock that is constructed from past consumptions.

To illustrate the differences between a state variable to depict habit persistence and the state variable that appears in our representation of preferences, suppose that the habit stock is constructed as a geometric weighted average:

$$h_t = (1 - \lambda)c_t + \lambda h_{t-1}, \tag{7.6}$$

for $0 < \lambda < 1$. Define the date t preferences using:

$$\tilde{V}_t = U(c_t, h_{t-1}) + \beta E \, (\tilde{V}_{t+1} | \mathcal{F}_t) \tag{7.7}$$

where (7.6) is used to build the habit stock from current and past consumption. A feature of (7.7) is that we may be able depict date t preferences in terms of consumption from date t forward and the habit stock h_{t-1} coming into time t. A state variable h_{t-1} is used to define the date t preferences, but this variable can be constructed mechanically from past consumption.

Consider now two consumption processes $\{c_t^1\}$ and $\{c_t^2\}$ that agree from date zero through date $\tau - 1$ and suppose that h_{-1} is fixed at some arbitrary number. Thus, $h_t^1 = h_t^2$ for $t = 0, 1, ..., \tau - 1$. If $\tilde{V}_\tau^1 \geq \tilde{V}_\tau^2$ with probability one, then $\tilde{V}_0^1 \geq \tilde{V}_0^2$ with probability one. This is the notion of time consistency in preferences used by Duffie and Epstein (1992) and others, appropriately extended to include a state variable. Habit persistent preferences are dynamically consistent in this sense, once we introduce an appropriate a state variable into the analysis. In contrast to the conditional entropy r_t, the habit stock state variable h_{t-1} can be formed mechanically from past consumptions. No separate optimization step beyond that needed to choose $\{c_t\}$ itself is needed to construct h_{t-1} when we compare consumption processes with particular attributes.

By way of contrast, our state variable r_τ cannot be formed mechanically in terms of past consumption. It is constructed through optimization and is therefore forward-looking. Some people might regard this feature as unattractive because it makes the date τ preferences look 'too endogenous'. The forward-looking nature of this variable makes it depend on unrealized alternatives. (See Epstein and Schneider, 2003 for an elaboration on this complaint.) Thus, our state variable r_τ can be said to play a rather different role than the h_τ that emerges under habits. In particular, if we condition on an initial r_0 and compare consumption processes that agree between dates zero and $\tau - 1$, we will not necessarily be led to use the same value of r_τ because the decision of how to allocate continuation entropy at date $\tau - 1$ will reflect forward-looking calculations. In particular, it will depend on how future consumption depends on events that might be realized in the future.

This complaint that our state variable r_τ is too endogenous does not especially disturb us. Proponents of habit persistence like to emphasize the endogeneity of the resulting preference ordering. While the habit stock state variable can be formed mechanically, along a chosen consumption path the realized habit stock will typically depend on beliefs about the future and be forward-looking. This feature is emphasized in models of 'rational addiction' and is an attribute for which no apologies are offered.[9]

Whenever we have history dependence in preference orders, along a chosen consumption path the date τ preference order will depend on 'unrealized alternatives' through the endogeneity of the state variable. Just as minimization induces this dependence in our investigation, utility maximization will induce it along a chosen path. In effect, the time consistency problem in preferences over consumption processes comes from studying only the minimizing player's half of a two-player, dynamic game.

7.9 WE DON'T LIKE TIME-AND-STATE SEPARABLE CONSTRAINTS ON ENTROPY

Our aim in studying preferences that can represent concerns about robustness is to explore extensions of rational expectations that accommodate model misspecification. We seek convenient ways to explore the consequences of decisions across dynamic models with similar observable implications. Statistical discrimination leads us to study relative likelihoods. Likelihood ratios for dynamic models intrinsically involve intertemporal tradeoffs.

Accommodating misspecification in a dynamic evolution equation using a separable specification would seem to require some form of state dependence in the constraints. For instance, many interesting misspecifications of a first-order autoregression would require a state-dependent restriction on the one-period conditional entropy. This state dependence is permitted by Chen and Epstein (2002) and Epstein and Schneider (2003) but its precise nature is in practice left to the researcher or decision-maker.[10] It is intractable to explore misspecification that might arise from arbitrary state dependence in the setting of η_t period-by-period. For this reason we have considered non-separable specifications of model misspecification with explicit intertemporal trade-offs.

We achieve computational tractability partly through our separable specification of an entropy-penalty for distorting q^*. (See the construction for W in 7.1.) But this differs from adopting a separable constraint on the date t conditional entropy:[11]

$$E\left[\log(q_{t+1}^*)q_{t+1}^*|\mathcal{F}_t\right] \le \eta_t.$$

A virtue of the robust control theory approach is that it delivers state dependence in the implied η_t's from a low parameter representation. For instance, we could back-solve η_t from our date zero commitment problem via the formula:

$$\eta_t = r_t - \beta E(q_{t+1}^* r_{t+1}|\mathcal{F}_t)$$

where $\{r_t\}$ is the date t continuation entropy. However, back-solving for the η's will typically not produce identical decisions and worst-case distortions as would emerge from simply exogenously specifying the η's. In the separable constraint specification, the minimization problem for q^*_{t+1} will take account of the fact this choice will alter the probabilities over constraints that will pertain in the future. That will result in different valuation processes and may well lead to substantively interesting differences between the two approaches.

Nevertheless, because of its links to maximum likelihood estimation and statistical detection, this back-solving remains interesting. See Anderson et al. (2000) for a discussion. Just as a Bayesian explores when a given decision rule is a Bayes rule and evaluates that rule by exploring the implicit prior, so we may wish to use the implied $\{\eta_t\}$ process better to understand the probability models that are admitted in robust control problems.[12]

7.10 CONCLUDING REMARKS

In all approaches to robustness and uncertainty aversion, the family of candidate models is ad hoc. Savage's single-prior theory and multi-prior generalizations of it are not rich enough to produce beliefs for alternative hypothetical environments. Advantages of rational expectations are that it delivers one well-defined endogenous specification of beliefs, and it predicts how beliefs change across environments. Robust control theory does too, although it is not clear that r_0 or η_t should have the status of a policy-invariant parameter to be transferred from one environment to another.[13] What is and what is not transportable under hypothetical interventions is an important question that can only be addressed with more structure or information from other sources.

Nevertheless, the development of computationally tractable tools for exploring model misspecification and its ramifications for modeling dynamic economies should focus on deciding what are the interesting classes of candidate models for applications. We believe that it would impede this endeavor if we were to remove robust control methods from the toolkit of economists. These methods have been designed to be tractable and we should not ignore them.

NOTES

*   We thank Sherwin Rosen for urging us to write this chapter. We thank Nan Li and Martin Schneider for useful comments on earlier drafts.

1. Especially Anderson et al. (2000), which builds extensively on Basar and Bernhard (1995), James (1992) and Petersen et al. (2000).
2. Hansen and Sargent (2001) characterize aspects of choices over which the constraint and multiplier preferences agree and disagree.
3. Also see Hansen and Sargent (2007), Chapter 7.
4. While we have changed notation relative to that used in section 7.2, there is a simple relation. Since q^* was a function of w before and could be chosen to depend on x, when evaluated at x_t and w_{t+1}, the earlier q^* is a $f_t + 1$ measurable random variable.
5. Below we consider a habit persistence specification in which past consumptions are used to construct a current habit stock that enters U.
6. Alternatively, Epstein and Schneider (2003) suggest that one might begin with a family of models constrained in accordance with difference equation (7.3) solved forward from date zero. One could then expand this family of models sufficiently to satisfy their dynamic consistency requirement. In particular, one might hope to find an implied choice of η_t's in (7.5) to support this construction. Unfortunately, this way of constructing the η_t's suffers from an analogous problem. The restrictions on the densities in future periods would be effectively removed so that the η_t's in (7.5) would have to be infinite. Therefore, Epstein and Schneider's proposed repair is uninteresting for our decision problem because the expanded set of probability models is too large.
7. This can be seen by computing a date-zero value for the $\{c_t^2\}$ using the minimizing distortions between date one and τ.
8. See also Epstein and Schneider (2003) for a closely related discussion of a weaker dynamic consistency axiom.
9. A form of commitment is also present in habit persistent models since the date τ decision-maker remains 'committed' to past experience as measured by the habit stock $h\tau - 1$.
10. Epstein and Schneider (2003) feature state dependence in one of their examples.
11. For sufficiently nice specifications of the state dependence, presumably tractable recursive computation methods can also be developed to solve separable-constraint models.
    By extending the notions of dynamic consistency used by Epstein and Schneider (2003) to include state variables like those that support habit persistence, we suspect that separability in the construction of this constraint will no longer be required. Instead of being specified exogenously, the η_t's will possibly also depend on the same state variables used to capture more familiar forms of time nonseparability. In particular, η_t might depend on past consumptions. Martin Schneider concurred with this guess in private correspondence.
12. Thus it might illuminate situations in which our continuation entropy approach is not very attractive relative to an approach with an exogenous specification of $\{\eta_t\}$. For instance, if it is optimal to 'zero out' the exposure to risk in some given date, the minimizing agent will chose not to distort beliefs at that date and approximation errors will be allocated in future dates. If the $\{\eta_t\}$ were instead exogenously set to be positive, then multiple beliefs would support the no-exposure solution and substantially change the pricing implications.
13. But since it can be viewed as a special case that sets $r_0 = 0$, the same qualification applies to rational expectations.

REFERENCES

Anderson, E., L.P. Hansen and T. Sargent (2000), 'Robustness, detection and the price of risk', Mimeo, March.
Anderson, E., L. Hansen and T. Sargent (2003), 'A quartet of semigroups for model specification, robustness, prices of risk, and model detection', *Journal of the European Economic Association*, **1** (1), 68–123.

Basar, T. and P. Bernhard (1995), H_∞-*Optimal Control and Related Minimax Design Problems*, Boston, MA: Birkhauser.

Blackwell, D. and M. Girshick (1954), *Theory of Games and Statistical Decisions*, New York: Wiley.

Chen, Z. and L.G. Epstein (2002), 'Ambiguity, risk and asset returns in continuous time', *Econometrica*, **70**, 1403–43.

Duffie, D. and L.G. Epstein (1992), 'Stochastic differential utility', *Econometrica*, **60** (2), 353–94.

Epstein, L. and M. Schneider (2003), 'Recursive multiple priors', *Journal of Economic Theory*, **113** (1), 1–31.

Gilboa, I. and D. Schmeidler (1989), 'Maxmin expected utility with non-unique prior', *Journal of Mathematical Economics*, **18**, 141–53.

Hansen, L.P., T. Sargent and T. Tallarini (1999), 'Robust permanent income and pricing', *Review of Economic Studies*, **66**, 873–907.

Hansen, L.P. and T.J. Sargent (2001), 'Robust control and model uncertainty', *American Economic Review*, **91**, 60–66.

Hansen, L.P. and T.J. Sargent (2007), *Robustness*, Princeton, NJ: Princeton University Press.

Hansen, L.P., T.J. Sargent, G.A. Turmuhambetova and N. Williams (2006), 'Robust control, min–max expected utility, and model misspecification', *Journal of Economic Theory*, **128**, 45–90.

James, M.R. (1992), 'Asymptotic analysis of nonlinear stochastic risk sensitive control and differential games', *Mathematics of Control, Signals, and Systems*, **5**, 401–17.

Johnsen, T.H. and J.B. Donaldson (1985), 'The structure of intertemporal preferences under uncertainty and time consistent plans', *Econometrica*, **53**, 1451–8.

Maccheroni, F., M. Marinacci and A Rustichini (2006a), 'Ambiguity aversion, robustness, and the variational representation of preferences', *Econometrica*, **74** (6), 1447–98.

Maccheroni, F., M. Marinacci and A. Rustichini (2006b), 'Dynamic variational preferences', *Journal of Economic Theory*, **128**, 4–44.

Petersen, I.R., M.R. James and P. Dupuis (2000), 'Minimax optimal control of stochastic uncertain systems with relative entropy constraints', *IEEE Transactions on Automatic Control*, **45**, 398–412.

Wang, T. (2003), 'Conditional preferences and updating', *Journal of Economic Theory*, **108**, 286–321.

8. A tale of two countries: innovation and incentives among great inventors in Britain and the United States, 1750–1930

B. Zorina Khan and Kenneth L. Sokoloff

Technological change comprises an integral input into economic growth. Contemporary debates about the advance and diffusion of technological knowledge echo historical concerns about the specific rules and standards that might encourage would-be inventors, innovators and investors. As in the nineteenth century, skepticism about patent institutions has increased of late. A number of economists have been persuaded by the results from theoretical models of prizes and subsidies and have begun to lobby for these policies as superior alternatives. Although the topic is of great concern, systematic empirical investigation has been limited and many of the key issues about the effects of different features of patent systems and prizes remain poorly understood. Fortunately, the variation in intellectual property regimes and non-patent awards that existed over the nineteenth century can be studied to evaluate the sources, consequences and evolution of knowledge-generating institutions.

At the core of nineteenth-century controversies over knowledge-generating institutions were questions about which segments of the population were capable of producing significant inventions, and whether patents or other types of incentives such as prizes, grants or subsidies could be effective in increasing the rate at which they made discoveries. In the leading countries of Europe the dominant view held that only a very narrow group of the population was capable of truly important contributions to technological knowledge. In other words, the basic conception was that broadening access to patent protection would do little or nothing for increasing the pace of advance of technical knowledge, and perhaps might even retard technological progress. By way of contrast, the framers of US intellectual property institutions believed that a wide range of individuals, whatever their social origins and standing, were responsive to material incentives and capable of making significant contributions to the advance of technological knowledge.

Nearly all of the innovations they made in setting up US patent institutions can be viewed as enhancing the asset value of patent grants, and making it easier for inventors of all classes to obtain them.

This chapter employs a new data set of 'great inventors' in Britain and America to test the hypothesis that the differences between the patent systems in the two countries were in part manifested in the socio-economic composition of those generating significant new technological knowledge, if not overall rates of invention more generally. In our view, the rules and standards of knowledge-generating institutions had important effects on whether technologically creative individuals chose to invest in the exploration of their ideas. The far more restricted access to patent grants in Britain was likely to affect the extent to which their inventors would be disproportionately drawn from wealthier backgrounds than their counterparts in the United States, and also held implications for the type of inventions that would be protected. We further examine the related issues of how well alternative social schemes for promoting invention (such as the award of prizes) performed, and whether they tended to work in favor of those from privileged backgrounds.

8.1 PATENT SYSTEMS AND INVENTIVE ACTIVITY IN BRITAIN AND THE US

The British approach to encouraging private agents to invest in discovering and developing new technologies reflected a view that significant advances in technical knowledge were primarily likely to emanate from those who already possessed large stocks of human or financial capital. Features such as onerous fees (over ten times per capita income), high transaction costs, a lack of examination of applications, and an anti-patent legal system implied that British patent institutions offered rather limited incentives to inventors without financial assets and to creators of incremental inventions (Khan, 2005). Prizes for technological discoveries were also common, in part due to the rationale that elite inventors were not very motivated by material incentives.

In response to the threat of American competition, in 1852 the British patent laws were revised in the first major adjustment of the system in two centuries. The patent application process was greatly simplified, and a renewal system was adopted, making it cheaper to obtain a patent initially. Before 1852 patent specifications were open to public inspection only on payment of a fee per patent but afterwards, following the US model, they were indexed and published. However, patents were still granted through registration rather than examination and this absence of an examination system may have been very important. Without examination, there was great uncertainty about what a patent was really worth, and this increased the transaction costs involved in either trading the rights to the underlying technology or in using the patent to mobilize capital. It is therefore not surprising that the prevalence of assignments (sales of patents) and licenses was significantly lower throughout the nineteenth century in Britain than in the US which had moved early to such a regime.

The framers of early US policies were intent on crafting a new type of patent system that would promote learning, technology and commercial development, as well as create a repository of information on prior art (Khan and Sokoloff, 2001). Their chosen approach to accomplishing these objectives was based on providing broad access to property rights in technology, which was deliberately achieved through low fees and an application process that was impersonal and relied on routine administrative procedures. Incentives for generating new technological knowledge were also fine-tuned by requiring that the patentee be 'the first and true inventor' anywhere in the world. Moreover, a condition of the patent award was that the specifications of the invention be available to the public immediately on issuance of the patent, in order to aid rapid diffusion and commercialization.

Another distinctive feature of the US system was the requirement that all applications be subject to an examination for novelty by technically trained examiners. Approval from technical experts reduced uncertainty about the validity of the patent, and meant that the inventor could more easily use the grant either to mobilize capital to develop the patented technology commercially, or to sell or license off the rights to an individual or firm better positioned to exploit it directly. Private parties could always expend the resources needed to make the same determination as the examiners, as they did under the registration systems prevailing in Europe, but there was a distributional impact, as well as scale economies and positive externalities, if the government absorbed the overhead costs of certifying a patent grant as legitimate and made the information public. Accordingly, one would expect technologically creative people without the capital to go into business and directly exploit the fruits of their ingenuity to be major beneficiaries under an examination system such as the one the US pioneered.

These variations in patent design over place and time provide a natural experiment to investigate the effects of intellectual property institutions. If technologically creative individuals respond to expected returns, then one would expect that the existence and specific design of a patent system would influence the rate and direction of inventive activity. An examination of patent records suggests that inventive activity in nineteenth-century

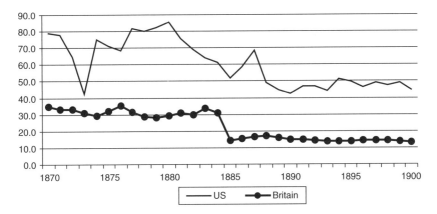

Sources: US Patent Office (various years), *Annual Report of the Commissioner of Patents.* Washington, DC: GPO, various years; and Great Britain Patent Office. *Annual report of the Commissioners of Patents [after 1883: Annual Report of the Comptroller-General of Patents, Designs and Trade Marks.]* London: H.M.S.O., various years.

Figure 8.1   *The ratio of all assignments to patents in the US as compared to the ratio of all assignments and licenses to patents in Britain, 1870–1900*

America was indeed responsive to material returns.[1] Another testament to this notion comprises the increase in per capita patenting in Britain after the 1852 change in that country's patent law. A key indication that the design of a patent system matters is apparent in the contrast between the US and Britain in the volume of trade in patented technologies. In Figure 8.1, the British numbers are biased upward by the inclusion of licenses as well as assignments, so it is all the more striking that trade in patents was still much more extensive – even on a per patent basis – in the US than in Britain.

We have long been interested in whether the different structures of intellectual property institutions between the US and Britain mattered for the relative involvement by different social groups in invention. In previous work with samples of ordinary patentees, we showed how individuals from elite backgrounds accounted for a much smaller proportion of patentees in the US than they did in countries such as Britain during the early nineteenth century (Khan and Sokoloff, 1998). This work was subject to the criticism, however, that not all patentees produce inventions of significance and some important technological discoveries are never patented. We therefore decided to collect information on the great inventors (and their inventions, patented or not) who were active in Britain and the United States. In the current chapter, we use the information on these great inventors to examine the hypothesis that the rules and standards of patent and other award institutions in the two leading industrializers were associated with significant differences between the US and Britain in the socioeconomic backgrounds of those responsible for generating significant new technological knowledge.

Our US sample consists primarily of all the individuals born before 1886 and listed in the *Dictionary of American Biography* on the basis of their career as an inventor. For each of the 409 US inventors (all men except for one woman), we collected biographical information including places and dates of birth and death; family background such as father's occupation; level and course of formal schooling; a series of variables reflecting work experience and means, if any, of realizing a return on inventions; total numbers of patents ever received and, for patentees, the years of first and last patent. We also collated the individual records of a proportion of the patents (roughly 4500 out of 16 900) they were awarded over their careers (roughly 97 percent received at least one). Our parallel sample of great inventors from Britain, primarily drawn from the *Oxford Dictionary of National Biography*, includes 434 men and one woman who made significant contributions to technological products and productivity between 1790 and 1930. It is significant that upwards of 85 percent of these eminent British inventors – increasing in the later cohorts – received a patent over their career. We further have information on all of the prizes or other sorts of official recognition the British great inventors received, including membership in the Royal Society.

Proxies for the social origins of the individuals who were making important discoveries include father's occupation and the educational attainment of the inventors. The comparison presented in Table 8.1 suggests that throughout most of the nineteenth century the great inventors in the US were indeed drawn from a much broader spectrum of the population than were their British counterparts. For example, among the great inventors born between roughly 1820 and 1845, nearly 43 percent of those in Britain had fathers who were in elite or professional occupations, whereas less than 19 percent of those in the US came from such privileged backgrounds. The substantial disparity in the social origins of those responsible for important inventions continued until the cohort born after 1865 – a group who would have been most active at invention after the major reforms of the British patent system during the 1880s and 1890s. It must be noted, however, that much of this convergence seems not to be attributable to a shift in the social origins of British great inventors, but rather because an increased proportion of their counterparts in the U.S had fathers who were of elite, professional or other white collar occupations. This reflects in part the growing importance for productive inventors of attaining a high level of formal

Table 8.1   Social backgrounds of great inventors in britain and the US: by birth cohorts, 1700 – 1910

Birth cohorts	Occupation of father					
	Farmer or ag. (%)	Professional or elite (%)	Manufacturers or skilled wk. (%)	Other white collar (%)	Unskilled workers or miscellaneous (%)	No.
Britain, distribution of inventors						
1709–80	10.0	45.7	21.4	10.0	12.9	70
1781–1820	7.8	37.9	38.8	11.2	4.3	116
1821–45	8.6	42.9	35.7	4.3	8.6	70
1846–70	7.3	45.5	21.8	18.2	7.3	55
1871–1910	5.0	57.5	12.5	7.5	17.5	40
United States, distribution of inventors weighted by patents						
1739–94	40.5	9.3	22.7	12.6	11.2	259
1795–1819	37.4	19.8	27.9	12.8	2.0	494
1820–45	39.0	18.7	32.1	7.0	3.2	918
1846–65	11.0	28.1	31.8	23.3	7.7	1115
1866–85	0.2	54.9	8.2	36.7	—	463

Notes and Sources: These estimates were computed for all of the great inventors included in the US and British samples, where we had information about the father's occupation. See the text for more information about the samples. Because many of the British great inventors did not obtain patents, we have reported the distribution of great inventors for Britain. However, we have reported the distribution of great inventors weighted by patents for the US, because only a small number (less than 5 percent) of the great inventors there did not obtain patents. As we had some information on British great inventors born up to 1906 (identified using the same procedures as those in the sample for Britain), we computed our estimates for the 1871–1910 cohort with these additional observations so as to increase our sample size for that cohort.

schooling, and the pattern that children of such fathers were more likely to attend institutions of higher learning than children of different backgrounds.

Indeed, another way of gauging the social class of the great inventors is to utilize the information we have on the formal schooling they received. For most of the eighteenth and nineteenth centuries, whether (and how far) an individual advanced beyond primary schooling was highly correlated with the income and social class of his parents. Another reason for examining the formal schooling attained by the great inventors is that it bears directly on the notion underlying many of the European intellectual property institutions of the nineteenth century – so ably depicted by Dava Sobel in her book *Longitude* – that people from humble backgrounds without

much in the way of formal schooling (or scientific knowledge) were generally not capable of making truly significant contributions to technological
knowledge. Those adhering to such views, as well as those who believe that
advances in science were the driving force behind the progress of early
industrialization, might well be surprised by the distributions of the US
great inventor patents.

Table 8.2 arrays the amount and type of formal schooling they received,
by birth cohort. It is striking that from the very earliest group (those born
between 1739 and 1794) through the birth cohort of 1820 to 1845, roughly
75 to 80 percent of patents went to those with only primary or secondary
schooling. So modest were the educational backgrounds of these first generations of great US inventors, that 70 percent of those born during
1739–94 had at best a primary education, with the proportion dropping to
only just above 59 percent among those who entered the world between
1795 and 1819. Given that these birth cohorts were active and, indeed,
dominant until the very last decades of the nineteenth century, these
numbers unambiguously indicate that people of rather humble backgrounds were capable of making important contributions to technological
knowledge. Up until the Second Industrial Revolution, the technologically
creative of this era seem to have been able to accumulate the skills and
knowledge necessary to operate at the frontier largely on their own, or
through their work experience as apprentices or younger employees.
Talented inventors such as Thomas Edison and James Eads were able to
realize large returns to their technological creativity by taking advantage
of the broad access to opportunity that the patent system and other
American institutions provided.

Our evidence does indeed suggest that these features of the US patent
system were highly beneficial to inventors, and especially to those whose
wealth would not have allowed them directly to exploit their inventions
through manufacturing or other business activity. As seen in Table 8.2, a
remarkably high proportion of the great inventors, generally near or above
half, extracted much of the income from their inventions by selling or
licensing off the rights to them. Moreover, it was just those groups that one
would expect to be most concerned to trade their intellectual property that
were indeed the most actively engaged in marketing their inventions.
Specifically, it was the great inventors with only a primary school education
who were most likely to realize the income from their inventions through
sale or licensing, whereas those with a college education in a non-technical
field were generally among the least likely to follow that strategy. Overall,
the reliance on sales and licensing was quite high among the first birth
cohort (51.4 percent on average), and remained high (62.1, 44, and 66
percent in the next three cohorts), until a marked decline among the last

Table 8.2   The distribution of US 'great inventor' patents by level of formal schooling and principal means by which the inventor extracted returns over his career: by birth cohorts, 1739–1885

Birth cohort	Level of education				
	Primary	Second.	College	Eng/NatSci.	Total
1739–94 (%)	69.5	6.8	12.5	11.3	400
Av. career patents	5.6	3.8	6.5	5.2	75
sell/license (col. %)	54.9	11.1	84.0	17.7	51.4%
prop/direct (col. %)	36.5	74.1	2.0	44.7	35.6%
employee (col. %)	6.2	7.4	—	—	4.8%
1795–1819 (%)	59.1	19.3	5.4	16.2	709
Av. career patents	20.0	14.4	17.3	12.1	80
sell/license (col. %)	58.2	81.0	42.1	60.4	62.1%
prop/direct (col. %)	33.2	10.2	47.4	24.3	28.1%
employee (col. %)	8.4	8.8	—	13.5	8.8%
1820–45 (%)	39.2	34.7	16.3	9.7	1221
Av. career patents	41.8	44.0	29.4	23.7	145
sell/license (col. %)	50.7	31.8	37.4	72.8	44.0%
prop/direct (col. %)	42.3	55.2	47.7	19.3	45.5%
employee (col. %)	7.7	13.0	14.9	7.0	10.2%
1846–65 (%)	22.2	24.5	20.9	32.4	1438
Av. career patents	158.3	73.6	78.6	55.3	80
sell/license (col. %)	94.5	68.5	46.2	57.1	66.0%
prop/direct (col. %)	5.5	18.6	52.8	16.9	22.6%
employee (col. %)	—	12.9	—	23.6	10.4%
1866–85 (%)	0.2	17.9	21.4	60.5	574
Av. career patents	—	144.5	53.6	155.7	26
sell/license (col. %)	—	1.0	46.3	40.1	34.3%
prop/direct (col. %)	100.0	98.1	49.6	18.7	39.7%
employee (col. %)	—	1.0	4.1	41.2	26.0%

Notes and Sources: See the text. Our overall sample of 'great inventors' was constructed in two waves. In the first (160 inventors), consisting primarily of those born before 1821, we collected the information for all of the patents they received through 1865, and retrieved the information on the number they received after 1865 for our estimates of the total career patents. In the second wave (249 inventors), we collected patents from every fifth year through 1930, and thus will be missing the patents received late in the careers of those of our inventors who were born in the 1870s and 1880s.

The table reports the distribution of US great inventor patents across the schooling class of the patentee, by the birth cohort of the inventor; the average number of patents received by each inventor, by birth cohort and schooling class; and the distribution of patents across the principal method of the inventor extracting income, by birth cohort and schooling class. The numbers of patents and great inventors are reported in italics for each birth cohort. We classified the way income was extracted after a close reading of the biographies, and this variable extends over the overall career of the inventor (all of his or her patents). The categories include: inventors who frequently sold or licensed the rights to the technologies they patented; those who sought to directly extract the returns by being a principal in a firm that used the technology in production or produced a patented product; and those who were employees of such a firm. We have omitted a category for those inventors who seem to have made no effort to extract income from their inventions.

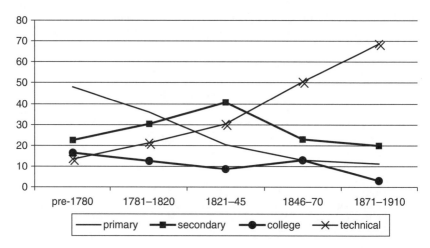

Figure 8.2   Distribution of British great inventors by level of schooling and birth cohort

birth cohort (those born between 1866 and 1885). The proportion of great inventors who relied extensively on sales or licensing of patented technologies then fell sharply, and there was a rise in the proportion that realized their returns through long-term associations (as either principals or employees) with a firm that directly exploited the technologies.

Consistent with what we would expect from the design of their patent system, British institutions do not appear to have been nearly as favorable to those who did not, or could not, attend universities. Despite Britain lagging behind the US considerably in literacy and other gauges of schooling amongst the general population (thus biasing the results against the case we are making), individuals with low levels of schooling were far less well represented, and those with university degrees in technical fields such as engineering, natural sciences or medicine far more represented, amongst the great inventors of that country than they were amongst those in the US (compare the results in Figure 8.2 for British great inventors with those in Table 8.2 for the American inventors, or Figure 8.3 for a succinct summary). Among the great inventors born in the US between 1820 and 1845, those with no more than a primary school education accounted for roughly 40 percent of the patents that were granted to that cohort, while those with university educations in a technical field garnered only 10 percent. The analogous shares for the British great inventors (computed over inventors because many did not patent) were roughly 20 percent and over 30 percent respectively. The contrast is dramatic, and the implication is that the great inventors in the US were much more likely to obtain their familiarity with the

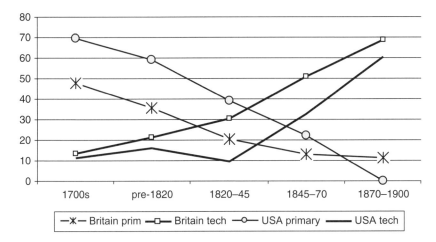

Figure 8.3   Proportions of British and US great inventors with only primary schooling and with only technical university degrees, by birth cohort

technological frontier through informal channels or institutions other than formal schools than were their British counterparts. This pattern is consistent with the view that a much narrower class of the population was involved in generating new technological knowledge in Britain than was the case in the US, especially since our evidence (see Figure 8.4) on the occupations of the fathers of the great inventors who attended university suggests that the universities in the former country recruited their students from far more privileged backgrounds than did those in the latter (particularly after 1820).

Circumstances changed over time with the evolution of technology. Knowledge of science clearly became increasingly important, particularly beginning in the late nineteenth century with the onset of the Second Industrial Revolution. Such knowledge enhanced contributions at the technological frontier and perhaps (when certified by university degrees in technical fields) facilitated access to the resources to carry out programs of research and development (R&D). This development is evident in the rapid rise to dominance of individuals with technical degrees amongst the later birth cohorts of great inventors in both countries. Although there is substantial convergence in the distributions of great inventors by formal schooling during this period, this likely overstates the extent to which the social origins of the inventors likewise converged. As reported above, the great inventors in Britain who received degrees at universities seem to have continued to be drawn overwhelmingly from extremely privileged backgrounds. The US educational institutions, which incorporated such

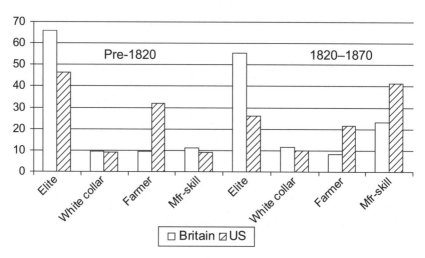

Figure 8.4   *Proportion of great inventors who attended college by*
                occupational class of father: for Britain and the US pre-1820
                and 1820–85 birth cohorts

innovations as land-grant universities, may have evolved more readily to
support broader admission to opportunities for gaining valuable training
in technical fields than did those in Britain. Britain was much slower in
extending access to educational opportunities, as well as in establishing new
universities, and the emphasis was decidedly on a more 'classical' orienta-
tion. Thus, even after the patent systems in the US and Britain became
much more similar, the contrasts in the social origins of those active at
invention may have persisted because of other institutional differences.

8.2   A FIRST LOOK AT HOW PRIZES WORKED

In recent years, economists have paid increasing attention to prizes as alternatives to patent institutions as a means of encouraging and rewarding
creativity and innovation without incurring deadweight losses.[2] The theoretical problems with prizes are well recognized, however, and they include
difficulties in assessing the value of the invention (such as those that arise
from asymmetric information, delays in the determination of value, and the
complexities of aggregating benefits which might accrue from sequential
innovations). Even if these were resolved, the credibility or efficiency of
bureaucrats in holding to contracted promises might be questioned, leading
to a diminution in the expected return from a prize. Much of this work has

relied on casual illustrative anecdotes, such as the prizes offered for margarine and food preservation, the process to make soda from sodium chloride, and the oft-cited case of John Harrison's notorious quest for the prize for a method of determining longitude at sea.[3]

In the United States numerous proposals were repeatedly submitted to Congress throughout the nineteenth century to replace the patent system with more centralized systems of national prizes, awards or subsidies by the government. Such proposals failed to persuade, because it was argued that the process of democratization was most likely to be attained through decentralized decision-making by inventors themselves, and through enforcement by judges confronting individual conflicts on a case-by-case basis. This was not the case in Europe, where extensive arrays of prizes were offered to 'deserving' inventors. But closer inspection of the historical records gives ample reason to question the efficacy of administered centralized awards, especially in the case of inventors who were not politically astute or who were more likely to have been drawn from the 'lower classes' than the great inventors.

The biographies of the British great inventors include information about honors and awards. Altogether, 171 of the inventors in our sample received such recognition, ranging from the recipients of gifts of silver plate from the Crown to two winners of the Nobel Prize (Sir Edward Appleton and Guglielmo Marconi). These data offer more systematic insights into the advantages and drawbacks of patents and alternative incentive and reward mechanisms. Table 8.3 presents the results of logistic regressions where the dependent variable is the likelihood that an inventor is also the recipient of at least one prize (we do not distinguish here between different types of awards). The coefficients on the independent variables report the antilog or the odds of having received a prize (rather than the log odds) conditional on the vector of independent variables. Prizes and medals, in particular, might be more effective than patents as inducements to the generation of significant new technological knowledge if scientist-inventors differed from patentees and were motivated by the recognition of their peers and less by financial incentives. However, the results indicate that prizes and medals tended to be awarded to the same individuals who had already received patents and, indeed, the likelihood of receiving a prize increased with the number of patents the individual received. That the marginal effects of these non-patent awards were low is supported by the observation that the majority of premia were made later in life to those who had already attained eminence.

The regressions also highlight the potential inefficiencies of administered awards, which might be subject to the possibility of bias, personal prejudices or even corruption. The likelihood that an inventor had received prizes and medals was higher for scientific men, more so for those who had

Table 8.3 *Logistic regressions with the probability of the British great inventor receiving at least one prize as the dependent variable*

	Point estimate of odds ratio			
	(1)	(2)	(3)	(4)
Time period				
Before 1800	0.32	0.34	0.34	0.28
	(8.97)***	(7.39)***	(6.51)**	(8.56)***
1800–1819	0.52	0.60	0.53	0.47
	(3.32)*	(1.81)	(2.49)	(3.11)
1820–39	0.38	0.41	0.36	0.27
	(9.16)***	(7.30)***	(7.78)***	(11.54)***
1840–49	0.52	0.54	0.60	0.56
	(2.56)	(2.02)	(1.18)	(1.42)
1850–59	0.51	0.48	0.58	0.46
	(3.52)*	(3.80)*	(1.66)	(3.04)
1860–69	0.96	0.99	0.96	0.78
	(0.01)	(0.00)	(0.01)	(0.28)
Total patents	1.01	1.01	1.01	1.01
	(4.54)**	(3.67)*	(3.03)*	(1.60)
Residence				
London & home Counties	—	2.14	2.10	1.97
		(11.89)***	(11.72)***	(7.64)***
Education				
Elite university	—	3.57	3.11	2.30
		(16.60)***	(10.16)***	(4.30)**
Science degree	—	—	1.03	0.75
			(0.00)	(0.63)
Technical degree	—	—	1.36	1.38
			(0.54)	(0.50)
Publications	—	—	—	2.10
				(7.70)***
Fellow of Royal Society	—	—	—	2.38
				(7.22)***
Employment				
Scientific	—	—	—	1.29
				(0.07)
Professional	—	—	—	0.90
				(0.13)
Engineering	—	—	—	0.87
				(0.03)
Manufacturing	—	—	—	1.47
				(0.19)

Table 8.3   (continued)

	Point estimate of odds ratio			
	(1)	(2)	(3)	(4)
N=	410	410	370	370
−2 Log L	522.78***	509.01***	446.92***	416.20***

Notes and Sources: The data draw on biographical information for the British great inventors. Prizes consist of non-patent awards including medals and *ex post* or *ex ante* cash grants. Total patents were determined by a search for all patents granted to the inventor through 1890, and co-invention was counted as one patent. Publications indicate articles in specialized journals and nonfiction books published. London and the Home Counties include Berkshire, Middlesex, Sussex, Essex, Kent, Oxford, Bedfordshire and Hertfordshire. Elite education refers to education at Cambridge, Oxford, Durham, the Royal Colleges, or graduate education in Germany. Science education includes college training in mathematics, sciences, or medicine, whereas Technical education comprises post-secondary education in engineering or metallurgy. Numbers in parentheses are Wald Chi-squared statistics.

*   Significant at 5% level.
**   Significant at 1% level.
***   Significant below 1% level.

gained recognition as famous scientists or Fellows of the Royal Society. An interesting facet of the relationship between privilege, science and technological achievement in Britain is reflected in the 90 great inventors who were also appointed as Fellows of the Royal Society. The Royal Society itself was the target of persistent criticism throughout this period, including scathing assessments by its own members such as Charles Babbage. Many were disillusioned with these award systems, attributing outcomes to arbitrary factors such as personal influence, the persistence of one's recommenders, or the self-interest of the institution making the award.[4] The bias towards elites was not limited to privileges for members of the Royal Society. The uneducated George Stephenson resolved the problem of a safety lamp using practical methods and received 100 guineas, whereas Sir Humphry Davy applied scientific principles and was rewarded with a public testimonial of £2000.

The grants of prizes among British great inventors seem to have been strongly related to elite status. The most important variable affecting the likelihood of receiving a prize was an Oxbridge or elite education, which doubled the odds of receiving an award (evaluated at the mean probability), despite the traditional hostility of such institutions to pragmatic or scientific pursuits. It is worth noting the contrast with specialized education or employment in science or technology, neither of which had much impact on the probability of getting a prize. Instead, such awards were far more closely linked to residence close to the capital, or to publications in the annals of the 'learned societies' which resembled gentlemen's social clubs where membership simply depended on connections and payment of significant dues. By 1900 the Council of the Royal Society decided to change its emphasis from the allocation of medals to the financing of research, and the growing disillusionment with prizes as an incentive for innovation is consistent with the coefficients on the time trend, which are no longer statistically significant after the second half of the nineteenth century. [5] Thus, the data here seem to support those who view the experience of the Longitude Prize as a cautionary tale, rather than an exemplary parable, because John Harrison's problems seem to have been more general than many have acknowledged.

8.3   CONCLUSION

In this preliminary analysis, we have begun to study parallel data sets of great inventors from Britain and the US to compare the patterns of inventive activity in these first two industrializers. Three results stand out in this exploration of patterns of intellectual property institutions. First, the inventors in the US were drawn from a much broader spectrum of the population than were their counterparts in Britain, consistent with the view that the narrower provision of property rights in new technological knowledge under the latter's patent system did matter for who was involved in inventive activity. Although other differences in institutions and economy-wide circumstances probably contributed to this pattern, it is striking that so much of the important invention in the US was carried out by individuals from humble backgrounds until very late in the nineteenth century.

Second, that so much of the important invention during the early stages of US industrialization came from individuals with only very limited formal schooling, raises questions about what sorts of technical or scientific knowledge were really required during that era to make a significant discovery, and how technologically creative individuals accumulated that knowledge. Job experience, especially in apprentice-like positions, seems to have been adequate for learning about the frontiers of technology prior to the Second Industrial Revolution, but in both countries great inventors born after 1860 depended on formal education at university in technical fields. The shift in academic credentials was, of course, more abrupt in the US, and focuses attention on what changed. In other work (Khan and Sokoloff, 2004) we have shown that the shift occurred at roughly the same time across all of the major industrial sectors. It may be that scientific advances had implications for all fields of technology, but the growing importance of academic credentials for securing long-term support of programs of inventive activity could also help account for the change (Lamoreaux and Sokoloff, 1996, 1999).

Finally, our examination of which of the British great inventors received prizes or honors for their discoveries provides little evidence that this approach toward encouraging private investment in inventive activity was superior to patent awards. On the contrary, the findings that some of the most decisive determinants for whether the inventor received a prize were which university he had graduated from and where he lived, support the view that the inordinate role of politics and/or social connections in selecting recipients tend to undermine the efficacy of the incentives offered under such schemes.

NOTES

1. Working with a general sample of patent records (and manufacturing firm data from 1820, 1832, 1850), Sokoloff (1988, 1992) argued that both the geographic and cyclical patterns of inventive activity in early industrial America were profoundly influenced by the extent of the market, and had measurable impacts on manufacturing productivity.
2. In the absence of asymmetries in information regarding costs and benefits, theoretical models suggest that prizes, public funding or payment on delivery might be preferable to the monopoly offered by intellectual property rights (Maurer and Scotchmer, 2004). Wright (1983) found that prizes are optimal if the success probability is moderately high, if the supply elasticity of inventions is low, and where awards can be adjusted ex post. Shavell and van Ypersele (2001) argued that subsidies might be the most effective means of calibrating rewards for innovations according to social value. Some versions of this subsidy mechanism center on discounting the price to consumers who value the patented product above its marginal cost. Kremer (1998) suggested an ingenious hybrid that transforms the patent into a prize that is auctioned to the highest bidder in a process that reveals the underlying value of the invention; the government would then engage in patent buyouts of high-valued discoveries and turn them over to the public domain.
3. See Sobel (1995) for more details. The Longitude Act awarded £20 000 for a means of determining longitude at sea. Candidacy for the award was judged by a Board of Longitude, members of which were drawn from the scientific, military and public elite, who were scornful of Harrison as a common uneducated artisan, and hindered his attempts to collect the prize, which was never actually awarded.
4. Sir William Robert Grove, a great inventor and member of the Royal Society, 'lambasted both the Royal Society and the increasingly influential specialist scientific societies for their nepotism and corruption', Gillispie (1980), Vol. 5, p. 559.
5. The Council stated that its experience in the award of medals had revealed that adding to the number of such awards would be 'neither to the advantage of the Society nor in the interests of the advancement of Natural Knowledge', MacLeod (1971), p. 105.

REFERENCES

Dictionary of American Biography (1928–36), New York: C. Scribner's.
Gillispie, Charles D. (ed.) (1980). *Dictionary of Scientific Biography*, 16 vols, New York: Scribner.
Khan, B. Zorina (2005), *The Democratization of Invention: Patents and Copyrights in American Economic Development, 1790–1920*. New York: Cambridge University Press.
Khan, B. Zorina and Kenneth L. Sokoloff (1998), 'Two paths to industrial development and technological change', in Maxine Berg and Kristine Bruland (eds), *Technological Revolutions in Europe, 1760–1860,* Cheltenham, UK and Lyme, USA: Edward Elgar: pp. 292–313.
Khan, B. Zorina and Kenneth L. Sokoloff (2001), 'The early development of intellectual property institutions in the United States', *Journal of Economic Perspectives*, **15** (3), 233–46.
Khan, B. Zorina and Kenneth L. Sokolloff (2004), 'Institutions and democratic invention in 19th Century America', *American Economic Review*, **94** (2) 395–401.
Kremer, Michael (1998), 'Patent buyouts: a mechanism for encouraging innovation', *Quarterly Journal of Economics*, **113** (4) 1137–67.
Lamoreaux, Naomi R. and Kenneth L. Sokoloff (1996), 'Long-Term Change in the Organization of Inventive Activity', *Proceedings of the National Academy of Sciences*, **93** (November), 12686–92.
Lamoreaux, Naomi R. and Kenneth L.Sokoloff (1999), 'Inventors, firms, and the market for technology in the late nineteenth and early twentieth centuries', in Naomi R. Lamoreaux, Daniel M.G. Raff and Peter Temin (eds), *Learning By Doing in Markets, Firms, and Countries*, Chicago, IL: University of Chicago Press pp.19–57.
MacLeod, Roy M. (1971), 'Of medals and men: a reward system in Victorian science, 1826–1914', *Notes and Records of the Royal Society of London*, **26** (1), 81–105.
Maurer, Stephen M. and Suzanne Scotchmer (2004), 'Procuring knowledge', in G. Libecap (ed.), *Intellectual Property and Entrepreneurship: Advances in the Study of Entrepreneurship, Innovation and Growth*, **15**, pp. 1–31.
Oxford Dictionary of National Biography (2007), http://www.oxforddnb.com.
Shavell, Steven and Tanguy van Ypersele (2001), 'Rewards versus intellectual property rights', *Journal of Law and Economics*, **44** (2), 525–47.
Sobel, Dava (1995), *Longitude: the True Story of a Lone Genius Who Solved the Greatest Scientific Problem of His Time*, New York: Penguin Books.
Sokoloff, Kenneth L. (1988), 'Inventive activity in early industrial America: evidence from patent records, 1790–1846', *Journal of Economic History*, **48** (December), 813–50.
Sokoloff, Kenneth L. (1992), 'Invention, innovation, and manufacturing productivity growth during the antebellum period', *The Standard of Living in Early 19th Century America*, Robert Gallman and John Wallis (eds.), Chicago, IL: University of Chicago Press, 345–378.
Wright, Brian D. (1983), 'The economics of invention incentives: patents, prizes, and research contracts', *American Economic Review*, **73** (4), 691–707.

9. Macroeconomics with intelligent autonomous agents

Peter Howitt

9.1 INTRODUCTION

Axel Leijonhufvud has spent much of his distinguished career investigating how a decentralized economy coordinates economic activities. The question is basically the same as the one Keynes (1934) once posed: To what extent, and under what circumstances, particularly under what policy regimes, is the economy self-adjusting? In recent years Leijonhufvud has advocated the use of agent-based computational economics as an approach to the problem.[1] The present chapter discusses this methodology and describes an ongoing research agenda aimed at implementing it.

As described by Tesfatsion (2006), agent-based computational economics is a set of techniques for studying a complex adaptive system involving many interacting agents with exogenously given behavioral rules. The idea motivating the approach is that complex systems, like economies or anthills, can exhibit behavioral patterns beyond what any of the individual agents in the system can comprehend. So instead of modelling the system as if everyone's actions and beliefs were coordinated in advance with everyone else's, as in rational expectations theory, the approach assumes simple behavioral rules and allows a coordinated equilibrium to be a possible emergent property of the system itself. The approach is used to explain system behavior by 'growing' it in the computer. Once one has devised a computer program that mimics the desired characteristics of the system in question one can then use the program as a 'culture dish' in which to perform experiments.

Now the first reaction of many economists upon first hearing about this methodology is that all economic models with an explicit microfoundation, which is to say almost all models that one sees in mainstream macroeconomic theory, are 'agent-based'. Some even have a multitude of heterogeneous agents (see Krusell and Smith, 1998 and Krebs, 2003, among others). So what's the big deal?

The big deal, as Tesfatsion has emphasized on many occasions, has to do with autonomy. An agent in a rational expectations equilibrium model has a behavioral rule that is not independent of what everyone else is doing. In any given situation, his or her actions will depend on some key variables (prices, availability of job offers, and so on) or the rational expectation thereof, that are endogenous to the economic system. These variables will change when we change the agent's environment, and hence his or her behavior cannot be specified independently of the others'. The household, for example, in a market clearing model of supply and demand cannot choose what quantity to demand until told what price will clear the market. Likewise the agent on a Lucas Island (a Phelps Island with rational expectors) cannot choose how much to sell until informed of the stochastic process determining aggregate and relative demand fluctuations.

The problem with assuming non-autonomous agents is that it leaves the model incomplete, and in a way that precludes a deep analysis of the coordination problem. For if the model does not allow people to act without knowing the equilibrium value of some variable, then someone must have computed that equilibrium value a priori. In such a model there is no way to describe out-of-equilibrium behavior, and the problem of reconciling people's independently conceived plans is assumed to be solved by some unspecified mechanism that uses no scarce resources. Autonomy is thus essential to the problems that Axel has done so much to keep alive since the rational expectations revolution.

Now under certain assumptions about common information, someone endowed with enough information could figure out on their own what the market clearing price is going to be, or what the rational expectation of the price level is, and in this sense could act autonomously even in a rational expectations equilibrium framework. But an economy full of agents that were autonomous in this sense would not be decentralized in the Hayekian sense, because no market would be needed to aggregate the diverse information of heterogeneous people, each of whom can do the aggregation in their head. Each would be capable of acting as the economy's central planner, although in this case the planner would not be needed. Moreover, such an economy would have no need for macroeconomists, because everyone would already know as much as could be known about the macroeconomy. The coordination problem would be trivial. So by 'autonomous' agents I mean agents that are endowed with behavioral rules that can tell them what to do in any given situation, independently of each others' rules, even when no one has access to a correct model of the economy.

The literature on learning in macroeconomics, recently surveyed by Evans and Honkapohja (2001), specifies autonomous agents according to this definition. For example the least-squares learner in the Cagan model of hyperinflation has a sequence of observations on past inflation and acts according to a rule that tells her to demand the quantity of money whose log is a given linear function of the rate of inflation predicted by the ordinary least squares (OLS) estimator. This function can be specified independently of what everyone else in the economy is doing. Of course there is the problem of specifying the time series model correctly, and this will depend on the nominal demand process driving inflation, in a way that someone lacking a correct model of the economy could not know for sure. Much of the literature supposes that people are endowed with knowledge of how to specify the model to be estimated in such a way that it will eventually be correct if the economy converges to a rational expectations equilibrium. But Evans and Honkapohja also cover the case of misspecified models, where the economy might or might not converge, and sometimes to an equilibrium that is not rational expectations. In such a case, the agents are indeed autonomous.

Although I believe that much can be learned from the macroeconomic learning literature, and have discussed this at length elsewhere (Howitt, 2006b), that literature does not come to grips with what I now see as one of the most salient aspects of how people behave in an economic environment that they do not understand, and that they know they do not understand. This aspect was an important theme of Keynes, who argued that people are not in a position to act according to the conventional theory of rational choice if they cannot attach numerical probabilities to all possible consequences of their decisions. Keynes argued that under such circumstances they tend to cope by falling back on custom and convention. They also devise institutions to insulate themselves from having to rely upon necessarily unreliable forecasts.

As Axel has argued, macroeconomic life is full of unquantifiable uncertainty. He once likened forecasting inflation to playing a game of chess refereed by someone who announces that: 'From now on bishops move like rooks and vice versa . . . and I'll be back with more later' (Leijonhufvud, 1981, p. 264). Hence a lot of economic decisions, particularly those involving risks of losses from inflation, are based on conventional or institutionalized rules of thumb.

Paul Davidson (1989, pp. 15–17) has also argued that money, in its role as a unit of account and standard of deferred payment, is an institution through which people cope with uncertainty without having to rely upon necessarily imperfect predictions of the future. In a money-using economy, firms and households are concerned not just with their 'real' economic profits, but also with their cash flow, for no matter what happens to the value of money they can at least stay out of the bankruptcy court as long as inflow exceeds outflow. Historical cost accounting helps firms to keep track of their cash flow better than would an indexed system, and nominal, non-indexed debt contracts allow them to insulate their cash flow from unpredictable fluctuations in the price level, especially in a world where their customers demand some assurance of predictable nominal prices. Controlling real cash flow would be the ideal objective if it were possible, but controlling nominal cash flow, with the aid of such devices as nominal debt and historical cost accounting, is at least a useful objective with the advantage of being reasonably attainable.

Likewise, one of the central themes of David Laidler's work is that money is a device for economizing on the costs of processing information. People use it as a buffer stock that automatically absorbs unforeseen changes in income and expenses without the need for deliberation. They also use it as a unit of account, measure of value and standard of deferred payment because it is convenient to use, conventional and easily understood, even if this seems to introduce biases and inefficiencies into their decision-making and even if economists can think of better measures and standards.[2]

From the point of view of mainstream macroeconomics, people that follow rules of behavior that have no obvious rationalization in terms of optimal choice appear to have 'bounded rationality'. Economists are socialized to be skeptical of any theory that relies on such limits to human intelligence. But the case can be made that using simple rules that seem to work reasonably well is actually a more intelligent way to arrange one's affairs in an uncertain world than the more conventional Bayesian alternative of fabricating a model of the world and choosing a plan that would be optimal under the incredible assumption that the model was a true representation of reality. Under the Bayesian alternative, not only would specification error be likely to lead the decision-maker astray, but Bellman's curse of dimensionality would render the task of implementing the strategy unworkable, since it would involve computing a solution to a very complicated model, unless the model was made tractable by other convenient heuristic devices, like assuming all agents to be identical, only two possible states of the world, Cobb–Douglas aggregate production functions, and so forth.

This view as to what constitutes intelligent behavior is explained vividly in the recent book by Andy Clark (1998) which I first learned about at Axel's 2006 Trento summer school. Clark's book is an account of recent developments in cognitive science and artificial intelligence, developments exemplified by the idea of 'neural networks'. His thesis is that human intelligence is not to be thought of as an abstract reasoning capability joined to a memory bank of facts, but rather as a device for controlling the body's varied set of adaptive behaviors in a way that helps the body cope with the particular environment it finds itself in. Clark calls this view 'embodied, environmentally embedded cognition'. It portrays intelligence not as a central computer program solving a well-defined maximization problem but as a decentralized network of autonomous neurons that interact with each other, often sending conflicting messages, and often competing to execute the same task. Intelligence emerges not from the capacity to solve planning problems but from simple chemical reactions that reinforce the neural processes that have been associated with improvements in the body's well-being and weaken the processes that have not.

Clark points out that the process of human adaptation is not guided by an internal model of the world which the brain takes as defining the constraint set for optimization, but rather it consists of simple rules for acting in ways that cope quickly and effectively with environmental hazards such as the presence of predators, the need for food, and so on. These rules may sometimes make use of internal representations but typically they need to operate much faster than the construction and use of any such representation would allow – people typically need to make economic decisions faster than would be possible by the use of dynamic programming. The intelligent individual is not the one capable of solving big analytical problems, but the one that has learned useful tricks and strategies with which to act quickly in a way that is well adapted to one's environment.

In short, if we are to study the economy's coordination mechanisms we must specify autonomous agents, and if we are to endow these autonomous agents with what commentators from Keynes to Clark have argued is the essence of intelligence, then we are driven to assume that they act according to simple rules. The key to agent-based modeling is not to make use of the classical distinction between estimation and optimization, but to find good, robust behavioral rules that map situations directly into actions. The distinction between these two modelling strategies is basically the same as that made in the literature on learning in games, between learning–optimization and stimulus–response. Although someone that first estimates a model and then optimizes subject to the estimated model will end up with a rule of the same general form as the person that adapts the rules directly to success in achieving their goals in the given environment, the former strategy has proven in artificial intelligence applications to produce brittle outcomes – behavior that makes no sense whatsoever when circumstances change in a way that violates the exclusion restrictions of the estimated model.

Axel once remarked that the real problem of macroeconomics was to understand how order can arise from the interactions of people following simple rules to cope with a complex environment, and contrasted that with much of mainstream macroeconomics which postulates people using complex decision procedures to deal with a simple environment.[3] This is the challenge I wish to take up: how to model the macroeconomy as a human anthill; one that organizes individuals' activities into patterns more complex than the individuals can fully comprehend, performs collective tasks that the individuals are hardly aware of, and adapts to shocks whose consequences none of the individuals can predict. Accounting for spontaneous order as an 'emergent property' of a complex system is one of the main themes of agent-based modeling, and the research agenda that Axel has been advocating is to apply this idea to the study of macroeconomic coordination, by modeling people not as rational maximizers but as intelligent autonomous agents.

9.2　MODELING THE COORDINATION PROCESS

Another question raised by the idea of autonomous agents is how anyone could possibly be autonomous when it takes two to tango. Surely in a complex economy such as ours, each person's behavior and well-being are inextricably linked with the others' behavior. What this question highlights is that assuming intelligent autonomous agents is just the starting point for studying the coordination problem. Economics being a social science, the really important issue is not so much how people behave as how they interact. An autonomous agent has simple rules for finding other people, sending communications to them and responding to their communications. What sort of exchange patterns emerge from the interaction between these rules, how orderly and stable they are, and how they evolve over time is the quaesitum of the research agenda Axel has proposed.

Several years ago, Robert Clower and I took this question up using what I now recognize as agent-based computational economics. We started from the observation that in the real world trades are coordinated by a self-organizing and self-regulating network of trade specialists – shops, brokers, middlemen, banks, realtors, lawyers, accountants, employers and so forth. Modern economic life is largely a sequence of exchanges with people outside one's own family and social circle. Almost every such exchange involves a specialized trader ('shopkeeper') on one side or the other of the market. Shopkeepers are the agents that undertake to match buyers and sellers, arrange terms of exchange and bear the costs of adjustment in the face of day-to-day imbalances between spending plans and productive capacity; in short, they are the real-world counterparts of the fictional auctioneer of general equilibrium theory.

In our (2000) paper we attempted to model in a crude way how such a network of coordinating shopkeepers might emerge spontaneously, from elementary interactions between people following simple opportunistic rules of behavior that represented what we considered to be the most salient activities of a decentralized economy. The idea was not to say this is how economic organization emerged, but rather that this is a model of economic organization that passes the minimal test of being self-organizing. If the organizational structure was not there, it would quite likely arise from the interaction of intelligent autonomous agents. Moreover, we showed that the organizational structure that emerged exhibited one of the most common features of real-world exchange mechanisms – their monetary structure. That is, whenever a stable network of shops emerged that supported a stable pattern of exchange activities, one of the tradeable objects would always emerge as a universal medium of exchange, being traded in every shop and involved in every act of exchange. The fact that this model can generate what we believe to be the most salient features of real-world coordination mechanisms gives us confidence that we can potentially use it as a platform with which to study various issues that interact with the coordination problem. What follows in this section is a sketch of that model and a summary of how it works.

The basic idea underlying the model is that trade is a useful but costly activity. People are motivated primarily by the goal of maximizing consumption, and they exhibit a tendency to wander and encounter each other, as in any random matching model. From time to time it occurs to someone that there are gains from trading with a randomly encountered stranger. However, the probability of meeting a stranger with whom there is a double coincidence of wants is so small, and the probability of meeting that stranger again in the absence of any institutionalized trading arrangements is so small, that a negligible amount of trade takes place until someone gets the idea to set up a trading facility that can easily be located, along with an idea for how to operate that facility. Sometimes such an idea does occur to someone, and this person (entrepreneur) perceives that acting on the idea might be more profitable than continuing to wander, because he or she could set a spread between buying and selling prices. People on each side of the market the entrepreneur would be creating might willingly pay for this spread in order to secure a reliable source of consumption rather than continuing to wander about looking for a random trading partner. As such facilities start to open, trading patterns start to form.

The economy has N perishable commodities and a discrete number of transactors, each one being *ex ante* identical except for type. A type (i, j) transactor is endowed with commodity i and can consume only commodity j. There is the same number of each type for each ordered pair of distinct commodities. The model focuses on five activities: entrepreneurship, search, exchange, business failure and price setting. The computer program (written in C++) to implement the model goes through a sequence of periods, in each of which these activities take place in the following sequence.

Entrepreneurship

Each transactor in turn has a probability μ of receiving an innovation – an idea for setting up and operating a shop. If the transactor is of type (i,j) then the shop will be one where commodities i and j can be traded for each other. There is however a fixed cost of setting the shop up, so before doing so the potential shopkeeper surveys a number of other transactors and inquires whether they would patronize the shop if it opened at prices determined according to the full-cost formula described below. If the shopkeeper finds any interest at all on either side of the market he or she will pay the set-up cost and open the shop. This 'market research' allows a form of simulated annealing (see Sargent, 1993 for a simple description) with an endogenous degree of cooling. This is important because it allows for lots of innovation to shake up the system when there are plenty of gains from trade still unexploited, but not to keep disturbing a system that has already exploited most of the gains.

The full-cost rule for price-setting takes into account the fixed set-up cost, as well as a fixed operating (overhead) cost, so it will depend on the amount of business the shopkeeper expects to be doing. After the shop has become established, these expectations will be revised in the light of experience, but at first the entrepreneur simply picks a number based on a parameter $xMax$ representing the average degree of optimism – what Keynes called animal spirits. More specifically, the initial estimate of how much will be delivered to the shop of each commodity it trades is chosen from a uniform distribution on the interval from 1 to $xMax$. The higher this initial guess the more the shopkeeper will offer in exchange for quantities delivered to the shop.

Search

Each transactor in turn visits one location and encounters a small sample of other transactors. If she finds a shop on that location or finds someone else who has formed a trading relationship with a shop, she learns of those shops, the commodities they trade, and their currently posted prices. At this point she has a sample of shops which include the ones she has just learned of and the ones with which she already has a relationship. From this sample she can choose to have a relationship with at most two shops. Each relationship will last until the shop exits or the transactor herself chooses to sever the relationship to form a different one. In choosing which relationships to form she chooses the shop, or pair of shops, that would maximize attainable consumption at currently posted prices.

Exchange

At this stage, each person in turn can visit the shops with which she has a trading relationship. A type (i,j) transactor having a trading relationship with a shop trading i and j will deliver her endowment of i to that shop (everyone has one unit of endowment per period) for p_i units of j, where p_i is the shop's offer price for i. Alternatively if she has a trading relationship with two shops, one trading i for some third commodity c and the other trading c for j, she will deliver her i to the first shop and then deliver the proceeds to the second shop, thus allowing her to consume $p_i p_c$ where p_i is the first shop's offer price for i and p_c is the second shop's offer price for c. In this chapter we evaded the stockout problem by assuming that the shop-keeper was capable of engaging in negative consumption when the amount of any commodity demanded by customers plus the amount needed to defray operating costs exceeded the amount delivered by suppliers. (This assumption captures, as best we could do in a model with no durable commodities, the idea that one of the services provided by specialist traders is the availability of ready stocks.)

Business Failure

At this point anyone who has set up a shop in the past has a chance to exit, and thereby avoid having to pay the fixed operating cost of a shop. Each shop will follow a rule that says exit with probability θ if its operating surplus in either of the commodities it trades (deliveries minus the quantity paid out for deliveries of the other commodity minus the amount needed to defray the fixed operating cost) is negative; otherwise stay in business with certainty.

Price Setting

Each shop that remains in business now sets its prices for the following period. The rule it follows for price setting is a variant on full-cost pricing: first estimate the quantity that will be delivered of each of its traded commodities, and then set prices that would allow it just to break even in each commodity; that is, to have an operating surplus just large enough to provide what the shopkeeper deems an appropriate compensation for having incurred the set-up cost of establishing the shop. The estimation of deliveries is done using simple adaptive expectations.

Emergence of Organization

Clower and I showed that, provided that animal spirits are not too large
and that the fixed set-up and operating costs are not too large, the model
has several absorbing states – that is, arrays of shops, prices, trading relationships and shopkeeper expectations that would persist indefinitely once
established. One such absorbing state is a 'barter steady state', in which
there are $n \cdot (n - 1)/2$ shops, one for each unordered pair of distinct commodities, and in which each person who is not a shopkeeper trades their
endowment directly for their consumption good each period. Another set
of absorbing states consists of 'monetary steady states', in which one commodity c has emerged as a universal medium of exchange and there are
$n - 1$ shops, one for each of the other commodities, trading the other commodity for c, each person that consumes or is endowed with c trades
directly with one shop each period, and each other person trades with two
shops each period using c as a medium of exchange.

A monetary stationary state is much like the monetary equilibrium
studied by Starr and Stinchcombe (1998, 1999) in their version of the
Shapley–Shubik trading post model. It constitutes a Pareto efficient allocation of resources given that all trading must occur through shops.
Aggregate gross domestic product (GDP) in the economy is total consumption. Capacity GDP is the sum of all endowments minus the operating costs of the shops. The smallest number of shops consistent with
everyone trading is $n - 1$, so that capacity GDP equals $N - (n - 1)f$, where
f is the operating cost of each shop. This is achieved in an equilibrium
because all endowments are delivered to a shop and either used to pay the
operating cost, or paid out to a customer who consumes it, or consumed
by the shop's owner to defray the set-up cost.

We ran experiments on the model by simulating it repeatedly, starting
from an initial situation of autarky; that is, a situation in which no shops
exist and hence no trading relationships exist. We found that very often the
economy converged to a stable situation in which every agent was either a
shopkeeper or else had a profitable trading relationship with one or two
shops. Moreover, when it did converge, it always converged to a monetary
stationary state, except in the limiting case where the cost of operating a
shop was zero.

Our explanation for the emergence of this monetary structure is based
on the network externality created by the fixed costs of shops. During the
early stages of a simulation, by chance one commodity (say wheat) will
come to be traded in enough shops that the survival chances of such shops
is much greater than those of shops not trading this commodity. This is
because a shop that opens trading apples for wheat can attract not just

people with a double coincidence of wants – making wheat and consuming apples or vice versa – but also anyone with a single coincidence who can engage in indirect exchange – someone making apples and having a relationship already with a shop trading wheat for her consumption good or consuming apples and having a relationship already with a shop trading wheat for her endowment good. Attracting more customers makes the shop more likely to survive because it makes it easier to cover the fixed operating cost of the shop. Thus once a 'standard' medium of exchange has emerged randomly it will tend to snowball; the more shops trade wheat, the greater the survival probability of a wheat-trading shop compared to one that does not trade wheat.

9.3   THE MULTIPLIER PROCESS

The Keynesian multiplier process is an example of a positive feedback loop, or what Axel has called a deviation-amplifying process, in which an initial departure from full-employment equilibrium cumulates instead of being corrected. The existence of some such positive feedback loop in actual economies is attested to by the typical hump-shaped impulse response pattern of GDP to a random shock in estimated time series models. For example, Chari et al. (2000) report that quarterly movements in the log of detrended US GDP are well approximated by the following AR2 process:

$$y_t = 1.30y_{t-1} - 0.38y_{t-2} \tag{9.1}$$

according to which a negative shock that reduces GDP by 1 percent this quarter is expected to reduced it by 1.3 percent next quarter, and by 1.31 percent the following quarter.

As originally formulated by Kahn and Keynes, and as described in most undergraduate textbooks, the multiplier process involves a coordination problem arising from non-price interactions between decentralized transactors. In a world of perfect price flexibility, a drop in planned spending would cause wages and prices to adjust instantaneously so as to keep aggregate demand fully coordinated with productive capacity. But when prices are slow to adjust, one person's drop in spending causes a drop in other people's incomes, causing a drop in their spending, and so on, resulting in a cumulative increase in the gap between demand and capacity.

The theoretical foundation of this multiplier process is still not well understood. Clower (1965) showed how such a process could arise in a Walrasian general equilibrium setting if price adjustment takes place in real transaction time; when labor is in excess supply, unemployed workers will not present their notional consumption demands to the auctioneer but will instead present demands that are constrained by realized sales income. These ideas were pursued at length in the literature on disequilibrium analysis that followed Clower's original contribution and culminated in the book by Barro and Grossman (1976). But this literature raised more questions than it answered, largely because it offered no explicit account of a decentralized market economy's coordination mechanisms. Instead, it modeled price adjustment as if it takes place just the same as in the idealized world of Walrasian economics, where it is led by a fictitious centralized auctioneer, and supposed that while the auctioneer is groping towards equilibrium, transactors are constrained to trade according to rationing rules that are imposed from outside the system by a process that was never even discussed.

One of the supposed advantages of the rational expectations equilibrium approach that quickly displaced disequilibrium analysis from its dominant position on the frontiers of macroeconomic theory in the early 1970s was that it did not have to deal with the thorny details of disequilibrium adjustment. Instead it was based on the premise that one can restrict attention exclusively to equilibrium states, in which everyone's beliefs and actions have somehow been coordinated with the beliefs and actions of everyone else. But by adopting this premise, the approach has taken the coordination problem out of macroeconomics, and has denied the very existence of the Keynesian multiplier process, a process which has to do with disequilibrium adjustment rather than with equilibrium behavior (see Leijonhufvud, 1968; Patinkin, 1976).

In Howitt (2006a) I re-examined the foundations of the multiplier process making use of the same agent-based model of the coordination mechanism that I have just described. This paper investigated the real-time dynamics of the model in the face of disturbances, under the assumption that a monetary stationary state has already been reached and with a particular commodity (again, wheat) having been established for long enough as the economy's medium of exchange that no entrepreneur ever considers opening a shop that does not trade wheat. I showed that these dynamics contain within them a multiplier process that produces a hump-shaped impulse-response pattern very similar to that of equation (9.1) that characterizes the US economy.

The multiplier process takes place because of an institutional factor not usually considered in the macroeconomics literature, namely the exit of trading facilities. A shock that disrupts normal trading relationships can cause some of the businesses that coordinate trades to fail, inducing people who formerly had employment (supplier) relationships with those businesses to curtail their expenditure for lack of money, which forces closing of other businesses in cumulative fashion.

In this paper I again simulated the model many times, this time starting from an initial position of a stationary monetary equilibrium and disturbing it in period 1 by a shock that induces some fraction of the population to switch from eating one good to another. To preserve the aggregate structure I supposed that the total number of each type remains constant, so that for every *i*-eater that becomes a *j*-eater there is a *j*-eater that switches to *i*. At the time of this shock, each switcher is suddenly without a consumption-shop (store), and her former store loses a customer. The switcher may continue to sell her manna to her employer (endowment-shop) but she does not spend her wages. GDP falls because of the reduced goods consumption of the switchers that no longer show up to their former stores, and because of the reduced wheat consumption of the entrepreneurs whose operating surplus in wheat suddenly falls.

Because their revenues have fallen, the former stores of switchers will reduce both their wages (offer price for the non-wheat commodity) and their retail prices (the inverse of their offer price for wheat). The fall in wages will help to offset their profit shortfall, but it will spread the shortfall to other shops, some of whose customers will now deliver less wheat because their wages have fallen. Meanwhile, the fall in wages and prices will do little by itself to raise GDP, which will stay below capacity until the switchers find new stores.

During this process, the luck of the draw may result in particularly large shortfalls for some shops. A shop whose wheat surplus has fallen below zero will be at risk of failure. If that happens then all of the former suppliers of the failed shops will be without an employer, and their sudden drop of wage income will result in a sudden drop in revenues to their respective stores, who may also now become at risk of failure. In this way, the collapse of shops can be self-reinforcing, leading to a cumulative fall in GDP as in the more familiar multiplier process of textbook macroeconomics.

Of course whenever a shop fails, new entrepreneurs will start entering, and employment relations will start to form again. But because of fixed costs, and because a lot of firms may enter the same market, there will be a 'shakeout period' which not all new entrants will survive. Thus the process of shop failures is likely to continue for some time before a new stable pattern of shops re-emerges and the economy begins to recover from the cumulative downturn.

9.4   UPGRADING THE MODEL

There are many features of the agent-based model described above that make it difficult to take to real data. The latest version (available at http://www.econ.brown/fac/Peter_Howitt) differs from the above in the following ways. First, to recognize that loss of a trading relation with one's employer (that is, unemployment) is typically a more significant event than loss of a trading relationship with a store, I allow everyone to have two distinct consumption goods, and a utility function over those two goods.

Next, I assume that all goods are perfectly storable instead of perishable. This allows me to deal directly with the stockout issue instead of evading it through the device of negative consumption by shopkeepers. In this model shopkeepers target a level of stocks equal to some multiple of target sales, and they execute all buy orders if their stocks permit. The fact that not all orders might be executed introduces a new consideration into people's search decisions. Specifically, an agent might have to choose between an employer offering a low wage and another offering a high wage but who has not been executing all sell orders, or between a store offering a high retail price and another offering a lower price but who has not been executing all buy orders. To deal with this complication I assume that each agent keeps track of their employer's 'effective' wage and of their stores' 'effective' inverse-retail prices, where in each case the effective price equals the actual price multiplied by the fraction of the agent's last order that was executed at that shop. During the search process all choices are made on the basis of effective rather than actual prices.

To make the monetary structure of the model look a little more like that of a modern real-world economy I suppose that the money commodity is a pure token, being neither produced nor consumed by the private agents. There is now a government sector regulating the stock of fiat money. The government also issues perpetual bonds, paying $1 per period, whose price is P_b, and levies taxes, at a proportional *ad valorem* rate τ on all purchases from a shopkeeper. There is still no private debt, but people can go to a bond market every period, before trading with shops begins, to trade money for bonds. The government regulates the nominal interest rate $r = 1/P_b$ according to a Taylor-like rule that makes P_b adjust gradually towards a target value which is an increasing function of the current level of nominal GDP. The government also regulates the tax rate according to a fiscal rule that makes τ adjust gradually towards a target value which is an increasing function of the outstanding value of government debt and of the current rate of change of government debt.

Because there are durable assets, there is now a non-trivial consumption–saving decision to be made. Accordingly I suppose that people spend a fixed fraction of current wealth on consumption each period, as they would in a conventional lifetime utility-maximization model with logarithmic preferences, where the fixed fraction would be the rate of time preference. This expenditure is allocated between the two consumption goods in such a way as to maximize the current period utility function if the agent has relations with a shop for each good, or else allocated all to the consumption good traded in the store with which the agent does have a relationship. In this consumption function, current wealth is calculated as the current market value of bond holdings plus a fixed fraction of the capitalized value of permanent income, discounted at the current nominal rate of interest.

Because they can save in two different forms (money and bonds) people also now have a non-trivial portfolio allocation problem to solve. Here I adopt a buffer-stock approach to the demand for money, following Laidler (1984), and implementing it in much the same way as Akerlof and Milbourne (1980). In this approach, people allow money holdings to absorb unexpected shocks to income and expenditure, thereby economizing on frequent small portfolio adjustments. Specifically, each agent has a target money stock, equal to four times current planned expenditure (I think of a period as a week). When current money-holdings exceed twice this target the agent visits the bond market and spends the excess on bonds. When current money holdings fall below current planned expenditure the agent visits the bond market and sells enough bonds to restore money holdings to the target; if not enough bonds are being held to do this, all bonds are sold. If the agent still does not have enough cash to pay for current planned expenditure, all money is allocated to current expenditure. In all other cases the agent stays away from the bond market.

Instead of the full-cost pricing assumption of the earlier version I treat wages and retail prices separately. For wages, I take seriously the concern for fairness emphasized by writers like Akerlof and Yellen (1990) and Bewley (1999) by supposing that whenever an employer's wages fall below 80 percent of the economy-wide average there is a confrontation between the employer and its workforce that results in an increase all the way up to the economy-wide average. Likewise if the employer's permanent income rises to 120 percent of the economy-wide average wage their posted wage is raised to the economy-wide average.

On top of these relatively infrequent corrections, each period the wage is adjusted by a percentage amount that is proportional to the percentage gap between target input and its virtual input. Target input is the amount of labor needed to produce the firm's expected sales (formed at first by animal spirits and then by simple adaptive expectations) plus a gradual adjustment towards its target inventory, and virtual input is the number of suppliers with which the shop has a relationship. (Actual input can differ from virtual if the shop runs out of money with which to buy labor.)

Prices are set as a fixed mark-up over current marginal cost, where the latter includes wages and taxes. The mark-up fraction is chosen by a shop, when it enters, from a uniform distribution that is centered on the mark-up that would be optimal if the firm's demand function was the same as if consumers had the same utility functions and the economy was in a symmetrical equilibrium with a constant number of customers. A profit-maximizing equilibrium is thus given a chance to emerge if the economy converges.

In this version, firms are not forced to take on redundant workers during the search process as they were in the earlier versions. That is, a searching agent cannot choose to form a relation with a shop trading her endowment good if that shop's virtual input already exceeds its target input.

Finally, I allow each relationship to break up with a fixed probability and each firm to exit with a fixed probability even if still profitable, and I set animal spirits high enough that from time to time firms will enter with overly optimistic sales expectations. The effect of all three of these modifications is to keep the system constantly subject to disturbances and to destroy the existence of any absorbing state to the stochastic process generated by the model. (These modifications were deliberately not made in the earlier version, in order to be able to tell with certainty when the computer simulation was converging and what equilibrium it was converging to.)

9.5   THE EFFECTS OF WAGE-FLEXIBILITY

Is increased wage flexibility stabilizing? This is the question that Keynes raised in Chapter 19 of his (1936) *General Theory*, where he argued that unemployment was not attributable to the failure of wages to respond, and that in fact if wages were more flexible the unemployment problem would be even worse, because of adverse distributional effects and the disruption of debt-deflation. As Axel's (1968) book showed us, this aspect of the economics of Keynes was in sharp contrast to what became called, and for the most part still is called, Keynesian economics, which from Modigliani to Taylor has attributed unemployment to wage and/or price rigidity.

In (Howitt 1986) I argued that wage flexibility could increase the volatility of real output in a fairly conventional rational expectations equilibrium model because of the depressing effect on aggregate demand of a reduction in the expected rate of inflation.[4] A fall in demand would give rise to a fall in expected inflation through a Phillips-type relationship which, under a given money supply rule, results in a rise in the real rate of interest and hence an amplification of the fall in aggregate demand, as in a conventional IS–LM system where the IS curve depends on the real rate of interest and the LM depends on the nominal rate. The greater the slope of this Phillips relationship, the more the rational expectation of inflation will fall with any given negative shock to aggregate demand, and hence the stronger will be this deviation-amplifying mechanism.

The analysis assumed a given path for the money supply, as was conventional in macro theory until recently. But this assumption does not correspond to the way monetary policy is actually conducted in most countries, where the rate of interest is the central bank's instrument and the money supply is typically not given much attention. Moreover, under the more realistic alternative assumption of an interest-rate rule the mechanism that I identified in my 1986 paper would not be at work unless the rule violated the famous 'Taylor principle' in an expectational sense. This principle requires that any change in expected inflation result in more than a one-for-one change in the rate of interest. Thus if a fall in aggregate demand generated a fall in expected inflation, the interest-rate rule would cause the nominal interest rate to fall by enough so as to cause a decrease in the real rate of interest. (If the interest-rate rule also responded directly to the fall in output caused by the demand shock then the real rate of interest would fall by even more.) Thus wage flexibility, by strengthening the reaction of expected inflation to a demand shock, would be unambiguously stabilizing.

The present model can deal with both of these issues. We have assumed that the monetary authority follows a Taylor-like rule in setting interest rates, but there is no one forming expectations of inflation. Instead, the effect of changing the degree of wage flexibility would be on the efficacy of the system's coordination mechanism. And as far as this is concerned, there is clearly a reason for having some flexibility but not too much. That is, without some wage flexibility there would be no way for shops to eliminate excess demands or supplies. On the other hand, as pointed out in the previous section, the propagation mechanism that I identified in my multiplier analysis is not something that is necessarily helped by having more wage flexibility. Indeed, by introducing extraneous movements in relative prices as the economy adjusts to shocks, increased wage flexibility could easily weaken the coordination mechanism, by inducing a lot of extraneous switching of trading relationships in pursuit of transitory wage and price differences, thus perhaps inducing too many business failures.

I have run the model under alternative speeds of wage adjustment, as measured by the coefficient in the wage-adjustment equation of the percentage gap between target and virtual input. The results as shown in Figure 9.1 below indicate that indeed macroeconomic stability is achieved at an intermediate level of flexibility. This figure shows the median value of the average end-of-year GDP when I ran the model for 100 years (5000 periods), 1000 times for each of six different values of the coefficient, along with the interquartile range.[5] So, for example, the P75 line indicates, for each coefficient value, the average end-of-year GDP over the 100 years of the run in which this average was the 250th-largest out of the 1000 runs

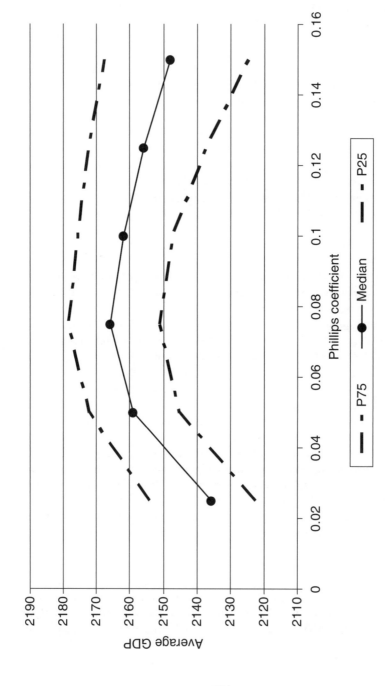

Figure 9.1   The effects of wage flexiblity

using that coefficient value. The figure indicates that as flexibility goes up, average GDP first rises and then falls.

9.6   CONCLUSION

The work I have outlined above is just the beginning of a research agenda aimed at characterizing the behavior of an economic system inhabited by intelligent autonomous agents, a system in which economic activities are coordinated by a self-organizing network of specialist traders. The ultimate goal of this agenda is to understand how, as Axel has said on many occasions,[6] a large complex economic system like that of the United States is capable of exhibiting such a high degree of coordination most of the time, and yet is also capable from time to time of departing drastically from such a coordinated state. Of course much work remains to be done. In particular, there are many free parameters in the latest version of the model, and as yet no attempt has been made to calibrate them to actual data. But the results so far indicate that the model is capable of addressing some of the questions that Axel has raised, and which a rational expectations equilibrium approach is incapable of addressing, such as how a multiplier process can cause cumulative deviations from equilibrium and how the degree of wage flexibility affects the ability of an economy to coordinate activities.

NOTES

1. Leijonhufvud (1993, 2006).
2. For example, Laidler (1974, 1984).
3. In (1993, pp. 1–2) he quoted Daniel Heymann as having 'remarked that practical men of affairs, if they know anything about economics, often distrust it because it seems to describe the behavior of incredibly smart people in unbelievably simple situations', and then went on to suggest 'asking how believably simple people cope with incredibly complex situations'.
4. A similar analysis was produced independently by DeLong and Summers (1986).
5. In each simulation there were 50 distinct commodities and 2400 separate transactors.
6. For example, Leijonhufvud (1976, 1981, 1993).

REFERENCES

Akerlof, George A. and Ross D. Milbourne (1980), 'Irving Fisher on his head II: the consequences of the timing of payments for the demand for money', *Quarterly Journal of Economics*, **95** (August), 145–57.
Akerlof, George A. and Janet L. Yellen (1990), 'The fair wage-effort hypothesis and unemployment', *Quarterly Journal of Economics*, **105** (May), 255–83.

Barro, Robert J. and Herschel I. Grossman (1976), *Money, Employment and Inflation*, New York: Cambridge University Press.
Bewley, Truman F. (1999), *Why Wages Don't Fall During a Recession*, Cambridge, MA: Harvard University Press.
Chari, V.V., Patrick J. Kehoe and Ellen R. McGrattan (2000), 'Sticky price models of the business cycle: can the contract multiplier solve the persistence problem?' *Econometrica*, **68** (September), 1151–79.
Clark, Andy (1998), *Being There: Putting Brain, Body and World Together Again*, Cambridge, MA: MIT Press.
Clower, Robert W. (1965), 'The Keynesian counter-revolution: a theoretical appraisal', in, Frank H. Hahn and Frank P.R. Brechling (eds), *The Theory of Interest Rates,* London: Macmillan, 103–25.
Davidson, Paul (1989), 'Keynes and Money', in Roger Hill (ed.), *Keynes, Money and Monetarism: The Eighth Keynes Seminar held at the University of Kent at Canterbury, 1987*, London: Macmillan, pp. 2–26.
DeLong, J. Bradford and Lawrence H. Summers (1986), 'Is increased price flexibility stabilizing?' *American Economic Review*, **76** (December), 1031–44.
Evans, George and Seppo Honkapohja (2001), *Learning and Expectations in Macroeconomics*, Princeton, NJ: Princeton University Press.
Howitt, Peter (1986), 'Wage flexibility and employment', *Eastern Economic Journal*, **12** (July–September), 237–42.
Howitt, Peter (2006a), 'The microfoundations of the Keynesian multiplier process', *Journal of Economic Interaction and Coordination,* **1** (May), 33–44.
Howitt, Peter (2006b), 'Monetary policy and the limitations of economic knowledge', in David Colander (ed.), *Post Walrasian Macroeconomics: Beyond the Dynamic Stochastic General Equilibrium Model*, New York, Cambridge University Press, pp. 347–67.
Howitt, Peter and Robert Clower (2000), 'The emergence of economic organization', *Journal of Economic Behavior and Organization*, **41** (January), 55–84.
Keynes, John Maynard (1934), 'Poverty in plenty: is the economic system self-adjusting?' in *The Collected Writings of John Maynard Keynes*, Vol. 13, London: Macmillan, for The Royal Economic Society, pp. 485–92.
Keynes, John Maynard (1936), *The General Theory of Employment, Interest, and Money*, London: Macmillan.
Krebs, Tom (2007), 'Growth and welfare effects of business cycles in economies with idiosyncratic human capital risk', *Review of Economic Dynamics*, **6**, 846–68.
Krusell, Per and Anthony A. Smith Jr. (1998), 'Income and wealth heterogeneity in the macroeconomy', *Journal of Political Economy* **106** (October), 867–96.
Laidler, David (1974), 'Information, money and the macroeconomics of inflation', *Swedish Journal of Economics*, **76** (March), 26–41.
Laidler, David (1984), 'The "buffer stock" notion in monetary economics', *Economic Journal* **94** (Supplement), 17–34.
Leijonhufvud, Axel (1968), *On Keynesian Economics and the Economics of Keynes: A Study in Monetary Theory*, New York: Oxford University Press.
Leijonhufvud, Axel (1976), 'Schools, "Revolutions", and research programmes in economic theory', in Spiro J. Latsis, (ed.), *Method and Appraisal in Economics*, Cambridge: Cambridge University Press, pp. 291–345.
Leijonhufvud, Axel (1981), *Information and Coordination.* New York: Oxford University Press.
Leijonhufvud, Axel (1993), 'Towards a not-too-rational macroeconomics'. *Southern Economic Journal,* **60** (July), 1–13.

Leijonhufvud, Axel (2006), 'Agent-based macro', in Leigh Tesfatsion and Kenneth L. Judd (eds), *Handbook of Computational Economics*, Vol. 2, Amsterdam: North-Holland, pp. 1625–37.

Patinkin, Don (1976), *Keynes' Monetary Thought: A Study of Its Development*, Durham, NC: Duke University Press.

Sargent, Thomas J, (1993), *Bounded Rationality in Macroeconomics*, Oxford: Clarendon Press.

Starr, Ross M. and Maxwell B. Stinchcombe (1998), 'Monetary equilibrium with pairwise trade and transaction costs', unpublished, University of California San Diego, September.

Starr, Ross M. and Maxwell B. Stinchcombe (1999), 'Exchange in a network of trading posts', in Graciela Chichilnisky (ed.), *Markets, Information and Uncertainty: Essays in Economic Theory in Honor of Kenneth J. Arrow.* Cambridge: Cambridge University Press, pp. 217–34.

Tesfatsion, Leigh (2006), 'Agent based computational economics: a constructive approach to economic theory', in Leigh Tesfatsion and Kenneth L. Judd(eds), *Handbook of Computational Economics*, Vol. 2, Amsterdam: North-Holland, pp. 831–80.

Axel Leijonhufvud: Publications

BOOKS

1. *On Keynesian Economics and the Economics of Keynes: A Study in Monetary Theory*, New York: Oxford University Press, 1968.
2. *Keynes and the Classics: Two Lectures*, London: Institute of Economic Affairs, 1969.
3. *Information and Coordination: Essays in Macroeconomic Theory*, (with Daniel Heymann), New York: Oxford University Press 1981.
4. *High Inflation*, (with Daniel Heymann), Oxford: Oxford University Press, 1995.
5. *Macroeconomic Instability and Coordination: Selected Essays*, (ed.) Cheltenham, UK and Northampton, MA, USA: Edward Elgar, 2000.
6. *Monetary Theory as a Basis for Monetary Policy*, (ed.), (Proceedings of a Conference of the International Economic Association), London: Palgrave, 2001.
7. *Monetary Theory and Policy Experience*, (Proceedings of a Conference of the International Economic Association, Vol. 2), London: Palgrave, 2001.
8. *Informazione, coordinamento e instabilità macroeconomica*, (a cura di Elisabetta De Antoni), Rome: Editori Laterza, 2004.
9. *Organización e inestabilidad económica: Ensayos elegidos*, Buenos Aires: TEMAS, 2006.

ARTICLES AND CHAPTERS IN PROCESS

10. 'So far from Ricardo, so close to Wicksell', paper given at Annual Conference of the Central Bank of Argentina, June 2007.
11. 'Natural rate and market rate of interest', (revised) to appear in Durlay, S. and Blume L. (eds) (2008) *The New Palgrave Dictionary of Economics*, 2nd edn, vol. 5, New York: Palgrave Macmillan, pp. 868–70.
12. 'The individual, the market and the division of labor in society', forthcoming in *Capitalism and Society*.

13. 'Moving on: Where to?' paper given at Post-Keynesian Conference in Kansas City, August 2006, to appear in *The Continuing Relevance of Keynes*, London: Palgrave.
14. 'Spreading the bread thin on the butter', to appear in Gustavo Piga and Lorenzo Pecchi (eds), Cambridge, MA: MIT Press.
15. 'The uses of the past', invited lecture at 2006 Meetings of the European History of Economic Thought (ESHET) Conference.

ARTICLES AND CHAPTERS

Recent

16. 'Monetary and financial stability', CEPR Policy Insight No 14.
17. 'The perils of inflation targeting', VoxEU.org, 26 October 2007.
18. 'Bubble, bubble, toil and trouble', VoxEU.org, 25 June 2007.
19. 'Understanding the great changes: a comment', *Capitalism and Society*, **1** (2), 2006.
20. 'Agent-based macro', in Leigh Tesfatsion and Kenneth L. Judd (eds), *Handbook of Computational Economics*, Vol. 2: *Agent-Based Computational Economics*, Amsterdam: North-Holland, 2006, pp. 1625–37.
21. 'Keynes as a Marshallian', in Roger Backhouse and Bradley Bateman (eds), *Cambridge Companion to Keynes*, Cambridge: Cambridge University Press, 2006.
22. 'Marshall on market adjustment', in T. Raffaelli, G. Becattini and M. Dardi (eds), *Elgar Companion to Alfred Marshall*, Cheltenham, UK and Northampton, MA, USA: Edward Elgar, 2006.
23. 'A century of macroeconomics', in David Colander (ed.), *Post-Walrasian Macroeconomics*, Cambridge: Cambridge University Press, 2006.

2001–05

24. 'Celebrating Ned', *Journal of Economic Literature*, **42** (September), 2004, pp. 811–21.
25. 'The metamorphoses of neoclassical economics', in Michel Bellet, Sandye Gloria-Palermo, Abdallah Zouache (eds), *Evolution of the Market Process: Austrian and Swedish Economics*, London: Routledge, 2004.
26. 'The long swings in economic understanding', in K. Vela Velupillai (ed.), *Macroeconomic Theory and Economic Policy: Essays in*

Honour of Jean-Paul Fitoussi, London: Routledge, 2004, pp. 115–127.

27. 'Review of Steven Horwitz, *Microfoundations and Macroeconomics: An Austrian Perspective*, London: Routledge, 2000', *Austrian Economics Review*, 2003, pp. 364–68.
28. 'Review of Randall E. Parker, *Reflections on the Great Depression*', *Economic Record*, **79** (September), 2003.
29. 'Reform and the fate of Russia', (with Earlene Craver), Observatoire Français Conjonctures Economiques (OFCE), Document de travail No 2001–03, May 2001.
30. 'Monetary theory and central banking', in A. Leijonhufvud (ed.), *Monetary Theory a Basis for Monetary Policy*, (Proceedings of a Conference of the International Economic Association), London: Palgrave, 2001.
31. 'Introduction', to A. Leijonhufvud (ed.), *Monetary Theory a Basis for Monetary Policy*, London: Palgrave, 2001.

1996–2000

32. 'Economic development from a division of labor perspective', in Satu Kähkönen and Mancur Olson (eds), *A New Institutional Approach: Achieving India's Full Potential*, Sage/India Press, 2000.
33. 'Involuntary unemployment once again: comment on DeVroey', in R.E. Backhouse, D.M. Hausman, U. Mäki and Andrea Salanti (eds), *Economics and Methodology: Crossing Boundaries*, London: Macmillan, 1998.
34. 'Un aporte para la comprensión de las crisis financieras', *Revista de Economia*, **6** (1), 1999, pp. 5–12.
35. 'Adaptive versus optimizing behavior: how to strike a balance?' in Peter Howitt, Elisabetta de Antoni and Axel Leijonhufvud (eds), *Money, Markets, Method: Essays in Honor of Robert W. Clower*, Cheltenham, UK and Lyme, USA: Edward Elgar, 1998.
36. 'Two types of crises', *Zagreb Journal of Economics*, December 1998.
37. 'Comment: involuntary unemployment one more time', in Roger E. Backhouse, Daniel M. Hausman, Uskali Mäki and Andrea Salanti (eds), *Economics and Methodology: Crossing Boundaries*, London: Macmillan and International Economic Association, 1998, pp. 225–35.
38. 'Mr Keynes and the Moderns', *European Journal of the History of Economic Thought*, 1998. Also in Luigi Pasinetti and Bertram Schefold (eds), *The Impact of Keynes on Economics in the 20th Century*, Cheltenham, UK and Lyme, USA: Edward Elgar, 1998.

39. 'Three items for the macroeconomic agenda', *Kyklos*, 1998.
40. 'Models and theories', *Journal of Economic Methodology*, $:2, Dec. 1997. 'Wicksell's Erbe', in *Vademecum zu Knut Wicksell's 'Geldzins und Güterpreise'*, Klassiker der Nationalökonomie (Bertram Schefold, ed.,), Düsseldorf: Verlag Wirtschaft und Finanzen, 1997. – English version: 'The Wicksellian heritage', *Economic Notes*, 26:1, 1997.
41. 'Russian dilemmas', (with Christof Rühl), *American Economic Review*, May 1997.
42. 'Models and Theories', *Journal of Economic Methodology*, **4**(2), 1997, pp. 193–8.
43. 'Macroeconomics and complexity: inflation theory', in W. Brian Arthur, Steven N. Durlauf and David A. Lane (eds), *The Economy as an Evolving Complex System II*, New York: Addison Wesley and the Santa Fe Institute, 1997.

1991–95

44. 'Review: Karl Brunner and Allan Meltzer, *Money and the Economy: Issues in Monetary Analysis*', in *Journal of Economic Literature*, **33** (September), 1995.
45. 'Monetary regimes and the effectiveness of monetary policy', in Wolfgang Gebauer (ed.), *Finanzmärkte und Zentralbankpolitik*, Frankfurt a.M.: Fritz Knapp Verlag 1995.
46. 'Adaptive behavior, market processes and the computable approach', *Revue Économique*, **46** (November), 1995, pp. 1497–1510.
47. 'The individual, the market, and the industrial division of labor', in Carlo Mongardini (ed.), *L'individuo e il mercato*, Rome: Bulzoni, 1995.
48. 'High inflations and the financial system', *Estudios Economicos*, **21** (December), 1994.
49. 'Hicks, Keynes, and Marshall', in H. Hagemann and O.F. Hamouda (eds), *The Legacy of Hicks*, London: Routledge, 1994, pp. 147–62.
50. 'The nature of the depression in the Former Soviet Union', *New Left Review*, **199** (May–June), 1993.
51. 'Towards a not-too-rational macroeconomics', *Southern Economic Journal*, **60** (1), 1993, pp. 1–13.
52. 'Problems of socialist transformation: Kazakhstan 1991', in Lazlo Somogyi, (eds), *The Political Economy of the Transition Process in Eastern Europe*, Aldershot, UK and Brookfield, US: Edward Elgar, 1993.
53. 'Whatever happened to Keynesian Economics?' in David A. Reese (ed.), *The Legacy of Keynes*, (Gustavus Adolphus College Nobel

Conference XXII Proceedings), San Francisco, CA: Harper & Row, 1987.

54.   'Rational expectations and monetary institutions', in Marcello de Cecco and Jean-Paul Fitoussi (eds), *Monetary Theory and Economic Institutions*, (Proceedings of a 1982 International Economic Association Conference), London: Macmillan, 1987.

55.   'Natural rate and market rate', in *The New Palgrave*, Vol. 3, 1987, pp. 1002–4. Also in *The New Palgrave Dictionary of Money and Finance*, London: Macmillan, 1991.

56.   'La Busqueda de la Estabilidad Monetaria: Una Perspectiva Norte-Americana', Economia Mexicana, 1986: No. 8. ('The Quest for Monetary Stability: A US Perspective,' paper delivered at 6th annual meetings of Latin-American Econometrics conference, Cordoba, Argentina, July 1986).

57.   'Capitalism and the factory system', in Richard Langlois (ed.), *Economics as a Process: Essays in the New Institutional Economics*, Cambridge: Cambridge University Press, 1986.

58.   'Time in theory and history – or why I am not a historian', *Agricultural History*, Winter 1986.

59.   'Rules with some discretion: comment on Barro', in C.D. Campbell and W.R. Dougan (eds), *Alternative Monetary Regimes*, Baltimore, MD: Johns Hopkins University Press, 1986.

60.   'Real and monetary factors in business fluctuations', *Cato Journal*, **6** (2), 1986, pp. 409–20.

1981–85

61.   'Ideology and analysis in macroeconomics', in Peter Koslowski (ed.), *Economics and Philosophy*, Tübingen: J.C.B. Mohr, 1985.

62.   'Buddhist values and Japanese growth: comment on Serge Kolm', in Peter Koslowski (ed.), *Economics and Philosophy*, Tübingen: J.C.B. Mohr, 1985.

63.   'Keynesianism at the Keynes Centennial', in Hellmuth Milde and Hans Monniesen (eds), *Rational Wirtschaftspolitik in komplexen Gesellshaften*, (Festschrift for Prof. Gerald Gäfgen), Stuttgart: Kohlhammer, 1985.

64.   'Statement on monetary policy, Federal Reserve accountability, and alternative institutional arrangements', *Monetary Reform and Economic Stability*, Joint Economic Committee, Washington, DC: Government Printing Office, 1984.

65.   'Ricordando Tarantelli', *Politica e Economia*, May 1985 Review: John Cunningham Wood, ed., John Maynard Keynes: Critical Assessments, Vols 1 4, in *Journal of Economic History*.

66. 'Hicks on time and money', *Oxford Economic Papers*, November 1984, Supplement. Also published as D.A. Collard, D.R. Helm, M. FG. Scott, and A.K. Sen (eds), *Economic Theory and Hicksian Themes*, Oxford: Oxford University Press, 1984.

67. 'Inflation and economic performance', in Barry N. Siegel (ed.), *Money in Crisis: The Federal Reserve, the Economy, and Monetary Reform*, Pacific Institute 1984. Review: Robert E. Lucas, Jr., Studies in Business-Cycle Theory, in Journal of Economic Literature, March 1983.

68. 'What would Keynes have thought of rational expectations?' in G.D.N. Worswick and J.S. Trevithick (eds), *Keynes and the Modern World*, Cambridge: Cambridge University Press, 1983.

69. 'Il mio Keynes un po' monetarista', *Politica ed Economia*, September 1983. 'Constitutional constraints on the monetary powers of government', *Scelte Pubbliche*, **1** (2), 1983.

70. 'Keynesianism, monetarism, and rational expectations: some reflections and conjectures', in Roman Frydman and Edmund S. Phelps (eds), *Individual Forecasting and Aggregate Outcomes: 'Rational Expectations' Examined*, New York: Cambridge University Press, 1983, pp. 203–22.

71. 'What was the matter with IS–LM?' in Jean-Paul Fitoussi (ed.), *Modern Macroeconomic Theory*, Oxford: Blackwell, 1983, pp. 64–90.

72. 'Preface to the Japanese Edition', *Information and Coordination*, 1983.

73. 'The Wicksell connection: variations on a theme' in *Information and Coordination: Essays in Macroeconomic Theory*, New York: Oxford University Press, 1981.

74. 'Expectations: policy-maker's dilemma', *Expectations and the Economy*: Essays submitted to the Joint Economic Committee, Congress of the United States, Washington, DC: Government Printing Office, 1981.

1976–80

75. 'Theories of stagflation', *Revue de L'Association Francaise de Finance*, December 1980. 'Stagflation', *Keizai Shushi*, January 1980 Review: Sir John Hicks, Economic Perspectives, Oxford 1977, in *Journal of Economic Literature*, June 1979.

76. 'Foreword to the Japanese edition', (*On Keynesian Economics and the Economics of Keynes*), 1978.

77. 'Costs and consequences of inflation', in G. Harcourt (ed.), *The Microeconomic Foundations of Macroeconomics*, (Proceedings of an

International Economic Association Conference), London: Macmillan, 1977.

78. 'Schools, "Revolutions", and research programmes', in Spiro Latsis (ed.), *Method and Appraisal in Economics*, (with Masanao Aoki), Cambridge: Cambridge University Press 1976.

79. 'Cybernetics and macroeconomics: a comment', *Economic Inquiry*, **14**, June 1976, pp. 251–8.

1971–75

80. 'The coordination of economic activities: a Keynesian perspective', (with R.W. Clower), *American Economic Review*, May 1975.

81. 'Statement of conduct of monetary policy', *Monetary Policy Oversight*, Committee on Banking, Housing and Urban Affairs, United States Senate, Washington, DC: Government Printing Office, 1975.

82. 'Keynes' employment function: comment', *History of Political Economy*, Summer 1974.

83. 'The varieties of price theory: what microfoundations for macrotheory?' UCLA Discussion Paper No. 44, January 1974.

84. 'Maximization and Marshall', 1974 Marshall Lectures at Cambridge University, unpublished.

85. 'Effective demand failures', *Swedish Economic Journal*, March 1973. (with R.W. Clower) 'Say's Principle: What It Means and Doesn't Mean', *Intermountain*.

86. *Economic Review*, Fall 1973. 'The backbending supply curve of labor: comment on Buchanan', *History of Political Economy*, Spring 1973.

87. 'Life among the Econ', *Western Economic Journal*, September 1973.

88. 'Aggregate demand', Interview in *Economics 73–74*, Guildford, CT: Dushkin Publishing Group, 1973.

89. 'Review: Donald Winch, *Economics and Policy: A Historical Study*, New York 1970', *Journal of Economic Literature*, September 1971.

90. 'Statement on monetary policy guidelines and open market operations', *Compendium on Monetary Policy Guidelines and Federal Reserve Structure*, Committee on Banking and Currency, House of Representatives, Washington, DC: Government Printing Office, 1968.

Prior to 1971

91. 'Notes on the theory of markets', *Intermountain Economic Review*, October 1970. Review: John F. Helliwell, Public Policies and Private Investment, Oxford 1968, in *Journal of Business*, January 1970.

92. Keynes and the Classics: Two Lectures, London: Institute of Economic Affairs, 1969 'Keynes and the Effectiveness of Monetary Policy', *Western Economic Journal*, March 1968.

93. 'Comment: is there a meaningful trade-off between inflation and unemployment?' *Journal of Political Economy*, Supplement, July/August 1968.

94. 'Keynes and the Keynesians: a suggested interpretation', *American Economic Review*, May 1967.

95. 'Review: David McCord Wright, *Growth and the Economy*, New York 1954', in *American Economic Review*, June 1967.

Index